SEN
CORRECTIONS, AND PRISONERS' RIGHTS
IN A NUTSHELL

Fourth Edition

By

LYNN S. BRANHAM
Professor of Law
Thomas M. Cooley Law School

SHELDON KRANTZ
Piper & Marbury
Washington D.C.

ST. PAUL, MINN.
WEST PUBLISHING CO.
1994

Nutshell Series, In a Nutshell, the Nutshell Logo and the WP symbol are registered trademarks of West Publishing Co. Registered in the U.S. Patent and Trademark Office.

COPYRIGHT © 1976, 1983, 1988 WEST PUBLISHING CO.
COPYRIGHT © 1994 By WEST PUBLISHING CO.
     610 Opperman Drive
     P.O. Box 64526
     St. Paul, MN 55164–0526
     1–800–328–9352

ISBN 0–314–04514–7

TEXT IS PRINTED ON 10% POST CONSUMER RECYCLED PAPER

PRINTED WITH SOY INK™

This book is dedicated to my parents, Ray and Ty Sanders, who instilled in me the firm conviction that if we each do our part, this world can indeed be a better place.

L.S.B.

*

PREFACE

This book is designed to provide students with a general overview of the law of sentencing and prisoners' rights. Much of the book is devoted to a discussion of the present state of the law—the rights of individuals during the sentencing process and the rights of individuals who have been incarcerated. The book also discusses the mechanics of litigating § 1983 suits and the remedies available to inmates whose constitutional rights have been violated.

The book is not, however, confined to a discussion of the present, but also looks towards the future. The book identifies some of the more critical constitutional questions in the areas of sentencing and correctional law which have yet to be resolved by the Supreme Court. In addition, the book discusses some key proposals for making the nation's corrections and sentencing systems more rational and cost-effective. Some of these proposals include the adoption by each state and the federal government of a comprehensive community corrections act, the use of rational, capacity-based sentencing guidelines, and the incorporation of victim-offender mediation programs into jurisdictions' sentencing and corrections systems.

Sheldon Krantz laid the important groundwork for this book by writing the first three editions of this Nutshell. I have attempted to build on this foundation by writing a Nutshell geared to the

PREFACE

needs of students who must assimilate an extensive amount of information on corrections and sentencing law. Since many of these students will be taught in courses using the casebook which Sheldon Krantz and I have written, *The Law of Sentencing, Corrections, and Prisoners' Rights* (West Publishing Company 1990 & Supp. 1993), this Nutshell tracks the format of that casebook.

I am indebted to Sheldon Krantz and my colleague, Professor Justin Brooks, for their comments on this book. I am also grateful to Randy Diamond, the information services librarian at the Thomas M. Cooley Law School, whose uncanny ability to quickly locate resource materials greatly facilitated my work. Finally, I would like to thank Dawn Beachnau, my secretary and very good friend, for her competent assistance in the preparation of this Nutshell.

LYNN S. BRANHAM

May, 1994

OUTLINE

PART THREE. PRISONERS' RIGHTS LITIGATION

TABLE OF CASES

References are to Pages

A

B

C

D

E

F

G

H

I

J

K

L

M

N

O

P

T

U

V

W

Z

*

SENTENCING, CORRECTIONS, AND PRISONERS' RIGHTS
IN A NUTSHELL

Fourth Edition

*

PART ONE
THE LAW OF SENTENCING

CHAPTER 1

INTRODUCTION TO SENTENCING

For most judges, some of the most difficult, and sometimes wrenching decisions that they must make concern the sentences to be imposed on persons convicted of crimes. The difficulty of these decisions is compounded by the fact that in most jurisdictions, judges still have very few sentencing options from which to choose. Their options are generally confined to incarceration in prison or jail, probation, or a fine. Fines, since they are often not means-based, may not be a viable option though, leaving a judge with only two choices—incarcerating a defendant or placing the defendant on probation.

The problem with this type of two-tiered sentencing structure is that criminal behavior often cannot be pigeonholed into one of only two slots. Crimes cover a wide spectrum of criminal behavior, which means that a wide array of criminal sanctions must be available if judges are to be able to impose the most appropriate penalty on a criminal offender. Probation may not be suitable in a particular case because of the seriousness of the defendant's crime or because the defendant requires a level of supervision greater than that accompanying probation in its traditional form. At the same time, however, incarceration may be unnecessary under the circumstances and in fact counterproductive because of its negative effects on incarcerated individuals and their families.

It is therefore critically important that sentencing systems be structured so that judges can impose the most appropriate sentence on criminal defendants. For what is ultimately at stake when devising the nation's sentencing systems is the public's safety, billions of dollars of taxpayers' money, and the very justness of the criminal justice system.

A. THE PURPOSES OF CRIMINAL SENTENCES

What penalty or penalties should be imposed on an individual for a crime depends on the purpose or purposes of a criminal sentence. Traditionally, it has been said in this country that criminal sanctions have four principal purposes.

The first touted purpose of punishment is to deter future crimes. This deterrent objective has two facets—what is known as specific deterrence and general deterrence. The focus of specific deterrence is on the actual offender; the goal is to impose a punishment that will dissuade the offender from committing crimes in the future. General deterrence, on the other hand, as its name suggests, has a broader objective—inducing the public to refrain from criminal conduct by using the defendant as an example of what will befall a person who violates the law.

The deterrent rationale for punishment, particularly punishment in the form of incarceration, has increasingly come under attack in recent years. Critics point to the extremely high recidivism rates of individuals released from prison as evidence of the lack of success of specific deterrence. They also emphasize that it is the certainty of apprehension and punishment, rather than the amount of punishment, that has the greatest effect in deterring crimes.

The second purpose of criminal punishment is incapacitation, which entails making it physically difficult or impossible for a defendant to commit further crimes—or at least crimes against the public—while serving a sentence. The primary means of incapacitation is incarceration, although some community-based sanctions, such as electronically-monitored home confinement, have some incapacitation benefits.

Incapacitation has become a rallying cry for incarceration proponents in recent years. These proponents argue that since imprisonment averts many crimes that would otherwise have been committed had prisoners remained within the community, all that we need to do to be safer is incarcerate more criminals.

The problem with this facile argument is that it exaggerates incarceration's incapacitation benefits while overlooking its drawbacks. To argue that we should just "lock them all up" ignores the fact that "they" are not all the same. A drug offender is not the same as a rapist; a thief is not the same as a murderer; and an embezzler is not the same as a pedophile in terms of the risks posed to the public's safety. So incapacitation benefits vary, depending on whom we are locking up. In addition, as the incapacitation net is expanded further, more and more marginal offenders, who would not have committed more crimes in the future or would have committed relatively minor crimes, are caught in its web.

It bears to remember also that the costs of incarcerating offenders for incapacitation purposes who could be effectively punished in the community are enormous, not only in terms of the billions of dollars spent building and operating the prisons to hold these offenders but also in terms of the destruction of families that often ensues when a family member is incarcerated. And the true irony is that incapacitation-driven sentencing policies may actually endanger the public's safety, depending on who is incarcerated, since there is some evidence that the recidivism rates of individuals after their release from prison are higher than the recidivism rates of individuals who have committed comparable crimes and have comparable criminal backgrounds, but are punished in the community. *See, e.g.*, Joan Petersilia et al., *Prison versus Probation in California: Implications for Crime and Offender Recidivism* (The RAND Corporation 1986).

A third reason cited for imposing criminal sanctions is rehabilitation. A certain penalty is imposed on an offender, such as mandatory drug treatment, to assist the offender in overcoming criminal propensities.

The rehabilitative objective of criminal sanctions has proven to be controversial when offenders are sent to prison, supposedly for rehabilitation purposes. Critics argue that to pretend that prison is somehow good for a person ignores the negative effects of incarceration, including the criminogenic influences to which prisoners are exposed. In addition, in recent years, correctional officials, both within and without prisons, have balked at the notion that they can somehow rehabilitate offenders. They argue that at most, they can provide offenders with the tools—such as an education and job skills—through which offenders can rehabilitate themselves.

The final purpose of punishment that is traditionally mentioned is retribution. Retribution is simply punishment for punishment's sake—punishment because the offender deserves to be punished. Many proponents of retribution, however, acknowledge that the retributive aim of punishment should be qualified by the notion of "just deserts." Although offenders may be punished because they deserve to be punished, they should be punished no more than is warranted by the severity of the crimes of which they were convicted.

The retributive aim of criminal sanctions is to be contrasted with a fifth purpose of sentencing that has been mentioned with increasing frequency in recent years, a purpose that is subsumed within the phrase, "restorative justice." The premise of restorative justice is that offenders should be held accountable for the harm caused by their crimes. Restorative justice therefore seeks to involve offenders in repairing the harm that they have caused victims, the community, and themselves through their criminal behavior.

Victim-offender mediation programs are one of the primary means through which restorative-justice principles are implemented. During the mediation process, an offender and the victim of the offender's crime meet together in the presence of a trained mediator. During the mediation session or sessions, the victim is given the opportunity to explain to the offender how the crime has affected the victim. The victim is also able to ask the offender questions about the crime that may have been troubling the victim, such as why the offender chose the victim's home to burglarize or what the victim might have done to avert the crime. Finally, the offender is given the opportunity to discuss his or her views about the crime. This discussion will often culminate in an expression of remorse for the crime.

The victim and the offender will then try to reach an agreement about what the offender can and should do to redress the harm caused by the offender's crime. This agreement may, for example, require the offender to pay restitution to the victim, to perform work for the victim, or to perform community service. The agreement may also require the offender to take steps to resolve some of the offender's personal problems which may have contributed to the offender's criminal behavior. The offender may, for example, agree to obtain substance-abuse treatment or to obtain a GED.

One of the chief advantages of victim-offender mediation programs is that they humanize the criminal justice process. During a mediation session, offenders often realize, for the first time, the human impact of their crimes, and they are less able, as they typically do, to rationalize their criminal behavior. At the same time, victims see the human side of the person otherwise impersonally known as "the offender" and gain an understanding of what that person is like and the factors that may have contributed to that person's criminal behavior. For additional information about victim-offender mediation programs, *see* Mark S. Umbreit & Robert B. Coates, *Victim Offender Mediation: An Analysis of Programs in Four States of the U.S.* (1992).

Not all of the purposes of criminal sanctions meld together very well, and in fact, some of them are conflicting. For example, sending a person to prison for incapacitation purposes may undermine the rehabilitation that might occur were the offender to be punished in the community. And imposing sanctions to satisfy retributive urges to "get back" at offenders because of their crimes is at odds with the premise of restorative justice that what is most important is that offenders "give back" to victims and the community because of their crimes.

B. PROPOSALS FOR REFORM

Even a cursory look at the nation's sentencing and corrections systems reveals that something is amiss. In this country, we incarcerate more people *per capita* than any other country in the world. Billions of dollars have been and are being diverted from educational, health, and other government programs to pay the costs of building and operating a burgeoning number of prisons and jails. And yet what is the payoff for this enormous diversion of resources? Crime continues unabated, recidivism rates are extremely high, and victims of crime feel unrequited and ignored by the criminal justice system. Inappropriately lenient or stringent sentences are often the norm in many jurisdictions where judges are offered just two choices when sentencing criminal offenders—"slap them on the wrist" or "lock them up and throw away the key." And the system is rocked by charges that it is racist, punishing African Americans and Hispanics more severely than white people.

In the pages that follow, you will be reading about some of the proposals that have been made, and in some cases implemented, to make the nation's sentencing and corrections systems more rational and cost-effective. Some of the proposals which have been made include the adoption of comprehensive community corrections acts by each state and the federal government; the adoption of rational, capacity-based sentencing guidelines that guide judges in the exercise of their sentencing discretion, encompass community-based sanctions, ensure that the criminal penalties imposed do not exceed the resources made available to the corrections system, and ensure that most nonviolent offenders can be and are punished, and punished effectively, in the community; the repeal of mandatory-minimum sentencing provisions; and the adoption of requirements that correctional impact statements be prepared before legislation is ever enacted that increases the number of people subject to a particular sanction, such as imprisonment.

These are just some examples of the many steps that can and, in the authors' opinion, need to be taken to improve the efficacy of the nation's corrections and sentencing systems. (For other suggestions for reform, *see* Lynn S. Branham, *The Use of Incarceration in the United States: A Look at the Present and the Future* 27–45 (1992)). The reader should keep in mind, however, that even if the nation's sentencing and corrections systems are reformed to better protect the public's safety and to provide meaningful and cost-effective responses to crime, crime itself will not be eradicated. We must remember that there are limits to what the criminal justice system can do to combat crime and that the solution to crime lies not in the criminal justice system nor even within any other governmental program, but within our own families and ultimately, within ourselves.

CHAPTER 2

GUILTY PLEAS AND PLEA BARGAINING

When a person is charged with a crime, that person can enter one of several different pleas to the charge—not guilty, guilty, or, in some jurisdictions, *nolo contendere*. A person who enters a plea of *nolo contendere* or "no contest" can be sentenced as if he or she pled guilty to the crime. The principal distinction between a no-contest plea and a guilty plea is that the former type of plea cannot be introduced as evidence in a civil trial, such as one brought by a victim to recoup losses caused by the crime.

Understanding guilty pleas is critical to the understanding of the criminal justice process, since guilty pleas play such a dominant role in the process. In fact, approximately ninety percent of the criminal cases in which charges are pursued result in a guilty plea. Bureau of Justice Statistics, U.S. Dep't of Justice, *The Prevalence of Guilty Pleas* 1 (1984).

There are basically two types of guilty pleas— "blind pleas" and negotiated pleas. A "blind plea" is one which is entered without any promise of a concession from either the prosecutor or the judge.

11

A negotiated plea, on the other hand, is part of a *quid pro quo*. A defendant may enter a plea of guilty, for example, in return for the prosecutor's agreement to refrain from bringing additional charges, to drop other pending charges, or to make a certain sentencing recommendation to the court. Alternatively, as part of the plea agreement, the prosecutor may agree to let the defendant plead guilty to a crime that is less serious than the one with which he or she was initially charged.

Negotiated pleas that are the outgrowth of the plea-bargaining process have been castigated by critics of that process. Some of the principal objections that have been levelled against plea bargaining include the following: (1) that the inducements offered to plead guilty pressure innocent defendants into entering pleas of guilty; (2) that the "rewarding" of those who plead guilty in effect penalizes those who exercise their constitutional right to go to trial; and (3) that public safety is jeopardized and correctional goals undermined by unduly lenient plea bargains. Critics have also noted that some prosecutors are much more willing to plea bargain when their cases are weak, thereby enhancing the chances of innocent people being convicted. Defense attorneys have also not escaped criticism for their role in the plea-bargaining process. "Quickly cop a plea and take the fee" seems to be the mantra of at least some defense attorneys.

Plea-bargaining proponents, on the other hand, argue that many benefits follow from plea bargaining. Plea bargaining, for example, expedites the processing of criminal cases, preventing the breakdown of court systems that would occur if very many more defendants insisted on going to trial. In addition, as cases are disposed of more quickly, defendants who are awaiting trial in jail simply because they do not have the money to post bail can be released, a benefit not only to themselves and their families but to the taxpayers who are paying the expensive tab for their pretrial incarceration. Plea bargaining can also relieve the stress on defendants and their families caused by not knowing what the outcome of a criminal case will be, and it can help them to avoid the expense of a criminal trial. Finally, plea bargaining can assist law enforcement as defendants provide information about the criminal activities of others in return for a favorable plea agreement.

A.   INTELLIGENT AND VOLUNTARY GUILTY PLEAS

In order for a guilty plea to be constitutional, the defendant must have entered it intelligently and voluntarily. Failure to meet either one of these requirements violates the tenets of due process.

When a defendant is challenging the validity of a guilty plea on appeal, a court cannot constitutionally presume that the defendant entered a valid plea. Instead, the record must contain an "affirmative showing" that the defendant's guilty plea was indeed rendered intelligently and voluntarily. *Boykin v. Alabama* (1969).

By contrast, the Supreme Court has said that when a defendant is challenging the validity of a guilty plea in a collateral proceeding, one which follows the exhaustion or relinquishment of direct appeal rights, a court can properly presume that the guilty plea was constitutional, at least to the extent that the burden can be placed on the defendant to introduce evidence of its unconstitutionality. *Parke v. Raley* (1992). Whether or not the ultimate burden of proof on the issue of a guilty plea's constitutionality can be placed on a defendant in a collateral proceeding was not resolved by the Court in *Parke v. Raley*, since the state statute whose constitutionality was at issue in that case placed the burden of proof on the prosecution. The Court did, however, say that the preponderance-of-the-evidence standard that this statute required the prosecution to meet clearly satisfied the requirements of due process. In other words, even if the government has the ultimate burden of proof in a collateral proceeding on the issue of a guilty plea's validity, the government can meet that burden by proving that it is more likely than not that the defendant's plea was entered intelligently and voluntarily.

The Supreme Court has not fully answered the question of what is required for a guilty plea to be considered "intelligent" in the constitutional sense. From its discussion in *Boykin*, it appears as though the defendant must at least be aware of the crime with which he or she has been charged, of the potential penalties that can be imposed for that crime, and of the rights that are being surrendered through entry of the guilty plea—the right to a jury trial, the right to confront and cross-examine adverse witnesses, and the privilege not to be compelled to incriminate oneself.

In addition, in at least some circumstances, a defendant must be apprised of at least some of the elements of the crime with which he or she has been charged. In *Henderson v. Morgan* (1976), a defendant charged with first-degree murder pled guilty to second-degree murder. Later, however, he contended that his guilty plea was invalid because he was never told that to be guilty of second-degree murder, a defendant must have acted with an intent to kill the victim.

In striking down the defendant's guilty plea, the Supreme Court underscored that it was not necessarily holding that in all criminal cases in which defendants plead guilty, the defendants must first be apprised of the elements of the crime with which they have been charged. The Court noted, however, that in this case, intent to kill was "such a critical element" of the crime of second-degree murder that the defendant must have been made aware of this element for his guilty plea to meet constitutional requirements.

The Court went on to observe that ordinarily, a court might properly presume that a defendant's attorney had informed the defendant in sufficient detail of the nature of the crime to which the defendant was pleading guilty. In this case, however, such a presumption was unwarranted since the district court had specifically found that the defense attorney had not apprised the defendant of the intent-to-kill element.

A defendant's guilty plea may be "intelligent" in the constitutional sense even though the defendant is unaware of weaknesses in the government's case, including constitutional problems in the way in which the case has been prosecuted. In *Brady v. United States* (1970), a defendant pled guilty to a kidnapping that had culminated in the victim's death, at least in part to avoid the death penalty that could have been imposed under a federal statute if he went to trial and was convicted. The Supreme Court later ruled that this statute was unconstitutional. *United States v. Jackson* (1968). The Supreme Court, however, spurned the defendant's argument in *Brady* that his guilty plea was therefore invalid because he would not have pled guilty if he had known that the death-penalty statute was unconstitutional. The Court observed that when a defendant has admitted having committed a crime in open court, the defendant cannot then retract the plea simply because the defendant's attorney failed to predict a future change in existing law.

At the same time, however, missteps of the defendant's attorney will, in some circumstances, lead to the invalidation of a guilty plea. When a defendant is represented by counsel, the defendant is entitled, under the sixth amendment, to the effective assistance of counsel when deciding whether or not to enter a plea of guilty. That does not mean that the defendant is entitled to perfect advice when making this decision. It is not even realistic to expect such perfect advice from a defense attorney because of the many vagaries in a criminal case; a defense attorney, for example, can often not predict with certainty whether or not a court will suppress certain evidence or which witnesses at trial the court or jury would find credible.

Although a defendant is not entitled to perfect advice from his or her attorney when deciding whether or not to plead guilty, the defendant is entitled to "reasonably competent advice." *McMann v. Richardson* (1970). Defendants who contend that they did not receive such advice, however, must rebut a "strong presumption" that their attorneys acted within the "wide range of reasonable professional assistance." *Strickland v. Washington* (1984).

Even if a defendant is successful in rebutting this presumption, that does not mean that the defendant's constitutional right to the effective assistance of counsel was violated and that the defendant's guilty plea will therefore be set aside. The defendant must in addition prove that he or she was prejudiced by counsel's deficient advice or performance. What this means in the guilty-plea context is that the defendant must prove that there is a "reasonable probability" that had the defendant received competent assistance from the defense attorney, the defendant would not have pled guilty and would instead have gone to trial. *Hill v. Lockhart* (1985).

When a defendant who entered a guilty plea received the effective assistance of counsel to which defendants are constitutionally entitled, the general rule discussed earlier kicks in: the defendant cannot challenge the validity of the guilty plea on due process grounds because of an independent violation of the defendant's constitutional rights that occurred sometime before the guilty plea was entered. Thus, in *Tollett v. Henderson* (1973), the Supreme Court held that the defendant's guilty plea was not constitutionally defective simply because the defendant was unaware, at the time the plea was entered, that the grand jury that had indicted him had been selected through an unconstitutional process that systematically excluded blacks. The Court noted that only if the failure of the defendant's attorney to apprise the defendant of this constitutional infirmity constituted ineffective assistance of counsel would the guilty plea be invalid.

The Supreme Court has carved out an exception to the general rule that independent constitutional claims cannot be raised after a defendant's guilty plea has been entered and accepted by a court. In *Menna v. New York* (1975), a defendant was sentenced to jail for thirty days after a court held the defendant in criminal contempt for refusing to answer questions posed by a grand jury. Later, the defendant was prosecuted for this same failure to cooperate with the grand jury. The defendant claimed that this prosecution was barred by the constitutional prohibition of double jeopardy, but when he was unsuccessful in getting the criminal case dismissed, he pleaded guilty. On appeal, he resurrected his double jeopardy claim.

The Supreme Court held that the defendant's submission of a guilty plea did not foreclose him from raising the double jeopardy claim on appeal. The Court noted that *Tollett v. Henderson* and other related Supreme Court cases did not rest on the notion that defendants waive their right to contest earlier constitutional violations upon entering a plea of guilty. These cases rather simply stand for the proposition that when a defendant pleads guilty, the defendant is admitting guilt, which makes most earlier constitutional violations irrelevant. In *Menna*, however, the Supreme Court said that the constitutional violation of which the defendant complained was not rendered irrelevant simply because the defendant had pled guilty, since the defendant was essentially claiming that no matter how clear his factual guilt, the government could not obtain a constitutional conviction.

The Court hastened to add in *Menna* that not all double jeopardy claims could necessarily be raised following the entry of a guilty plea. The meaning of that caveat later became clear in *United States v. Broce* (1989). In that case, several defendants pled guilty to two separate counts of conspiracy. Later, they sought to set aside one of their sentences on the grounds that they had in fact been involved in only one conspiracy that overlapped both charges. Their dual convictions, they contended, therefore violated their right not to be twice placed in jeopardy for the same crime.

The Supreme Court, however, refused to consider their double jeopardy claim, distinguishing *Menna v. New York* in the process. The Court noted that in *Menna*, the double jeopardy violation was apparent from the record. By contrast, in *Broce*, to resolve the double jeopardy issue, a court would have to have delved outside the record to determine whether the defendants had committed only one or really two conspiracies. The exception to the general rule barring collateral review of constitutional violations that preceded the entry of a guilty plea is thus a very narrow one; the exception only applies when "on the face of the record the court had no power to enter the conviction or impose the sentence."

As mentioned earlier, in addition to the requirement that a guilty plea be intelligently rendered, a guilty plea must be voluntary to satisfy due process. In *Brady v. United States* (1970), the Supreme Court considered whether entering a guilty plea in order to avoid the death penalty automatically makes the plea involuntary. The Court concluded that it does not—that all of the circumstances surrounding the entry of a guilty plea must be examined in determining the plea's voluntariness. The Court noted that to hold otherwise—to hold that entering a guilty plea in order to avoid a heavier penalty, in this case death, invalidates the plea—would conflict with the very underpinnings of the plea bargaining that is countenanced by the criminal justice system. The Court then concluded that Brady's guilty plea in this case was voluntary based on all of the circumstances, including the fact that he was represented by a competent attorney and that the state's case against him was quite strong.

Even when a defendant professes innocence at the time a guilty plea is entered, that plea may still be valid. In *North Carolina v. Alford* (1970), the Supreme Court upheld a guilty plea to second-degree murder entered by a defendant who insisted that he was innocent of the crime. At the same time, however, the Court emphasized that there was "strong evidence" in the record that the defendant had indeed committed the murder. This strong factual basis helped to confirm that the defendant's guilty plea was "intelligently" made in the constitutional sense.

North Carolina v. Alford therefore seems to suggest that a factual basis, if not a strong factual basis, must exist for a guilty plea accompanied by a protestation of innocence to be valid. Most courts, however, have held that due process does not otherwise normally require that there be a factual basis for a guilty plea. *See, e.g., Rodriguez v. Ricketts* (9th Cir.1985). A factual basis, however, may be, and often is, required by statutes or court rules governing the proceedings surrounding the entry of a guilty plea. *See, e.g.,* Fed. R. Crim. P. 11(f). These statutes and rules often impose requirements that must be met for a guilty plea to be valid that go beyond the constitutional minima.

While the Supreme Court in *North Carolina v. Alford* concluded that a guilty plea may be valid even though the defendant entering the plea insists that he or she is innocent, the Court at the same time emphasized that its decision did not mean that a trial court must accept the guilty plea of such a defendant. Whether or not to accept a defendant's plea of guilty generally falls within a court's discretion, and the refusal to accept the guilty plea of a defendant who professes innocence will not usually be considered an abuse of discretion. *United States v. Cox* (7th Cir.1991).

B. BREACHES OF PLEA AGREEMENTS

A plea bargain, as discussed earlier, is an agreement in which the defendant agrees to plead guilty in return for some concessions from the prosecutor. But what happens if one of the parties reneges on his or her part of the agreement?

Santobello v. New York (1971) addressed this question in a case involving a noncompliant prosecutor. In *Santobello*, a prosecutor had agreed to make no recommendation as to the sentence to be imposed for the gambling offense to which the defendant pled guilty. A different prosecutor, however, was assigned to handle the case at the sentencing hearing, and at that hearing, the prosecutor asked that the maximum prison sentence be imposed on the defendant. The sentencing judge ultimately imposed the maximum sentence, although he insisted that his decision was based on the defendant's criminal record and not influenced at all by the prosecutor's sentencing recommendation.

Nonetheless, the Supreme Court concluded that the defendant had a right to relief because of the prosecution's failure to live up to its obligations. The Court, however, left to the lower court the decision as to what remedy would be appropriate under the circumstances of the case. The state court was left to choose between requiring specific performance of the agreement, which would mean that the defendant would be resentenced by a different judge with no sentencing recommendation tendered by the prosecutor, or permitting the defendant to withdraw his guilty plea. After withdrawing his guilty plea, the defendant could then decide whether to negotiate anew with the prosecutor or go to trial.

The Supreme Court's decision in *Santobello* is to be contrasted with its subsequent decision in *United States v. Benchimol* (1985). In *Benchimol*, the defendant pled guilty after the prosecutor agreed to recommend that the defendant be placed on probation. The prosecutor, however, apparently made a lackluster recommendation and also failed to explain why the government believed that a sentence to probation was appropriate. The court then sentenced the defendant to prison for six years.

The defendant argued that the government had failed to live up to the terms of its agreement, but the Supreme Court disagreed. Noting that the prosecutor had not promised to make the sentencing recommendation enthusiastically or to state reasons for the recommendation at the sentencing hearing, the Court was unwilling to read such terms into the agreement. Instead, the Court observed that if a defendant wants a prosecutor to make a sentencing recommendation in a certain way, the defendant must obtain an explicit commitment from the prosecutor to do so as part of the plea agreement.

The Supreme Court also distinguished *Santobello* in *Mabry v. Johnson* (1984). In *Mabry*, a prosecutor offered to recommend a 21–year prison sentence to be served concurrently with two other prison sentences being served by the defendant if the defendant agreed to plead guilty to the crime of being an accessory after a felony murder. The defendant, through his attorney, later accepted the offer, but the prosecutor then announced that he had made a mistake and that the offer was now a 21–year prison sentence to be served consecutively with the defendant's other prison sentences. The defendant eventually, though reluctantly, accepted this offer, and the court imposed the 21–year consecutive sentence.

Later though, the defendant sought to hold the government to its original offer, arguing that the defendant's due process rights were violated when the government backtracked from an offer after its acceptance by the defendant. The Supreme Court, however, concluded that the defendant's due process rights had not been abridged. The critical fact for the Court was that at the time the defendant pled guilty, he knew that the prosecutor would only recommend a consecutive sentence. The defendant's guilty plea therefore, unlike the plea in *San-*

tobello, did not rest on an "unfulfilled promise" of the prosecutor.

As is evident from the Supreme Court's decision in *Ricketts v. Adamson* (1987), defendants also have an enforceable obligation to abide by the terms of a plea agreement. In that case, a defendant charged with first-degree murder entered into a plea agreement under which he pled guilty to second-degree murder and received a prison sentence in return for testifying at the trials of two accomplices. The defendant did testify at their trials, but when his co-defendants' convictions were reversed on appeal, the defendant refused to testify at their retrials unless the government agreed to release him from prison after he testified. The government responded by charging the defendant once again with first-degree murder, a charge of which he was ultimately convicted and for which he received a death sentence. To the defendant's argument that his prosecution for first-degree murder was barred by the constitutional prohibition against double jeopardy, the Court responded that under the terms of the plea agreement, the agreement was null and void if the defendant refused to testify at the trials of his co-defendants. By refusing to testify at the retrials of his co-defendants, the defendant therefore, according to the Court, assumed the risk that he would be found in breach of the plea agreement, thereby exposing himself to prosecution for first-degree murder.

Defense attorneys can draw two important lessons from *Ricketts,* as well as *United States v.*

Benchimol. First, counsel must take great care to ensure that a plea agreement specifically and clearly outlines the obligations of both the prosecutor and the defendant under the agreement. And second, should there still for some reason later be doubt regarding the scope of the defendant's obligations under a plea agreement, the defense attorney should seek clarification from the court as to the meaning of the plea agreement rather than relying on the defense attorney's own, and possibly erroneous, interpretation of the agreement.

C. CONSTRAINTS ON THE GOVERNMENT DURING AND AFTER THE PLEA PROCESS

A prosecutor can put a tremendous amount of pressure on a defendant to plead guilty without necessarily violating constitutional strictures. Of that there can be no doubt after the Supreme Court's decision in *Bordenkircher v. Hayes* (1978).

Bordenkircher involved a defendant who had been charged with forging a check in the amount of $88.30, a crime for which he could be sent to prison for two to ten years. The prosecutor offered to recommend a five-year prison sentence if the defendant pled guilty. The prosecutor furthermore informed the defendant that if he refused to plead guilty, the prosecutor would prosecute him under the state's habitual-offender law because of his two prior felony convictions. Under this law, a person convicted of three felonies was subject to a mandatory life sentence in prison.

The defendant refused the prosecutor's offer and went to trial. After being convicted of the forgery offense and found to be an habitual offender, he was sentenced to life in prison.

The defendant argued that the prosecutor had unconstitutionally retaliated against him for having exercised his constitutional right to go to trial. In support of this argument, the defendant cited two Supreme Court cases—*North Carolina v. Pearce* (1969) and *Blackledge v. Perry* (1974). In *North Carolina v. Pearce*, the Supreme Court had held that when a judge imposes a higher sentence on a defendant following the successful appeal of a conviction in order to retaliate against the defendant for having taken an appeal, the defendant's right to due process of law is violated. And in *Blackledge*, the Supreme Court had held that a defendant's due process rights were violated when a prosecutor retaliated against the defendant by charging him with felony assault after the defendant had sought a new trial following his conviction of misdemeanor assault.

The Supreme Court repeated in *Bordenkircher* that it violates due process to punish a defendant for exercising his or her legal rights. The Court, however, then went on to say that such punishment does not, in its opinion, occur when a prosecutor is exerting leverage on a defendant during the "give-and-take" plea-bargaining process, since the defendant is free to either accept or reject the prosecutor's plea offer. To hold otherwise, the Court noted, would lead to the invalidation of plea bargaining, since prosecutors often offer defendants strong inducements to plead guilty.

The dissenters in *Bordenkircher* responded that there was a way to retain plea bargaining while limiting the risk that the prosecutorial vindictiveness that offends due process has occurred—require prosecutors, if they wish to plea bargain, to bargain down from the charges initially filed. Charging decisions would then not hinge on defendants' willingness to forego constitutional rights. The dissenters recognized, however, that as a practical matter, this rule might simply lead some prosecutors to overcharge at the outset of a case. The dissenters still believed though that in order to detect and prevent abusive prosecutorial practices during plea bargaining, it was better to have the pressures that had been exerted on a defendant to plead guilty apparent in the public record rather than be hidden in the form of undisclosed threats by a prosecutor.

Two assumptions underlay the Supreme Court's conclusion in *Bordenkircher* that the type of pressure exerted on the defendant to plead guilty in that case did not violate due process. First, the Court posited that when engaging in plea bargaining, the prosecutor and the defendant "arguably possess relatively equal bargaining power," a dubious proposition in light of the personal interests that are at stake when an individual is charged with a crime. Second, the Court assumed that as long as a defendant is represented by a competent attorney and afforded the procedural safeguards that customarily surround the taking of a guilty plea, a defendant would be "unlikely to be driven to false self-condemnation" by the inducements to plead guilty offered by the prosecutor. One might equally argue, however, that a defendant facing, for example, a possible life sentence if the defendant does not plead guilty might agree to plead guilty in order to receive a vastly diminished prison sentence, even though the defendant is innocent and even though the defendant is represented by counsel.

Bordenkircher does not mean that there are no constitutional limits on the tactics that can be employed by a prosecutor when attempting to extract a guilty plea from a defendant. Even in *Bordenkircher*, the Court inserted some potentially important caveats into its opinion. The Court noted, for example, that the threat to file habitual-offender charges against the defendant was not unwarranted; the defendant could properly be charged as an habitual offender. The Court also seemed to suggest that the result of the case might have been different if the prosecutor had tried to sway the defendant into pleading guilty by offering to treat someone other than the defendant, such as a relative, more leniently if the defendant pled guilty or more severely if the defendant did not.

Another point emphasized by the Court in *Bordenkircher* was that the defendant was aware when he rejected the prosecutor's offer of the potential consequences ensuing from his decision to plead not guilty. This was not a case, the Court emphasized, where the prosecutor, without notice, sprang a more serious charge upon the defendant after plea negotiations had failed.

Despite that remonstration, however, the Supreme Court later concluded in *United States v. Goodwin* (1982) that a prosecutor can, before trial, bring more serious charges against a defendant after unsuccessful plea negotiations, even if the defendant was not made aware during negotiations of the possibility of more serious charges being filed. The Court rejected the argument that there should be a presumption of prosecutorial vindictiveness under such circumstances that the prosecutor has to rebut to avoid a finding of a due process violation. The Court explained that there is much less basis for assuming, in the pretrial context, that additional charges have been filed for vindictive reasons than there is in the posttrial context, where a presumption of vindictiveness is warranted. *Blackledge v. Perry* (1974). In the pretrial setting, when the prosecutor is still putting the government's case together, it is to be expected that the prosecutor may discover information that suggests that more serious charges should be filed against the defendant.

Alabama v. Smith (1989) is another case where the Supreme Court refused to apply a presumption of vindictiveness. In that case, a defendant received two concurrent 30–year prison sentences after pleading guilty to rape and burglary in return for dismissal of a sodomy charge. After securing the reversal of his convictions on appeal because his guilty pleas were invalid, he went to trial and was convicted on all three counts. In sentencing the defendant, the trial judge stated that the trial had revealed facts about the case of which the judge was previously unaware, such as that the defendant had raped the victim five times. The judge then sentenced the defendant to two concurrent life sentences in prison for the sodomy and burglary and imposed an additional 150–year sentence for the rape, to be served consecutively with the other two sentences.

The question for the Supreme Court was whether an increased sentence following the setting aside of a guilty plea creates a presumption that the judge was retaliating against the defendant for exercising the right to contest the validity of the guilty plea. The Court said that for there to be such a presumption, there would have to be a "reasonable likelihood" that increased sentences following the setting aside of guilty pleas are due to judicial vindictiveness. The Court, however, was convinced that this "reasonable likelihood" of vindictiveness does not exist when a defendant was first sentenced following entry of a guilty plea and then resentenced following a trial. *Compare North Carolina v. Pearce* (1969) as it was construed in *Texas v. McCullough* (1986) (presumption of vindictiveness when conviction following a trial is reversed on appeal and higher sentence is then imposed by the same judge who initially sentenced the defendant). The Court noted that during a trial, a judge would generally find out information about a crime and the defendant that was not revealed to the judge when earlier accepting the defendant's guilty plea—information that would often suggest that the defendant should receive a more severe sentence than that initially imposed.

The Supreme Court noted in *Alabama v. Smith* that if the defendant could prove that his enhanced sentences were actually imposed, not because of such new information, but because the judge was retaliating against the defendant for exercising the right to contest the validity of his guilty pleas, the defendant could still prevail on his due process claim. But the point of the Supreme Court in *Alabama v. Smith* was that the defendant could not avail himself of a presumption of vindictiveness. Instead, to prevail on his due process claim, the defendant had to assume the difficult task of proving the existence of actual vindictiveness.

The Supreme Court has not only condoned substantial prosecutorial inducements tendered to a defendant to plead guilty, but also substantial legislative inducements. In *Corbitt v. New Jersey* (1978), the Court upheld a statute that required imposition of a life sentence when a defendant convicted of first-degree murder had gone to trial but permitted imposition of either a 30–year prison sentence or a life sentence if the defendant pled *nolo contendere* to the murder charge. The defendant argued that this sentencing scheme unconstitutionally penalized him for exercising his constitutional right to go to trial. The Supreme Court responded, however, that there is nothing inherently unconstitutional about offering a defendant an incentive to plead guilty, as demonstrated by the Court's decision in *Bordenkircher v. Hayes* (1978). In the Court's opinion, offering a defendant the possibility of more lenient treatment in return for a plea of guilty does not mean that the defendant is being punished if the defendant goes to trial and the prospect of more lenient treatment is withheld.

The Supreme Court in *Corbitt* pointed to another case that helps to clarify at least somewhat the distinction between constitutional and unconstitutional pressures that can be exerted on a defendant to plead guilty—*United States v. Jackson* (1968). In *Jackson*, the Supreme Court struck down a statute that authorized imposition of the death penalty if a defendant was convicted after a jury trial, but permitted imposition, at most, of a prison sentence for life if a defendant pled guilty or was convicted after a bench trial. According to the Court, the statute unconstitutionally impinged upon defendants' due process right to plead not guilty and their sixth amendment right to a jury trial.

In *Corbitt v. New Jersey*, the Supreme Court noted two distinctions between this statute and the statute before the Court in *Corbitt*. First, the possible price of demanding a jury trial under the statute in *Jackson* was death, a penalty "unique in its severity and irrevocability." And second, a defendant, under the statute at issue in *Jackson*, could totally avoid the maximum penalty—death—by entering a plea of guilty. By contrast, under the statute upheld in *Corbitt*, the maximum sentence—life in prison—might be imposed even if the defendant pled guilty.

CHAPTER 3

THE SENTENCING PROCESS

A. RIGHTS DURING SENTENCING

Defendants in criminal trials have an array of constitutional rights. They have, for example, the right to call witnesses to testify in their own behalf, the right to confront and cross-examine adverse witnesses, and the right to be found not guilty if the government fails to prove their guilt beyond a reasonable doubt. By contrast, the constitutional rights of prisoners during sentencing proceedings, or at least the rights recognized thus far by the Supreme Court, are few.

Defendants do have the right, under the sixth amendment, to have their attorneys assist them during sentencing hearings. *Mempa v. Rhay* (1967). Many defendants, however, do not have the funds to hire their own attorneys and are unable to persuade an attorney to represent them free of charge, so the question of the scope of the right of indigent defendants under the sixth amendment to appointed counsel is an important one.

In *Scott v. Illinois* (1979), the Supreme Court, in a 5–4 decision, held that the right to appointed counsel at trial hinges on the actual penalty ultimately imposed on a defendant. If the penalty included some period of incarceration, then an indigent defendant had the right to appointed counsel at trial. If the penalty did not include incarceration, then the defendant had no such right.

Although *Scott v. Illinois* involved a defendant convicted of a misdemeanor, the language of the Supreme Court's opinion seemed to suggest that the actual-incarceration standard is to be applied in all criminal cases, those involving felonies as well as misdemeanors. In a subsequent decision, however, the Court observed, though in *dictum*, that indigent defendants have the right to appointed counsel in all felony cases. *Nichols v. United States* (1994).

The Supreme Court has yet to address the scope of the right to appointed counsel at a sentencing hearing. Unless the Court overrules *Scott v. Illinois*, however, it seems most likely that the Court will apply the actual-incarceration standard to sentencing proceedings in misdemeanor cases, since it is difficult to fathom the Court recognizing a broader right to appointed counsel at a sentencing hearing than exists at trial.

The sixth amendment right to counsel at sentencing hearings includes, logically, the right to the effective assistance of counsel. In determining whether that right has been abridged during a sentencing proceeding, at least in a capital case, courts apply a two-part test. *Strickland v. Washington* (1984). The Supreme Court in *Strickland* specifically left open the question whether the same two-part test is to be applied to ineffectiveness claims based on the performance of counsel during sentencing proceedings in noncapital cases.

Under the two-part test that applies at least to sentencing proceedings in capital cases, the defense attorney must have failed to render reasonable professional assistance during the proceeding. The courts, however, apply a "strong presumption" that an attorney acted reasonably, and it is incumbent on a defendant to rebut this presumption.

To prevail on an ineffectiveness claim, a defendant must also prove that he or she was prejudiced by the attorney's incompetent performance. There are two facets to this inquiry. First, the defendant must prove, at least in a case in which the death penalty was imposed, that there is a "reasonable probability" that the defendant would have received a more lenient sentence had the attorney rendered reasonable professional assistance. In other words, in a capital case, a defendant must prove that there is a reasonable probability that had the defense attorney acted competently, the defendant would not have received the death penalty. The burden of proof which must be met—reasonable probability—is not as high as a preponderance-of-the-evidence standard, which would require that it be more likely than not that the defendant was prejudiced by the errors made by defense counsel.

The second component of the prejudice inquiry was discussed by the Court in *Lockhart v. Fretwell* (1993). In that case, the defendant's attorney failed to make an objection that would have prevented imposition of the death penalty on the defendant based on the caselaw that then prevailed. The case upon which an objection could have been founded, however, was later overruled. Even though the defendant would not have received the death penalty if his attorney had made the appropriate objection, the Supreme Court concluded that the defendant was not unconstitutionally prejudiced. According to the Court, the existence of prejudice depends not only on the effect that counsel's deficient performance had on the sentence imposed but also on whether that sentence was "fundamentally unfair or unreliable." In this case, the Court concluded, there was no such unfairness or unreliability because the defendant had only been deprived of the opportunity to have the sentencing court make a mistake.

The sixth amendment right to the assistance of counsel during sentencing proceedings includes the right, in at least some circumstances, to have the defense attorney notified before the defendant is interviewed about matters that may affect the sentence imposed. In *Estelle v. Smith* (1981), the defendant in a capital murder case was examined by a psychiatrist to determine whether he was competent to stand trial. To the defendant's surprise, the psychiatrist later testified for the prosecution at the defendant's sentencing hearing, describing the defendant as a sociopath. Holding that the defendant's sixth amendment right to counsel had been violated, the Supreme Court unanimously agreed that the defendant's attorney should have been notified that the psychiatrist's examination would encompass not only questions concerning the defendant's competency to stand trial but also the subject of his future dangerousness. *See also Lankford v. Idaho* (1991) (defendant sentenced to death had a due process right to be notified that the judge was still considering imposing the death penalty despite the government's announced decision not to seek the death penalty).

While defendants have a sixth amendment right to the assistance of counsel during sentencing proceedings, most of the other procedural safeguards to which they are or may be entitled during sentencing proceedings stem from the constitutional right to due process of law. The due process guarantee in the fifth amendment applies in federal prosecutions, while its counterpart in the fourteenth amendment provides protection to defendants in state and local prosecutions.

Traditionally, the Supreme Court has balanced three factors when determining whether a particular procedural safeguard is required by due process. The first is the private interest that is at stake. The more weighty the private interest, the more likely it is that the safeguard is an element of due process. The second factor is the governmental interests that would be affected if the safeguard had to be provided and the way in which they would be affected. To the extent that an important governmental interest would be adversely affected by provision of the safeguard, it is less likely that the safeguard is constitutionally mandated. On the other hand, to the extent that a significant governmental interest would be furthered by incorporating a procedural safeguard into the process through which an individual is deprived of life, liberty, or property, it is more likely that the safeguard is required by due process. The final factor to be weighed when determining whether a procedural safeguard is constitutionally mandated is the value of the safeguard in terms of its ability to avert an erroneous deprivation of the private interest that is at stake. The higher the risk that individuals will be erroneously deprived of their life, liberty, or property without the safeguard, the more likely it is that the safeguard is a component of due process. *See Mathews v. Eldridge* (1976).

Gardner v. Florida (1977) illustrates how the Court has applied the three-part test known as the *Mathews* balancing test in the sentencing context. In *Gardner*, the defendant was sentenced to death based in part on confidential information in a presentence investigation report that was not disclosed to either the defendant or his attorney. The state argued that disclosing such confidential information would adversely affect a number of important governmental interests. The state argued, for example, that without a promise of confidentiality, people would be less inclined to provide the information about a defendant upon which a sound sentencing decision is dependent. The Supreme Court responded, however, that the interest in maximizing the quantity of information made available to the sentencer about the defendant and the defendant's crime was counterbalanced by the interest in ensuring that the information provided was true—an interest that would be furthered by affording the defendant the opportunity to be informed of and respond to the information submitted to the sentencer. In addition, the Supreme Court emphasized the centrality of the interest that was at stake in *Gardner*—the defendant's very life.

The state in *Gardner* also argued that the full disclosure of the contents of presentence investigation reports would unduly delay sentencing proceedings as defendants contested the contents of these reports. The Supreme Court, however, was unconvinced by this argument. The Court was confident that presentence investigation reports are generally reliable, so defendants will not usually challenge their contents. Even if they do, the Supreme Court noted that a sentencing judge can avoid a protracted hearing on the issue in dispute by refusing to consider the disputed material when sentencing a defendant. Finally, the Court observed that to the extent that some time must be expended to ensure that a sentencing decision is predicated only on reliable information, that time is well-spent when the defendant's life is at stake.

The state finally argued that fully disclosing the contents of a presentence investigation report would at times impede a defendant's rehabilitation, since the reports sometimes include sensitive information concerning the results of a psychiatric or psychological evaluation of the defendant. The Supreme Court, however, considered this argument to be specious in a case where the state had, by seeking the death penalty, abandoned any pretense of pursuing a rehabilitative objective. In addition, the Court expressed doubt that the state's concern, even if legitimate, would justify refusing to disclose the sensitive information to the defendant's attorney.

According to the Supreme Court, the due process violation in *Gardner* stemmed not only from the failure to permit either the defendant or his attorney to review portions of the presentence investigation report, but also from the failure to afford the defendant the opportunity to "deny or explain" the information contained within the report. *See also Simmons v. South Carolina* (1994) (due process violated in capital sentencing hearing when prosecutor argued defendant's future dangerousness warranted imposition of the death penalty, but defendant was not permitted to inform jury that if not sentenced to death, he would receive a life sentence without the chance of parole). The Supreme Court did not elaborate, however, on what would be considered a constitutionally adequate opportunity to respond to the contents of a presentence investigation report. Is there only a right to have the defense attorney comment on the report's contents, or does the defendant also have the right to make a statement to the Court? Does the defendant have the right to call witnesses to refute statements made in the presentence investigation report, and does the defendant, in addition, have the right to confront and cross-examine adverse witnesses?

The Supreme Court, in other cases, has provided answers to at least some of these questions. In *Hill v. United States* (1962), the Court considered whether defendants have a constitutional right of allocution at a sentencing hearing—the right to make a statement to the court before sentence is imposed. The Court held that there was no such right, but in the course of rendering this opinion, noted that there were some special facts in the case. The defendant in *Hill* was represented by an attorney at the sentencing hearing, and the sentencing judge had not refused a request of the defendant to make a statement to the court. The court had simply failed to ask the defendant if there was anything he wanted to say to the court before he was sentenced. The question, of course, is whether any of these facts should make a difference to the question of whether or not a defendant has a constitutional right of allocution. *Cf. Green v. United States* (1961), a case where the Supreme Court, in the course of discussing the right of allocution under Rule 32(a) of the Federal Rules of Criminal Procedure, said, "The most persuasive counsel may not be able to speak for a defendant as the defendant might, with halting eloquence, speak for himself."

In at least some instances, defendants have the right to call witnesses to testify on their behalf at a sentencing hearing. In *Green v. Georgia* (1979), for example, the Supreme Court held that the defendant's right to due process of law was violated when the defendant was not permitted to call a witness to testify at his capital sentencing hearing. The witness would have testified about an admission of a co-defendant that he had in fact killed the victim whom the defendant had been convicted of murdering. The Court, however, emphasized that the witness's testimony was "highly relevant" to a "critical" sentencing issue and that there were "substantial reasons" for crediting the witness's statement. It must also be remembered that *Green* was a capital case. Whether or not the right to call witnesses extends beyond the confines of the special facts of *Green* remains in doubt. *See also Ake v. Oklahoma* (1985) (indigent defendant who had raised an insanity defense in a capital case had a due process right to receive the assistance of an appointed psychiatrist to testify on the subject of his future dangerousness, a "significant factor" at his sentencing hearing).

One question concerning the scope of defendants' procedural rights during sentencing proceedings about which there is no doubt, at least at the present, concerns the right to confront and cross-examine adverse witnesses at the sentencing hearing. In *Williams v. New York* (1949), another capital case, the Supreme Court held that there is no such right. The Court's rationale rested in part on the tradition of maximizing the flow of information to the sentencer about the defendant and the defendant's crime. The Court was concerned that some individuals with information that would be helpful to the sentencing decision would refrain from providing that information if they then had to face the defendant and be subjected to questioning. The Court also expressed a concern that according defendants a right of confrontation and cross-examination would unduly prolong sentencing hearings.

The lower courts have also held that, at least generally, due process does not require a sentencing judge to provide a defendant with a statement recounting the reasons why a particular sentence was imposed. *See, e.g., United States v. Golomb* (2d Cir.1985). One notable exception to this general rule is when a conviction obtained following a trial is reversed on appeal, the defendant is reconvicted, and the same judge who initially sentenced the defendant imposes a higher sentence the second time around. See *North Carolina v. Pearce* (1969) as construed by the Supreme Court in *Texas v. McCullough* (1986). In this situation, there is a presumption that the judge unconstitutionally imposed the increased sentence to retaliate against the defendant for having appealed the conviction. Unless this presumption is rebutted by legitimate reasons for the increased sentence which "affirmatively appear" on the record, the increased sentence will be vacated and the defendant resentenced because of the violation of the defendant's right to due process of law.

The cases holding that there is generally no due process right to a statement of reasons for the sentence imposed seem to at least arguably conflict with decisions of the Supreme Court requiring a statement of reasons in other contexts. For example, in *Morrissey v. Brewer* (1972), the Supreme

Court held that a parolee has the constitutional right to a written statement outlining the reasons why his or her parole was revoked. In addition, a prisoner whose good-time credits are revoked because of a disciplinary infraction has a right to receive a written statement outlining the evidence upon which the disciplinary decisionmaker relied and the reasons for the disciplinary action taken. *Wolff v. McDonnell* (1974).

Ultimately, the decision as to whether or not defendants have the constitutional right to a statement of reasons for the sentence imposed rests on the results of applying the *Mathews* balancing test. It would seem though that the interest in avoiding an inappropriate correctional placement is even greater in the case of a person who is being initially sentenced for a crime as compared to a person who has already been sent to or released from prison. Even if the lower courts are correct, however, that there is generally no constitutional right to a statement of reasons for the sentence imposed, such a right may of course be accorded by statute or court rule, as can other rights that are not constitutionally mandated.

During a sentencing hearing, a prosecutor will customarily point to aggravating factors that suggest that a more stringent sentence should be imposed on a defendant, while the defendant will cite mitigating factors which support imposition of a more lenient sentence. The Supreme Court has held that the burden of proving the existence of a mitigating circumstance can constitutionally be placed on a defendant, even in a capital case. *Walton v. Arizona* (1990). This conclusion makes sense when one remembers that defendants have much readier access to much of the information commonly presented to mitigate a sentence, such as facts about the defendant's health, employment record, and educational background.

In *McMillan v. Pennsylvania* (1986), the Supreme Court answered some of the questions concerning the burden of proving aggravating factors. *McMillan* involved a challenge to a state statute that required a sentencing judge to impose a minimum sentence of five years in prison on a defendant convicted of one of several crimes delineated in the statute if the judge found by a preponderance of the evidence—in other words, that it was more likely than not—that the defendant had "visibly possessed a firearm" at the time of the crime. The defendants contended that this statute violated due process of law for two reasons. First, they argued that the visible possession of a firearm that triggered the mandatory five-year prison term constituted an element of the crimes with which they were charged, which meant that the requisite possession had to be proven beyond a reasonable doubt.

The Supreme Court, however, disagreed. The Court noted that the Pennsylvania legislature had specifically said that visible possession of a firearm was not to be considered an element of the crime, but simply a sentencing factor. While the Court acknowledged that there were limits to the extent that a legislature could denominate a fact to be a sentencing factor rather than an element of the crime, the Court was convinced that those limits, whatever they might be, had not been exceeded in this case. The Court underscored, for example, that the state statute did not increase the maximum penalty that could be imposed on a person convicted of one of the crimes delineated in the statute. Instead, the statute simply defined, as the legislature, according to the Court, had the prerogative to do, the weight to be given a particular sentencing factor when sentencing a defendant within the prescribed sentencing range.

The defendants in *McMillan* also argued that even if visible possession of a firearm could properly be considered a sentencing factor, the prosecution's burden of proving the existence of this factor under the statute—by a preponderance of the evidence—was too low. The defendants contended that due process required that a defendant's visible possession of a firearm at the time of the crime be established by at least clear and convincing evidence, a standard of proof higher than a preponderance although not as high as proof beyond a reasonable doubt.

The Supreme Court, however, summarily dismissed this claim. Noting that defendants at sentencing hearings have already been found guilty beyond a reasonable doubt, the Court observed that traditionally there has been no required burden of proof at sentencing hearings. In the Court's opinion, the preponderance-of-the-evidence standard that had to be met under the statute therefore clearly satisfied, and may very well have exceeded, the requirements of the Constitution.

The Supreme Court in *McMillan v. Pennsylvania* rejected one other claim concerning the Pennsylvania mandatory-minimum sentencing statute—one grounded on the sixth amendment right to a jury trial. The defendants contended that they had a right to have a jury, and not a judge, make the determination whether they visibly possessed a firearm at the time of the crimes of which they were convicted. The Court, however, simply responded that there is no right to have the question of one's sentence, as opposed to one's guilt or innocence, decided by a jury. Even in a capital case, there is no constitutional right to be sentenced by a jury. *Spaziano v. Florida* (1984) (death penalty imposed by judge upheld even though advisory jury recommended life sentence in prison).

B. FACTORS CONSIDERED AT SENTENCING

Traditionally, the courts have emphasized the breadth of information about an offender and the offender's crime that can be introduced at a sentencing hearing to ensure that the most appropriate penalty is imposed on an offender. Several Supreme Court cases illustrate the expansive scope of the information that can be considered by a sentencing judge. In *Williams v. New York* (1949), for example, the Court condoned consideration by a sentencing judge of a number of burglaries allegedly committed by the defendant but of which the defendant had not been convicted. The lower courts have gone even further, permitting consideration at sentencing hearings of crimes of which defendants have been acquitted. *See, e.g., United States v. Boney* (D.C.Cir.1992). As these courts point out, an acquittal simply means that the government was unable to prove guilt beyond a reasonable doubt. Since this high standard of proof does not apply at sentencing hearings, evidence about the criminal conduct may constitutionally be admitted at a sentencing hearing.

Williams v. New York laid the foundation for the Supreme Court's subsequent decision in *United States v. Grayson* (1978). In *Grayson*, the sentencing judge had imposed a more severe sentence on a defendant because the judge believed that the defendant had perjured himself when testifying at his trial. The defendant contended that for two reasons, consideration of his alleged perjury as an aggravating factor at the time of sentencing violated his right to due process of law. First, he argued that he was in effect being punished for a crime of which he had not even been convicted. The Supreme Court, however, responded that a defendant's willingness to commit the crime of perjury is relevant to the question of what is the appropriate sentence for the crime of which he has been convicted, since a person who is willing to lie while under oath may be a less suitable candidate for rehabilitation.

The defendant in *Grayson* also argued that to enhance a sentence because of a defendant's suspected perjury at trial would unconstitutionally "chill" the exercise by defendants of their right to testify in their own behalf at trial. The Court, however, responded that to the extent that defendants have a right to testify at trial, that right only means the right to testify truthfully. So if consideration by sentencing judges of defendants' perjury when testifying at trial dissuades some defendants from taking the stand and testifying falsely, that chilling effect is constitutionally permissible. *See also United States v. Dunnigan* (1993) (constitutional to increase sentence under federal sentencing guidelines for "willfully obstructing or impeding proceedings" by committing perjury at trial).

A defendant's refusal to cooperate with authorities by providing information about the criminal activities of others can also, in some circumstances, properly be considered as an aggravating sentencing factor. In *Roberts v. United States* (1980), a defendant who had been charged with several drug offenses refused to name his drug suppliers. This refusal prompted the sentencing judge to impose a heavier sentence on the defendant. The Supreme Court acknowledged that the defendant may have had legitimate reasons for refusing to cooperate with the authorities. By disclosing the requested information he might have implicated himself in additional crimes, or he may have feared retaliation from his suppliers. The problem from the Supreme Court's perspective though was that the defendant had failed to assert any of these reasons for refusing to cooperate at the time of sentencing. If he had, the judge could have assessed the legitimacy of the defendant's concerns about incriminating himself and his fears for his safety. Since the defendant had failed to explain to the sentencing judge why he was reluctant to cooperate with the authorities, he could not now complain of the court's consideration of his lack of cooperation when sentencing him.

A prior misdemeanor conviction, obtained when an indigent defendant was not represented by counsel, but which did not result in incarceration, can also constitutionally be considered as an aggravating factor when sentencing the defendant in a subsequent criminal case. *Nichols v. United States* (1994). According to the Supreme Court, the uncounseled misdemeanor conviction, constitutional because of the actual-incarceration standard discussed earlier, can be used to enhance the defendant's sentence, even though the defendant will be imprisoned for a lengthier period of time because of that conviction.

While the scope of the information that may be introduced during sentencing hearings about defendants and their crimes is quite vast, the Constitution does place some limits on the information that can be considered when sentencing a criminal defendant. *Townsend v. Burke* (1948) is a case in point. *Townsend* involved a defendant who was sentenced to prison for a minimum of ten years and a maximum of twenty for burglary and robbery. The length of the sentence was due in large part to a string of prior convictions cited by the sentencing judge. In fact, however, the defendant had not received convictions in the cases to which the judge alluded. The criminal charges had been dismissed in one of those cases, and he had been acquitted in two others.

The Supreme Court held that under the circumstances, the defendant's right to due process of law had been violated. *Townsend*, however, does not stand for the proposition that a constitutional violation ensues whenever false information is introduced at a sentencing hearing. In *Townsend*, the Supreme Court emphasized that the information upon which the defendant's sentence was based was not only false, but "extensively and materially false." *Compare United States v. Addonizio* (1979) (judge's erroneous prediction of when the defendant would be released on parole was not "misinformation of constitutional magnitude" since the judge's expectations were unenforceable against the parole board). In addition, the sentencing judge must actually have relied on the material misinformation in order for a due process violation to result. *United States v. Talavera* (1st Cir.1982). It is for this reason that Rule 32 (c)(3)(D) of the Federal Rules of Criminal Procedure directs judges faced with a defendant's challenge to the accuracy of information in a presentence investigation report to either resolve the factual dispute or confirm in writing that the disputed information was not taken into account when sentencing the defendant.

United States v. Tucker (1972) dealt with the validity of a sentence that was grounded on three prior convictions of the defendant, two of which were later determined to have been obtained unconstitutionally, in violation of the defendant's sixth amendment right to counsel. The Court held that the defendant, who had received the maximum sentence for his crime, was entitled to be resentenced since his sentence was based at least in part on "misinformation of constitutional magnitude." The Court observed that if the sentencing judge had been aware that the defendant had spent ten years of his life illegally confined in prison, the judge might very well have imposed a different sentence. *See also Johnson v. Mississippi* (1988) (death sentence based in part on a conviction that was later vacated violated eighth amendment's prohibition of cruel and unusual punishments).

United States v. Tucker was later narrowly construed by the Supreme Court in *Custis v. United States* (1994). The defendant in *Custis* was sentenced under the Armed Career Criminal Act, a federal statute requiring imposition of a minimum prison sentence of fifteen years on a person with three prior convictions for a "violent felony" or a "serious drug offense" who was then convicted of possession of a firearm by a felon. 18 U.S.C.A. § 924(e). The defendant contended, however, that two of the prior convictions upon which his enhanced sentence was based had been obtained in violation of his constitutional rights. Specifically, he maintained that his convictions had been obtained in violation of due process of law and without the effective assistance of counsel to which he was constitutionally entitled. The federal sentencing judge, however, refused to delve into the question of whether the prior state convictions upon which the defendant's enhanced sentence was based were in fact unconstitutional.

One of the questions before the Supreme Court in *Custis* was whether the defendant had a due process right to challenge the constitutionality of his prior convictions when being sentenced under the Armed Career Criminal Act. The Supreme Court concluded that he did not. One of the Court's concerns was that requiring such collateral review of prior convictions would unduly delay and encumber sentencing proceedings under the Armed Career Criminal Act. Federal courts would be forced at the time of sentencing to sift through the records of state convictions, assuming that those records, many of which concerned convictions obtained many years ago, still existed.

The Court was not convinced that *United States v. Tucker* required a contrary result. The defendant's prior convictions in *Tucker* upon which his sentence had been based had been unconstitutional since he was not afforded the assistance of an attorney when those convictions were obtained. Describing this total failure to appoint counsel to represent an indigent defendant as a "unique constitutional defect," the Court in *Custis* concluded that a defendant being sentenced under the Armed Career Criminal Act has a due process right to challenge a prior conviction only when the defendant has suffered such a total abridgement of the sixth amendment right to counsel.

The dissenting judges in *Custis*—Justices Souter, Blackmun, and Stevens—lambasted the majority of the Court for the distinction it erected between violations of the sixth amendment right to counsel due to a total failure to appoint counsel to represent a defendant and other constitutional violations. They pointed out, for example, that defendants who have not received effective assistance from their attorneys are in as bad a predicament as defendants who have received no assistance whatsoever.

The Court in *Custis* did emphasize that while the defendant had no constitutional right to challenge the constitutionality of his prior convictions when being sentenced under the Armed Career Criminal Act, he was not necessarily left remediless. According to the Court, the defendant could challenge the constitutionality of his prior convictions in a state postconviction proceeding or a federal habeas corpus action. If he was successful in getting any of these convictions set aside, he could then apply to the federal court to have his enhanced sentence under the Armed Career Criminal Act reduced.

Another question which has yet to be resolved by the Supreme Court concerns the admissibility of illegally obtained evidence during a sentencing hearing. The brunt of the litigation on this question has concerned evidence seized in violation of the fourth amendment's proscription of unreasonable searches and seizures. Most of the lower courts have held that such evidence is usually admissible during a sentencing hearing. *See, e.g., United States v. Tejada* (2d Cir.1992) ("Absent a showing that officers obtained evidence expressly to enhance a sentence, a district judge may not refuse to consider relevant evidence at sentencing, even if that evidence has been seized in violation of the Fourth Amendment."). In arriving at this conclusion, the courts have weighed the costs of applying the fourth amendment exclusionary rule against the benefits of applying the rule in the sentencing context. Some costs include the withholding of probative and reliable evidence from sentencers, which can in turn lead to the imposition of inappropriate penalties on defendants.

The lower courts have concluded that these costs generally outweigh any benefit of exclusion in terms of deterring violations of the fourth amendment by police officers. These courts reason that to the extent that the suppression of evidence has a deterrent effect on police officers, they will generally be dissuaded from violating the fourth amendment by the prospect that illegally seized evidence will be inadmissible at trial. The inadmissibility of the evidence at a sentencing hearing will not therefore usually yield much, if any, additional benefit in terms of deterrence, unless the constitutional violation occurred for the express purpose of locating evidence to enhance the defendant's sentence.

One issue on which the Supreme Court has vacillated back and forth in recent years has concerned the admissibility of victim impact statements in capital sentencing proceedings. The Court first confronted this issue in *Booth v. Maryland* (1987). In that case, a victim impact statement was introduced and considered by a jury which sentenced the defendant to death for murdering an elderly man and his wife. In that statement, the victims' relatives described what the victims were like and how traumatized the relatives were by the murders. In addition, the family members expressed their views about the crimes, reviling the defendant for, for example, having "butchered" the victims "like animals."

The Supreme Court in *Booth* concluded that the introduction of this victim impact evidence in a capital sentencing hearing had violated the defendant's right under the eighth amendment not to be subjected to cruel and unusual punishment. The Court gave several reasons why evidence about a victim's personal characteristics and the impact of a murder on the victim's survivors was inadmissible. First, the Court opined that such evidence was simply irrelevant because it did not bear on the defendant's blameworthiness. The Court pointed out that defendants were often unaware of what their victims were like or whether or not they had families at the time they decided to murder the victims.

Second, the Court was concerned that the introduction of this type of victim impact evidence would create a risk of unconstitutional proportions that the death penalty would be imposed arbitrarily.

The Court objected to having the decision to put a defendant to death hinge on whether the victim was portrayed as and perceived to be a "sterling member of the community." The Court was also concerned that some defendants might be sentenced to death simply because some family members were more articulate than others in describing their grief. In a dissenting opinion though, Justice White spurned this latter argument as a specious one, noting that variation in the persuasiveness of the testimony of witnesses and the arguments made by different prosecutors is the norm in criminal cases and is unavoidable.

Third, the Supreme Court was disturbed that victim impact evidence would sidetrack sentencing juries from their primary and critical mission of determining whether defendants, based on their personal attributes and the circumstances of their crimes, should be put to death. The Court also pointed to the difficulty that defendants would often have rebutting victim impact evidence. For example, it would often be strategically unwise for a defendant to cast aspersions on the character of a person that he or she had killed.

As far as the issue of the admissibility of the opinions of family members about the crime, the Court concluded, rather summarily, that such opinions were introduced only for one reason—to inflame the jury. Consequently, such opinions had no proper place in a capital sentencing hearing.

The Supreme Court partially overruled *Booth v. Maryland* only four years after its decision in that case. In *Payne v. Tennessee* (1991), the Court concluded that it had erred in *Booth* when holding that it violates the eighth amendment to introduce evidence about a victim's personal characteristics and the impact of a murder on family members in a capital sentencing hearing. The Court observed that upon further reflection, it was convinced that this type of evidence did in fact bear on the defendant's blameworthiness since defendants have always been held responsible for the harm caused by their criminal behavior. In addition, the Court was no longer concerned that introduction of victim impact evidence would inappropriately shift the jury's attention away from the defendant. Instead, the Court noted that this evidence would appropriately expand the jury's focus, permitting the jury to see that just as the defendant is a unique individual, so was his or her victim. To do otherwise—to permit a defendant at a capital sentencing hearing to introduce any mitigating evidence whatsoever while treating the victim as a "faceless stranger"— in the Court's opinion "unfairly weighted the scales" in a capital sentencing hearing.

The Supreme Court also dismissed other concerns that had been expressed by the Court in *Booth*. The Court insisted that information about what a victim was like was not introduced to show that the victim was more worthy than others and that a defendant was therefore more deserving of death. This evidence was instead admitted to show the victim's "uniqueness as an individual human being" and the ensuing unique loss to the community caused by his or her death.

Nor was the Court concerned about the dilemma faced by defendants considering whether or not to rebut victim impact evidence. The Court simply noted that this decision was no more difficult than other decisions that had to be made by a defendant during the litigation process.

The Supreme Court did observe in *Payne v. Tennessee* that while the introduction of victim impact evidence would normally present no constitutional problem, sometimes such evidence might be "so unduly prejudicial" as to make the sentencing proceeding "fundamentally unfair," thereby violating the dictates of due process. The Court also noted that it was not overruling that portion of *Booth v. Maryland* that had held unconstitutional the admission of family members' descriptions and opinions of the defendant's crimes, since no such evidence had been presented during the sentencing hearing in this case.

CHAPTER 4

COMMUNITY–BASED SANCTIONS

As was mentioned in Chapter 1, one of the central problems with most of the sentencing systems in this country is that they offer judges too few sentencing options. The end result is that inappropriate penalties are imposed on criminal offenders—ones that are either too lax or overly stringent. If corrections and sentencing systems are to be rational, just, and cost-effective then, a broad spectrum of sanctions must be incorporated into them so that judges can impose, in each case, the most appropriate sanction under the circumstances.

Community-based sanctions, if properly structured, offer many advantages—to victims, to the public, and to offenders and their families. Some of those advantages include the following: (1) Such sanctions are generally cheaper, and often substantially cheaper, than incarceration in either prison or jail. (2) By punishing offenders in the community, family ties can be preserved, which in turn will enhance the likelihood of success of rehabilitative endeavors. In addition, the severe emotional trauma that ensues, particularly in children, when a close family member is incarcerated can be avoided. (3) If offenders are punished within the community, they can, if they are employed, continue to work, enhancing their rehabilitation prospects and the likelihood that they will be able to pay restitution to the victims of their crimes. (4) The economic burden on taxpayers that stems from the punishment of criminal offenders can furthermore be dissipated as those offenders working within the community pay taxes and support their families instead of having the public support them through welfare payments. (5) By serving their sentences in the community, offenders can avoid the criminogenic influences that seem to prevail in prisons and jails as well as the dependency that incarceration inculcates. (6) By imposing community-based sanctions on those offenders who can safely and effectively be punished in the community, crowding in prisons and jails can be alleviated, thereby making the correctional facilities safer and easier to manage and less likely to be embroiled in litigation. In addition, the efficacy of prison and jail work, educational, training, and treatment programs can be enhanced as the number of inmates who have needs to be met by such programs is reduced.

At the same time, however, community-based sanctions can be punishing, as studies of the reactions of offenders offered the choice between going to prison and being subjected to a community-based sanction have confirmed. Researchers have found in some studies that up to one quarter of offenders, once informed of the rigorous conditions of intensive supervision programs in the community, have opted instead to go to prison. *See, e.g.,* Joan Petersilia & Susan Turner, *Diverting Prisoners to Intensive Probation: Results of an Experiment in Oregon* 31 (1990).

A. COMMUNITY–BASED SENTENCING OPTIONS

Some of the sanctions to be found in a comprehensive community corrections system include standard supervised probation, intensive supervision probation, community service, home confinement without electronic monitoring, electronically-monitored home confinement, outpatient treatment programs, inpatient treatment programs, day fines, restitution, and day reporting centers. In addition, a comprehensive community corrections system would generally include a victim-offender mediation program as well as a pretrial services program whose purpose is to ensure that only those individuals who pose a substantial risk of not appearing at trial or of endangering the public are confined in jail while awaiting trial. Some of the sanctions mentioned above are briefly described below.

1. Probation

Probation is the most frequently imposed criminal sanction. When offenders are placed on probation, they are required to abide by certain conditions of their probation. If they violate any of these conditions, the terms of their probation may be modified to increase the level of supervision or the amount of restrictions to which they are subject.

Alternatively, their probation sentences may be revoked and prison sentences imposed in their stead.

Probation is not a monolithic sentence. Probation sentences can vary tremendously in terms of the constraints that are imposed on probationers. Probation often entails only perfunctory supervision, if any, of a probationer. A probationer may, for example, only be required to meet with a probation officer once a month or talk on the telephone with the probation officer once a week. In recent years, however, a form of probation known as intensive supervision probation has gained popularity for offenders needing a greater level of supervision within the community. Offenders sentenced to intensive supervision probation are generally required to meet with their probation officers a number of times each week, and they may be subjected to unannounced home visits and random drug urinalysis tests. Intensive supervision probationers are also frequently required to undergo substance-abuse treatment and to work or go to school.

Sentencing courts have traditionally been accorded broad discretion when defining the conditions of a probation sentence. As long as those conditions are reasonably related to the penological goals of probation, they have generally been held to be constitutional.

The rights of probationers are not only limited because of the probation conditions to which they are subject but also because the Constitution applies differently to them than it does to ordinary citizens. In *Griffin v. Wisconsin* (1987), the Supreme Court upheld a search of a probationer's apartment that was effected without a warrant and without probable cause. The search was conducted by probation officers, but several police officers were also present while the search was being conducted.

In determining whether the warrantless search of the probationer's apartment without probable cause violated the fourth amendment, the Supreme Court applied the fourth amendment balancing test under which the nature of the intrusion is balanced against the need for the intrusion—in this case, the need for a warrantless search and one predicated on something less than probable cause. With respect to the nature of the intrusion in this case, the Court felt that the intrusion on probationers was dissipated because probation officers, in the Court's opinion, are not total adversaries of probationers but act with the best interests of the probationers in mind. And as far as the need for the intrusion, the Court concluded that warrant and probable-cause requirements would unduly encumber the effective supervision of probationers. In the Court's opinion, requiring probation officers to first obtain a warrant before searching a probationer's home would interfere with the functioning of probation systems by having judges, rather than probation officers, determine how closely probationers should be supervised. In addition, a warrant requirement would cause delay in the search of probationers' homes, impeding the ability of probation officers to act quickly in response to concerns that probationers are not abiding by the conditions of their probation. Warrant and probable-cause requirements would also, in the Court's opinion, undermine the ability of probation systems to deter probationers from violating the conditions of their probation, since probationers would know that significant limitations have been placed on the authority of probation officers to enter into their homes and conduct a search.

The Court also emphasized in *Griffin* that the probation officers in that case were acting under a state statute that required "reasonable grounds" to believe contraband was in a probationer's home before a warrantless search could be conducted. Left open after *Griffin* then are the questions of whether a search conducted in the absence of such a statute is constitutional and if so, whether at least reasonable and articulable suspicion, a standard that is lower than probable cause, must exist for the search of a probationer's home to be constitutional.

Probation sentences can be combined in a variety of ways with incarcerative sentences. One common combination is what is known as a "split sentence"—a sentence to prison or jail followed by a period of probation.

Shock incarceration programs are also gaining in popularity. These programs, which are typified by boot camps, involve confinement for usually three to six months in a military-type setting. During this time period, offenders are generally subjected to strict discipline, physical exercise, and hard labor, and they participate in drills and ceremonies. If they successfully complete the program, they are resentenced to probation, avoiding confinement in prison. Research has confirmed, however, that any benefits of boot-camp programs will be short-lived unless there is intensive follow-up of boot-camp participants upon their return to their communities to assist them in their efforts to adopt a crime-free lifestyle.

2. Day Reporting Centers

Day reporting centers provide another way of intensively supervising offenders in the community. These centers are fairly new sanctioning options, and they vary in the way in which they are operated. A common pattern is for offenders to report to a center each day, where they must then write down their itineraries for the day—where they will be at all times. Staff members then, throughout the day, confirm, through telephone calls and visits, that the offenders are where they are supposed to be. Offenders can, however, be required to spend a great deal of time at the day reporting center itself, where they may participate in mandated educational, treatment, or counseling programs. When not at the center or at work, they can also be required to do community service.

3. Home Confinement

Another community-based sanction that is being used with increasing frequency across the country is home confinement. Home confinement is also a sanction notable for its diversity. Offenders can be required to stay at home for a few hours each day, or they may be confined to their homes for up to twenty-four hours a day. In addition, home confinement may or may not be electronically monitored. If it is electronically monitored, a variety of devices can be used to enforce the home-confinement sanction. Offenders may, for example, be required to wear a radio transmitter that constantly sends a signal confirming their presence in their homes to a central computer. If the offenders leave their homes, the computer alerts officials, who can then track them down. In addition, the computer can be programmed to alert officials if offenders attempt to remove the radio transmitter.

Another monitoring system uses a computer to call offenders' homes at random intervals. Offenders then confirm their presence in the home, by inserting a wristlet they are required to wear in a verifier box attached to the phone, through a voice-verification process, or through other means. Measures can be employed with this type of monitoring system as well to prevent or detect offenders' attempts to foil monitoring by removing their wristlets or otherwise tampering with the monitoring equipment.

4. Economic Sanctions

One way to punish criminal offenders is to impose a financial burden on them for their transgressions. A common means of doing this is through a fine.

In Europe, it has been widely recognized that fines can be a tough and effective form of punishment. The use of fines is also advantageous because it frees up resources that can be used for the supervision or incarceration of offenders for whom such supervision or incarceration is necessary.

In this country, however, the potential of fines as meaningful and effective punishments has not been realized. Fines have been underutilized, in part because of the way in which fine systems are structured in this country. Generally, judges in this country adopt one of two approaches when imposing a fine. One approach is a tariff system under which a set fine is imposed for a certain offense. Since the amount of the fine is the same regardless of an offender's financial means, the tariff system results in fines that are both too high and too low. Poor offenders may be unable to pay the designated amount, while the fine may be so low as to constitute almost no punishment at all for wealthier offenders.

The other approach commonly taken when imposing a fine is an *ad hoc* approach under which a judge imposes a fine based on a guesstimate of what an offender is able to pay. Having obtained information about, for example, where the offender lives, whether or not the offender is employed, and how many dependents the offender must support, the judge then selects the fine amount. The problem with this gut-feeling approach to the imposition of fines is that, as with a tariff system, it often leads to the imposition of fines that are too high or too low to meet their penological objectives. In addition, this approach leads to a great deal of disparity in the amount of the fines imposed on similarly situated offenders.

To avoid these problems of sentencing disparity and fines that are too high or too low to meet their penological objectives, many European countries and a few jurisdictions in this country have adopted day-fine systems, thereby greatly expanding the utility and effectiveness of fines as criminal sanctions. For example, in West Germany in 1968, just before a day-fine system was implemented, 113,000 custodial sentences of less than six months were imposed, but by 1976, that number had declined to less than 11,000. During this same time period, the proportion of criminal offenders in West Germany who were fined increased from 63% to 83%. Hillsman et al., *Fines in Sentencing: A Study of the Use of the Fine as a Criminal Sanction—Executive Summary* 17 (National Institute of Justice 1984).

The computation of a day fine is a two-step process. First, the sentencing judge determines how many units of punishment should be imposed on a particular offender. One unit in a particular jurisdiction may, for example, be the equivalent of a day's worth of income or a certain fraction of that income. This part of the sentencing decision is made without regard to the offender's financial means. A judge may, for example, decide that the number of units that equals one week's worth of income should be imposed on a particular offender for a particular crime.

The judge must then translate this unit number into a financial figure based on information about an offender's financial means. If the sentence mentioned above—one week's worth of income—is to be imposed, for example, the judge must determine the offender's weekly income and then set that amount as the fine. The end result is a rough equivalency in the fines imposed on criminal offenders since the units of punishment are selected without regard to an offender's financial means. At the same time, however, since the fines are then interpreted to reflect offenders' actual financial situation, it is less likely that fines that are unrealistically high or palpably low for particular offenders will be imposed.

If fines are not closely calibrated to offenders' ability to pay them, then the end result will frequently be nonpayment of the fines. The question arises as to whether there are any limits placed by the Constitution on what government officials can do in response to such nonpayment.

In *Williams v. Illinois* (1970), the Supreme Court answered this question in the affirmative. In *Williams*, the defendant, who was convicted of petty theft, was sentenced to jail for one year, the statutory maximum, and ordered to pay a $500 fine and $5 in court costs. The defendant, however, was unable to pay the fine and court costs. He was indigent and, due to his incarceration, unemployed. He was therefore required to stay in jail an extra 101 days under a state statute that authorized fines to be "worked off" at the rate of $5 for every one day in jail.

The Supreme Court concluded that the incarceration of the defendant because of his indigence beyond the maximum period of time that a nonindigent person could be confined in jail for theft violated the defendant's fourteenth amendment right to be afforded the equal protection of the law. The Supreme Court arrived at the same conclusion the next year in *Tate v. Short* (1971), a case involving an indigent defendant who had failed to pay fines imposed for traffic offenses that were not even punishable by incarceration and was then incarcerated "solely because of his indigence."

Williams and *Tate* set the stage for *Bearden v. Georgia* (1983), a case in which the Supreme Court addressed the constitutional constraints on the revocation of probation for failure to pay a fine. The Supreme Court, however, sidestepped the equal protection issue raised by such revocation and instead focused on the requirements of due process of law. The Court began by noting that the automatic revocation of probation for failure to pay a fine is fundamentally unfair and therefore violates due process. The Court added that pragmatic considerations also counsel against such automatic revocation, since indigent probationers facing the prospect of incarceration if they fail to pay their fines might commit crimes to obtain the funds needed to pay their fines.

The Supreme Court held in *Bearden* that before probation can be revoked for failure to pay a fine, a court must determine the answers to a series of questions. First, did the probationer deliberately refuse to pay the fine despite having the means to do so? If so, the probation sentence can constitutionally be revoked. If not, the court must turn to the next question: did the probationer make adequate *bona fide* efforts to obtain the money to pay off the fine by, for example, attempting to secure employment or borrow money? If the probationer failed to make such *bona fide* efforts, revocation of probation is again constitutionally permissible. If the probationer, however, made such *bona fide* efforts but still failed to procure the necessary funds, then the court must determine whether there are any adequate alternative ways of punishing the probationer other than incarceration. If there are such viable alternatives, then the incarceration of the probationer for failure to pay a fine violates due process. If there are no such alternatives though, incarceration for failure to pay a fine is constitutionally permissible because, as the Court said in *Bearden*, "[a] defendant's poverty in no way immunizes him from punishment." Of course, in a well-structured, comprehensive community corrections system, adequate alternative means of punishing an offender who was initially fined will usually exist.

Another economic sanction commonly imposed on criminal offenders is restitution. Restitution differs from a fine in that it is paid to the victim of the crime rather than the government. Its primary purpose is to compensate the victim for certain injuries caused by the crime. The offender may, for example, be required to pay for the victim's medical expenses stemming from the crime, for income lost while recuperating from injuries caused by the crime, or for the value of property stolen or destroyed during the crime's commission.

While one of the purposes of restitution is compensation, it is still considered a criminal penalty rather than a civil remedy. The ordering of restitution by a judge therefore does not abridge the constitutional right under the seventh amendment to a jury trial in a common-law suit where the amount in controversy exceeds twenty dollars. *United States v. Palma* (3d Cir.1985).

As is true with other economic sanctions, the challenge for a court that wishes to order the payment of restitution is to craft a restitution order that does not impede the offender's rehabilitation. If the restitution amount exceeds the defendant's resources, there is a very real risk that the order will literally induce the offender to "rob Peter to pay Paul."

Mindful of this problem, most restitution statutes direct judges to consider the defendant's financial resources and needs when calculating the amount of restitution. *See, e.g.,* 18 U.S.C.A. § 3664(a). Another tack is suggested by the *American Bar Association Guidelines Governing Restitution to Victims of Criminal Conduct* (1988). Under these guidelines, judges are to enter restitution orders that fully cover the victim's losses. Payment of part or all of the restitution award can then be stayed because of the defendant's present financial situation. If the defendant's financial status changes for the better in the future, however, the stay can be lifted, and the defendant will then have to pay the remaining sum due.

Some additional economic sanctions have been added to the sanctions menu in recent years. One is to deny individuals convicted of certain crimes of certain government benefits, such as student loans. *See, e.g.*, 21 U.S.C.A. § 862. Another is to require offenders to defray the costs of the sanctions imposed on them. Some examples of the fees that are now assessed on criminal offenders include: residential fees for offenders staying in work-release centers or other community correctional residential facilities; restitution-collection fees; substance-abuse assessment fees for the evaluation of offenders for drug or alcohol problems; substance-abuse treatment fees; counseling fees; probation-supervision fees; community-service fees; home-confinement fees; and court costs. Because of the danger mentioned earlier that offenders may be overwhelmed by unrealistic economic demands placed upon them, to both their and the public's detriment, it is imperative that these fees and assessments, as well as all other economic sanctions, be coordinated and integrated into a coherent and rational punishment package.

5. Community Service

Community service is a sanction through which offenders pay back the community for the harm caused by their criminal behavior by doing work that benefits the public. The range of tasks that offenders can be ordered to perform is almost endless. Offenders can be required, for example, to plant trees, pick up litter, refurbish buildings in low-income areas that are particularly ravaged by crime, and assist charitable and other non-profit organizations. But while the advantages that the public can reap from community-service sentences are great, this sanction, like many other community-based sanctions, is not widely used and when used in a jurisdiction, is often used only sporadically. One of the chief roadblocks to the widespread imposition of this sanction is the lack of a central agency in many jurisdictions responsible for coordinating the imposition and implementation of this sanction.

B. COMPREHENSIVE COMMUNITY CORRECTIONS ACTS

While it is important that judges have an array of sanctions from which to choose when sentencing criminal offenders so that the most appropriate penalty is imposed in each case, it is equally important that a structure be put in place to ensure that these sanctions are achieving their objectives and that community corrections systems are operating as cost-effectively as possible. In recent years, a number of states have adopted comprehensive community corrections acts to ensure that this structure is in place.

In 1992, the American Bar Association adopted a resolution calling on each state and United States territory to adopt a comprehensive community corrections act. At the same time, the ABA promulgated a Model Adult Community Corrections Act to provide guidance to states enacting or revising their own comprehensive community corrections acts. While the ABA Model Act contemplates that its provisions may have to be modified to fit the contours of a particular state's sentencing and corrections systems, there are certain key provisions in the Model Act that are considered central to the goal of making sentencing and corrections systems more rational and cost-effective. Some of these key ingredients include the following:

1. provision for a wide array of community-based sanctions that includes, but is not limited to, unsupervised probation, standard supervised probation, intensive supervision probation, community service, home confinement with and without electronic monitoring, outpatient treatment programs, inpatient treatment programs, day reporting centers, day fines, and restitution;

2. establishment of a rebuttable presumption that a community-based sanction is the most appropriate penalty for the following types of offenders: those convicted of misdemeanors; those convicted of nonviolent felonies, including drug

offenses; and those who violate a condition of their probation, parole, or other community sanction and whose violation is either noncriminal or, if charged as a crime, would be a misdemeanor or a nonviolent felony;

3. the development of a statewide community corrections plan by a broad-based group comprised of individuals from key constituency groups within the criminal justice system, such as law enforcement, prosecution, defense, judges, community corrections, and institutional corrections, as well as members of the public;

4. implementation of the community corrections act at the local level by a similarly broad-based community corrections board;

5. technical assistance and training to facilitate the achievement of the act's goals and to avoid unnecessary and costly duplication of efforts when community corrections programs are being established and revamped;

6. monitoring of the act's implementation at both the state and local level;

7. provision for the adequate funding of community sanctions; and

8. provision for the education of the public about community-based sanctions—about how punishing they can be, about how they can be structured to reduce, although not eliminate, risks to the public's safety, and about their costs relative to incarceration.

This latter requirement is particularly critical if community corrections programs are to reach their potential. Studies have shown that what an informed public wants, in terms of the punishment of criminals, varies greatly from the desires of an uninformed public. For example, 422 adults in Alabama were asked during a survey conducted in 1988 about the penalty they would impose in twenty-three hypothetical cases. Initially, when given the choice between only prison and probation, the respondents opted for incarceration in eighteen of the cases. When later given five other sentencing options from which to choose and about which they had been informed, however, the respondents chose imprisonment in only four of the cases. Intermediate sanctions were preferred for even very serious crimes, such as a third drug-dealing conviction, embezzlement of $250,000 and the commission of an unarmed burglary for the second time. *See* John Doble & Josh Klein, *Punishing Criminals: The Public's View—An Alabama Survey* (1989). *See also* the similar findings in John Doble et al., *Punishing Criminals: The People of Delaware Consider the Options* (1991).

With the aid of a comprehensive community corrections act, a sentencing system can be structured which provides offenders with incentives to work towards rehabilitating themselves. In a thought-provoking article, former Delaware Governor Pierre du Pont proposed that multi-tiered sentencing systems be created under which offenders would be assigned to one of ten different levels that vary in terms of the amount of supervision to which an offender is subjected and the number of privileges enjoyed. Offenders who conform to the requirements of their sentences can work their way down the tiers, gradually enjoying greater freedom, while the level of supervision can be increased and more privileges withheld if offenders do not abide by the requirements that have been imposed on them. *See* Pierre S. du Pont, *Expanding Sentencing Options: A Governor's Perspective* (National Institute of Justice 1985). A grid that reflects how such a multi-tiered sentencing system would work can be found on the next page.

Restrictions	Level I	Level II	Level III	Level IV	Level V	Level VI	Level VII	Level VIII	Level IX	Level X
Mobility in the community [1]	100 percent (unrestricted)	100 percent (unrestricted)	90 percent (restricted 0-10 hours/week)	80 percent (restricted 10-30 hours/week)	60 percent (restricted 30-40 hours/week)	30 percent (restricted 50-100 hours/week)	20 percent (restricted 100-140 hours/week)	10 percent (90 percent of time incarcerated)	Incarcerated	Incarcerated
Amount of supervision	None	Monthly written report	1-2 face-to-face/month; 1-2 weekly phone contact	3-6 face-to-face/month; weekly phone contact	2-6 face-to-face/week; daily phone contact; weekly written reports	Daily phone contact; daily face-to-face; weekly written reports	Daily onsite supervision 8-16 hours/day	Daily onsite supervision 24 hours/day	Daily onsite supervision 24 hours/day	Daily onsite supervision 24 hours/day
Privileges withheld or special conditions [2]	100 percent (same as prior conviction)	100 percent (same as prior conviction)	1-2 privileges withheld	1-4 privileges withheld	1-2 privileges withheld	1-10 privileges withheld	1-12 privileges withheld	5-15 privileges withheld	15-19 privileges withheld	20 or more privileges withheld
Financial obligations [3]	Fine, court costs may be applied (0- to 2-day fine)	Fine, court costs, restitution, probation (supervisory) fee may be applied; 1- to 3-day fine)	Same (increase probation fee by $5-10/month; 2- to 4-day fine)	Same (increase probation fee by $5-10/month; 3- to 5-day fine)	Same (pay partial cost of food/lodging/supervision fee; 4- to 7-day fine)	Same as Level V (8- to 10-day fine)	Same as Level V (11- to 12-day fine)	Fine, court costs, restitution payable upon release to Level VII or lower (12- to 15-day fine)	Same as Level VIII	Same as Level VIII
Examples (Note: many other scenarios could be constructed meeting the requirements at each level)	$50 fine, court costs; 6 months unsupervised probation	$50 fine, court costs, restitution; 6 months supervised probation, $10 monthly fee; written report	Fine, court costs, restitution; 1 year probation; weekend community service; no drinking	Weekend community service or mandatory treatment 5 hours/day; $30 month probation fee; no out-of-State trips	Mandatory rehabilitation skills program 8 hours/day; restitution; $40/month restitution; no drinking; curfew	Work release: pay portion of food/lodging; restitution; no kitchen privileges outside mealtimes; no drinking, no sex, weekends home	Residential treatment program; pay portion of program costs; limited privileges	Minimum-security prison	Medium-security prison	Maximum-security prison

1. Restrictions on freedom structure an offender's time, controlling his or her schedule, whereabouts, and activities for a designated period. To the extent that monitoring is not standard or consistent or to the extent that no sanctions accrue for failure or for meeting the part of the offender, the time is *not* structured. It could consist of residential, part-time residential, community service, or other specific methods for meeting the designated hours. The judge could order that the hours be met daily (e.g., 2 hours/day) or in one period (e.g., weekend in jail.

2. Privileges/conditions: choice of job, choice of residence, mobility within setting, driving, drinking (possible use of Antabuse), out-of-State trips, phone calls, curfew, mail, visitation, association, areas off limits.

3. As a more equitable guide to appropriate fines, the amount would be measured in units of equivalent daily income, such as 1 day's salary ("1-day fine."

Source: Pierre S. du Pont, *Expanding Sentencing Options: A Governor's Perspective* (National Institute of Justice 1986).

CHAPTER 5

SENTENCING STATUTES AND GUIDELINES

There are two central decisions that must be made when sentencing a criminal defendant. The first is known as the in-out decision. Should the defendant be sentenced to prison or jail, or should the defendant instead be punished in the community? The second decision concerns the length, amount, and conditions of the defendant's sentence. If the defendant is to be incarcerated, how long should that incarceration last? Alternatively, if a community-based sanction is to be imposed on the defendant, how long should that sanction last (or, in the case of an economic sanction, how much should the defendant pay), and what conditions should accompany that sanction?

Sentencing systems vary as to how discretion in sentencing criminal defendants is allocated. The systems can be differentiated based on the roles played by legislatures, judges, sentencing commissions, and parole boards in the sentencing of criminal defendants.

Sentencing systems can be divided into at least three general categories—those in which indeterminate-sentencing statutes predominate; those in which determinate-sentencing statutes prevail; and those in which sentencing guidelines are applied. But even within these broad categories, there is a great deal of variation in sentencing structures. There is also some overlap between the categories. Mandatory-sentencing statutes, for example, which are discussed later in this chapter and which are considered a form of determinate sentencing, can often be found in jurisdictions with indeterminate-sentencing statutes as well as in jurisdictions that employ sentencing guidelines.

In a jurisdiction characterized by indeterminate sentencing, a judge sentences a person to prison for a range of time falling within parameters set by the legislature. A judge might, for example, sentence an armed robber to prison for a minimum of two and a maximum of fifteen years. A parole board then decides how much time the individual is actually confined in prison. The parole board might decide that the person is ready to be released from prison after two years. The parole board might, however, decide that the person must remain in prison for the full fifteen years or might decide to release the prisoner from prison sometime in between the two-year minimum and the fifteen-year maximum period.

One of the argued advantages of parole systems is that parole boards, drawing on the advice of correctional officials who have been able to closely observe prisoners during their confinement, can best determine when a prisoner is ready to be safely released back into the community. This argument is, however, somewhat belied by the high recidivism rates of prisoners released on parole, although these high recidivism rates might also be due to other problems in correctional systems, including the lack of adequate plans and programs to facilitate inmates' successful reintegration into the community.

Another claimed benefit of parole systems is that they can help to relieve crowding in prisons. When a state's prisons become too crowded, the parole board can ease population pressures by releasing additional prisoners on parole. This touted benefit of parole, however, is often cited by critics as one of its chief drawbacks. The premature release of prisoners, they argue, jeopardizes the public's safety and undermines the other penological goals of incarceration.

There are two other major problems that stem from indeterminate-sentencing structures. First, the uncertainty spawned by indeterminate sentences as to exactly how long inmates will be imprisoned can cause stress and tension in prisoners that in turn interferes with rehabilitation efforts and compounds the already difficult problem of managing prisoners. This stress and tension may also be accompanied by resentment as inmates observe other inmates whom they believe to be comparable to themselves being released on parole while they are left to languish in prison.

The other problem with indeterminate sentences is the enormous amount of disparity in sentences that can result when the discretion to determine how much time a person will spend in prison is remitted to a parole board. This disparity, as well as the psychological pressures mentioned earlier, can be mitigated somewhat by parole guidelines that guide parole boards in the exercise of their discretion and require them to justify release decisions that depart from the guidelines. Parole guidelines, however, cannot totally eliminate the disparity that accompanies indeterminate sentencing, since they only govern decisions concerning when prisoners will be released from prison. They have no application to the initial decision of judges as to whether or not to send individuals to prison in the first place. Thus, a community-based sanction may be imposed on one person for a crime, while another person, with a comparable criminal background who has committed a comparable crime, is sent to prison.

Determinate-sentencing statutes avoid some of the problems of indeterminate sentences, but they have some of their own unique drawbacks. The nature and extent of those drawbacks depend on the type of determinate-sentencing statute in question.

Under a determinate-discretionary sentencing statute, a judge selects a sentence, when imprisoning an offender, from a range provided by the legislature. The difference between a determinate-discretionary sentencing structure and an indeterminate-sentencing system is that the judge, and not a parole board, defines the amount of time that a person will be confined behind bars. For example, if the legislature authorizes a prison sentence of no less than one year and no more than fifteen years for an armed robbery, the sentencing judge picks a number within that range, such as four years, eight years, or ten years.

Two caveats must be added though to this description of determinate-discretionary sentencing statutes. First, although such statutes delineate the range from which a judge will select a finite prison sentence for a particular crime, other statutes often authorize the judge to impose a community-based sanction if imprisonment is considered unnecessary. Second, while a judge under a determinate-discretionary statute imposes a finite prison term on an offender, the actual time that the offender remains behind bars may often be reduced by the earning of what are called good-time credits. With good-time credits, a prisoner's sentence is reduced by a prescribed amount of time for every day or month that the inmate refrains from violating prison rules or regulations. For example, a prisoner might have one day lopped off his or her prison sentence for every day of good behavior. In recent years though, there has been a movement in some jurisdictions towards what is called "earned time." With earned time, inmates must do something more than just refrain from misconduct to earn credits that reduce their prison sentences; they must work, go to school, or participate in other programs that will make it more likely that they will refrain from committing crimes after their release from prison.

Determinate-discretionary sentencing statutes offer the advantage of certainty. They avoid the tension felt by prisoners sentenced under indeterminate-sentencing statutes who do not know how much time they will have to be confined in prison. But as with indeterminate-sentencing schemes, determinate-discretionary sentencing structures are characterized by sentencing disparity, and sometimes gross sentencing disparity, as judges pick and choose numbers within the imprisonment range defined by the legislature.

One way to reduce this disparity is through another type of determinate-sentencing statute—a presumptive-sentencing statute. A presumptive-sentencing statute defines the presumptive sentence that the legislature wants imposed for a particular crime. If there are aggravating factors in a case, the statute generally outlines how far above the presumptive sentence the judge may go in imposing a sentence, and the judge's discretion is similarly circumscribed when a sentence more lenient than the presumptive sentence is imposed because of mitigating factors.

One of the problems with presumptive-sentencing statutes is that they tend to fall prey to political pressures. Presumptive sentences are not selected after thoughtful and careful consideration, guided by research, as to what would be the most appropriate sentences from a penological standpoint. Instead, they are generally the reflexive response of legislators competing to demonstrate to the public how "tough" they are on crime. Over the years, these legislatively prescribed presumptive sentences tend to be continually ratcheted up as the outgrowth of this ongoing competition between legislators.

This same criticism has been leveled against another form of determinate-sentencing statute— those prescribing mandatory-minimum sentences. As their name suggests, mandatory-minimum sentencing statutes require that offenders serve at least a certain specified amount of time in prison for particular crimes. Many of these statutes are directed against drug offenders and require prison sentences of five years, ten years, fifteen years, and sometimes even life in prison, depending on the amount of drugs involved.

The appeal of mandatory minimums to legislators is that by enacting them, the legislators can appear, to an uninformed public, to be sending a tough message to prospective criminals: "If you commit this crime, you will spend this amount of time in prison, no matter what." In truth, however, mandatory-minimum sentences are readily, and very often, circumvented. A study conducted by the United States Sentencing Commission in 1991, for example, revealed that about 40% of the federal offenders whose crimes should have triggered mandatory-minimum sentences were able to avoid these mandatory penalties. United States Sentencing Commission, *Special Report to the Congress: Mandatory Minimum Penalties in the Federal Criminal Justice System* 89 (1991). And what is particularly disconcerting about these statistics is that the disparity in the enforcement of mandatory-minimum sentences has racial and ethnic overtones; white defendants are much more likely to avoid mandatory penalties than are black and Hispanic defendants. *See, e.g., id.* at 76, 80–82.

The reason why mandatory-minimum sentences are so often circumvented is because their very rigidity can lead to the imposition of unjust sentences. While a particular penalty may generally be appropriate for most individuals who commit a particular crime, there will always be some individuals who don't fit the prototype. For example, a mother who is arrested for growing marijuana to be used to ease the suffering of her terminally ill son is unlike the typical defendant who grows marijuana for personal use or to make a profit. Even serious, violent offenders cannot always be typecast into a single mold. A woman who kills her husband after finding pictures of him sexually molesting their children, for example, is unlike a hired killer or a bloodthirsty sociopath.

Mandatory-minimum sentences can be circumvented in a variety of ways. Prosecutors can, for example, file charges that do not trigger a mandatory minimum, even though the defendant's actual crime falls within the scope of a mandatory-minimum sentencing provision. Alternatively, police may not arrest someone for a crime or judges may dismiss charges or acquit someone of a crime to avoid application of what is perceived to be an unjust mandatory penalty. The point is that there will always be discretion exercised in the imposition of criminal punishment. Mandatory-minimum sentencing provisions do not, as they purport to, eliminate sentencing discretion. They simply remove the exercise of that discretion from the public eye, causing disparity in the sentencing of criminal defendants in the process.

Sentencing guidelines, if properly structured, can avoid many of the pitfalls of determinate and indeterminate-sentencing statutes. The Minnesota sentencing guidelines, the first adopted in this country, exemplify how sentencing guidelines can work. Sentences are calculated under the guidelines by employing a sentencing guidelines grid which identifies what the presumptive sentence is for a person who has committed a crime of a certain severity level and who has a certain criminal history score. *See* page 92. An offender's criminal history score depends not only on the number and the severity of prior adult convictions, but also on the offender's juvenile record and on whether the offender was awaiting sentencing for another crime, on probation or parole, or confined for a felony or gross misdemeanor at the time the felony was committed for which the offender is now being sentenced.

There is a dark black line that divides the Minnesota sentencing-guidelines grid into two parts. There is a presumption that the sentences to the left of the black line will be stayed. A number of conditions can be attached to those stayed sentences, but as long as offenders abide by those conditions, they will not be sent to prison. On the other hand, there is a presumption that the sen-

MINNESOTA SENTENCING GUIDELINES GRID

IV. SENTENCING GUIDELINES GRID

Presumptive Sentence Lengths in Months

Italicized numbers within the grid denote the range within which a judge may sentence without the sentence being deemed a departure.

Offenders with nonimprisonment felony sentences are subject to jail time according to law.

SEVERITY LEVELS OF CONVICTION OFFENSE		CRIMINAL HISTORY SCORE						
		0	1	2	3	4	5	6 or more
Sale of a Simulated Controlled Substance	I	12*	12*	12*	13	15	17	19 18-20
Theft Related Crimes ($2500 or less) Check Forgery ($200-$2500)	II	12*	12*	13	15	17	19	21 20-22
Theft Crimes ($2500 or less)	III	12*	13	15	17	19 18-20	22 21-23	25 24-26
Nonresidential Burglary Theft Crimes (over $2500)	IV	12*	15	18	21	25 24-26	32 30-34	41 37-45
Residential Burglary Simple Robbery	V	18	23	27	30 29-31	38 36-40	46 43-49	54 50-58
Criminal Sexual Conduct 2nd Degree (a) & (b)	VI	21	26	30	34 33-35	44 42-46	54 50-58	65 60-70
Aggravated Robbery	VII	48 44-52	58 54-62	68 64-72	78 74-82	88 84-92	98 94-102	108 104-112
Criminal Sexual Conduct, 1st Degree Assault, 1st Degree	VIII	86 81-91	98 93-103	110 105-115	122 117-127	134 129-139	146 141-151	158 153-163
Murder, 3rd Degree Murder, 2nd Degree (felony murder)	IX	150 144-156	165 159-171	180 174-186	195 189-201	210 204-216	225 219-231	240 234-246
Murder, 2nd Degree (with intent)	X	306 299-313	326 319-333	346 339-353	366 359-373	386 379-393	406 399-413	426 419-433

Presumptive stayed sentence; at the discretion of the judge, up to a year in jail and/or other non-jail sanctions can be imposed as conditions of probation. However, certain offenses in this section of the grid always carry a presumptive commitment to a state prison.[1] These offenses include Criminal Vehicular Homicide. Third Degree Controlled Substance Crimes when the offender has a prior felony drug conviction, Burglary of an Occupied Dwelling when the offender has a prior felony burglary conviction, second and subsequent Criminal Sexual Conduct offenses and offenses carrying a mandatory minimum prison term due to the use of a dangerous weapon (e.g., Second Degree Assault).

Presumptive commitment to state imprisonment.

[1. The sentences for these offenses are not presumptively stayed since state statutes requires a mandatory imprisonment for these offenses.]

* one year and one day

tences to the right of the black line will be executed—in other words, that the individuals who receive such sentences will actually be sent to prison.

Judges can impose a sentence other than the presumptive sentence under the Minnesota sentencing guidelines when there are "substantial and compelling" reasons for a departure. When a judge departs from the presumptive sentence, however, the judge must explain in writing the reasons for the departure.

There are two types of departures possible under the Minnesota sentencing guidelines—a dispositional departure and a durational departure. If a judge sends a person to prison when, under the guidelines, the presumption is that the sentence will be stayed, the departure is a dispositional one. Similarly, if a judge stays a sentence that should presumptively be executed, a dispositional departure has occurred. On the other hand, if the judge imposes a sentence that is either longer or shorter than the presumptive sentence under the grid, a durational departure has occurred. If the sentence imposed represents both a durational and a dispositional departure, the judge must separately explain the rationale for both departures.

While sentencing commissions, and sometimes judges, draft sentencing guidelines, legislatures still play a role in the sentencing process. Statutes outline the general range of sentences for a particular crime within which the guidelines must operate, and legislatures are generally given the opportunity to approve or disapprove sentencing guidelines and revisions to those guidelines before they go into effect.

Sentencing guidelines, if drafted properly, offer a number of advantages to jurisdictions which adopt them. First, by identifying the penalty that should generally be imposed for a crime committed by an individual with a particular criminal background, the guidelines help to avert the sentencing disparity that plagues so many other types of sentencing systems. At the same time, however, by allowing departures from presumptive sentences, well-drafted sentencing guidelines offer judges the flexibility they need to ensure that appropriate sentences are imposed in atypical cases.

Another advantage of sentencing guidelines that are properly structured is that they can help to ensure that a jurisdiction's sentencing system is rational and cost-effective. The comprehensive overview of sentences that occurs when sentencing guidelines are drafted can, for example, help to ensure that the sentencing system is characterized by proportionality, an integral component of any rational sentencing system. When proportionality principles prevail, more serious crimes are punished more severely, and individuals with more serious criminal histories are punished more severely than those with low criminal-history scores.

The Minnesota sentencing guidelines are a case in point. When the Minnesota Sentencing Guidelines Commission first embarked on its mission to craft sentencing guidelines, the Commission recognized that prison space is a finite and very expensive resource and that therefore the guidelines should be selective as to who is sent to prison. In establishing the priorities for the use of prison space, the Commission came to two conclusions: first, that prison should generally be reserved for individuals who have committed serious, violent crimes or who have a lengthy history of criminal activity and second, that other offenders could be punished effectively, and if need be severely, in the community.

Another advantage of sentencing guidelines is that sentencing commissions continually monitor their implementation and can therefore finetune them based on the information gathered so that they better meet their objectives. Through this ongoing monitoring function, sentencing commissions can also avert crowding in a jurisdiction's prisons. But instead of taking crude measures like lopping the same amount of time off of all prisoners' sentences to alleviate crowding, sentencing commissions can carefully calibrate the guidelines to ease crowding while taking care not to compromise the public's safety. If, for example, there is a rash of armed robberies in a state leading to an unexpected influx of these violent offenders into the state's prisons, the sentencing commission can modify somewhat the guidelines applicable to some less serious offenders to make room for the armed robbers.

When modifying sentencing guidelines as well as sentencing laws, care must be taken, however, to avoid violating the prohibition in the Constitution of *ex post facto* laws. U.S. Const. art. I, § 10. A law or guideline which increases the punishment for a crime after the crime has been committed violates this *ex post facto* prohibition. *See, e.g., Miller v. Florida* (1987) (unconstitutional to impose presumptive sentence under guidelines that was higher than presumptive sentence in effect at time of crime); *Weaver v. Graham* (1981) (unconstitutional to decrease rate at which good-time credits accumulate after the date of defendant's crime). Consequently, the Minnesota sentencing guidelines provide that changes in the guidelines only apply to offenders who committed their crimes on or after the date that the changes went into effect.

Not all sentencing guidelines yield the advantages mentioned earlier. The federal sentencing guidelines in particular have been the subject of harsh criticism. One criticism leveled against them is that they are based on the incorrect premise that incarceration is the only form of tough punishment. As a result, the majority of federal prisoners are in prison for nonviolent crimes even though many of these offenders could be punished effectively, and much more cheaply, in a comprehensive community corrections system.

Another fundamental problem with the federal sentencing guidelines is that they were drafted without regard to available prison resources. The result has been an explosion in the number of federal offenders now sent to prison and an enormous financial burden on the taxpayers forced to pay the costs of building and operating the new prisons needed to accommodate this influx of prisoners.

Even those sentencing guidelines that were drafted with an eye towards available prison resources and which carefully establish priorities in the use of those resources are not, however, problem-free. The Minnesota sentencing guidelines, for example, define when offenders should generally be imprisoned and for how long. They do not, however, guide judges in the exercise of their discretion when imposing community-based sanctions on offenders. The end result is disparity in the sentences of offenders serving their sentences in the community. One offender may, for example, receive a probation sentence of one length while another almost identical offender is placed on probation for a much longer or shorter period of time.

One way in which to alleviate this problem is through the use of non-imprisonment guidelines that employ what are called sanctioning units. Kay Knapp, the former director of the Minnesota Sentencing Guidelines Commission, has described how a sanction units exchange system would work:

Such an approach rests on the development of two concepts: (1) sanctioning levels; and (2) exchange rates. The first concept, sanctioning level, is substituted in the guidelines system for the more traditional sanction. Thus, instead of defining six months imprisonment as the proper presumptive sentence for a particular category of offenders, the policy would prescribe a sanctioning level of six units (or eight or ten or twelve). The concept of exchange rates would be used to translate units into specific sanctions, such that one unit translates into 40 community service hours, or a month in jail, or two months on probation, or two weeks in residential treatment. Essentially the court would be provided with a menu of sanctions from which to fashion a sentence to meet the sanctioning level prescribed by policy.

Kay A. Knapp, "Next Step: Non–Imprisonment Guidelines," *Perspectives* 10 (American Probation and Parole Association; Winter, 1988).

The use of sanction units exchange systems would help to avert disparity in the imposition of community-based sanctions. Incorporating a broad range of sanctions into these systems would also help to ensure that judges have the flexibility they need to impose the most appropriate type of penalty on a criminal offender.

Another problem with sentencing guidelines is that prosecutors, if they do not agree with them, often try to circumvent them. They may, for example, charge a defendant with a different crime than a defendant might normally be charged with in order to avoid a presumptive sentence that they believe is too high.

One way to curtail the effects of this exercise of prosecutorial discretion is to base the presumptive sentence on the "real offense" rather than the offense of conviction. The sentence imposed for the "real offense," however, cannot exceed the maximum sentence for the offense of conviction.

One criticism of "real-offense" sentencing concerns its practical effects; sentencing hearings can become bogged down as judges, during those hearings, try to determine what crimes defendants actually committed. More fundamentally, critics have charged that "real-offense" sentencing denigrates the importance of criminal trials and generates perceptions of unfairness as defendants are sentenced based on criminal conduct with which they have not even been charged and of which they may even have been acquitted. Because of these problems with "real-offense" sentencing, other ways are being devised to limit prosecutors' ability to circumvent sentencing guidelines. One of those ways is through the use of prosecutorial guidelines which circumscribe prosecutors' discretion when they file charges and engage in plea bargaining.

CHAPTER 6

THE DEATH PENALTY

Few areas of criminal justice have prompted as much controversy and debate as the death penalty. Is the death penalty constitutional and if so, in what circumstances? And even if it is constitutional, when, if ever, should society ever resort to the imposition of this penalty?

In 1972, the Supreme Court in *Furman v. Georgia* (1972) struck down Georgia's death-penalty statute. The Court held that the statute violated the eighth amendment's prohibition of cruel and unusual punishments since it left the decision whether or not to impose the death penalty within the unconfined discretion of the sentencing judge or jury. The end result was such arbitrary imposition of the death penalty that those individuals who received the death penalty could not readily be distinguished from those who did not.

After *Furman*, states across the country, including Georgia, scrambled to enact death-penalty statutes that would pass constitutional muster. In *Gregg v. Georgia* (1976), the Supreme Court was asked to decide whether Georgia had succeeded in achieving this objective. The Court first, however, addressed the threshold question of whether the death penalty can ever be constitutional for the crime of murder.

In answering this question, the Supreme Court said that it must begin by presuming that a penalty selected by the legislature is constitutional. A "heavy burden," the Court observed, rests on those who seek to rebut this presumption. Ultimately, the Court concluded that this burden had not been met in this case. In other words, the death penalty is not *per se* unconstitutional.

In the course of arriving at this conclusion, the Court first examined whether the death penalty contravenes society's "evolving standards of decency." The Court concluded that it did not, citing several reasons for this conclusion.

First, from the text of the Constitution, it is evident that the framers of the Constitution had contemplated that death would be imposed as a penalty for some crimes. The due process clauses in the fifth and fourteenth amendments, for example, require that due process be afforded individuals deprived of "*life*, liberty, or property." In addition, the fifth amendment's double jeopardy prohibition refers to persons being placed in jeopardy twice of "*life* or limb," and the same amendment commands that indictments be obtained in "capital" cases.

Second, the Supreme Court cited the history of the death penalty—its long acceptance, up through the present, as a penalty for murder. In fact, under the common law, the mandatory penalty for murder was death.

Third, the Court noted the response of state legislatures to *Furman*. When it became apparent from *Furman* that death-penalty statutes throughout the country were unconstitutional, a wave of new death-penalty legislation, as mentioned earlier, was enacted. At least thirty-five states enacted new death-penalty laws, a strong indicator, in the Court's mind, that the death penalty in some circumstances comports with societal standards of decency.

Fourth, the Court mentioned the results of public-opinion surveys that revealed that a majority of Americans favor the death penalty. In a dissenting opinion though, Justice Marshall rejoined that support for the death penalty diminishes substantially when the public is fully informed about the penalty and its consequences. In other words, the views of an informed public vary greatly from those of an uninformed public.

Finally, the Court relied on the willingness of juries to sometimes return verdicts of death as another indicator that the death penalty does not inherently conflict with societal standards of decency.

Concluding that the death penalty for murder does not conflict with societal standards of decency did not, however, end the Supreme Court's analysis under the eighth amendment. The Court noted that even if the death penalty comported with societal standards of decency as reflected by such objective indicators as the statutes enacted by legislatures and the sentencing practices of juries, the death penalty would still be unconstitutional if it was "excessive." The Court essentially was saying that while the opinion of legislatures would be given great weight when assessing the constitutionality of a penalty, their opinions would not, and could not, be conclusive if the cruel and unusual punishment clause, which was designed to serve as a check on the penchant of legislatures to sometimes overreact to the problem of crime, is to have any meaning.

According to the Supreme Court in *Gregg v. Georgia*, the death penalty would be unconstitutionally excessive if it involved the "unnecessary and wanton infliction of pain" or was a grossly disproportionate penalty for the crime committed. The dissenters argued that the death penalty in fact constituted the unnecessary and wanton infliction of pain since there was a viable and less drastic alternative way of punishing murderers other than killing them—confining them for the rest of their lives in prison. The majority responded, however, that there is no least-drastic-alternative requirement subsumed within the eighth amendment. The death penalty would therefore only be considered the unnecessary and wanton infliction of pain if it was so devoid of any penological justification as to constitute the "gratuitous infliction of suffering."

According to the Supreme Court, this requirement was not met though because three penological objectives are furthered or arguably furthered by the death penalty. The first is retribution. Some people, the Court observed, might legitimately feel that death is the only appropriate penalty for certain particularly opprobrious crimes.

The second penological objective served by the death penalty that the Court alluded to is incapacitation. Simply put, once people are dead, they can and will commit no further crimes.

Finally, the Court noted the argued deterrent function of the death penalty—using the prospect of death as a punishment to dissuade people from committing murders. Although the Court acknowledged that the empirical evidence regarding the death penalty's claimed deterrent effects is inconclusive, the Court refused to discount this penological objective as a reason for upholding the death penalty, saying that it was up to legislatures to resolve the questions concerning whether the death penalty is an effective deterrent.

The Supreme Court ended its eighth amendment analysis of the generic question—can the death penalty ever be constitutionally imposed for the crime of murder—by concluding that the penalty is not grossly disproportionate in every case involving the deliberate taking of a life. The Court then turned to the question of whether the death-penalty statute before the Court was constitutional.

The Supreme Court answered this question in the affirmative. The Court held that this statute, unlike the statute that the Court struck down in *Furman v. Georgia*, contained safeguards that, in the Court's view, were adequate to prevent the arbitrary and capricious imposition of death as a penalty for the crime of murder. Particularly significant to the Court was the way in which the statute circumscribed the discretion of the sentencing jury or judge by requiring that the sentencer find beyond a reasonable doubt that at least one of ten aggravating factors delineated in the statute existed before the death penalty could be imposed. The Court also emphasized the presence of another procedural safeguard designed to avert the arbitrary imposition of the death penalty—automatic review by the Georgia Supreme Court of all death sentences.

Although the Supreme Court in *Gregg v. Georgia* seemed confident that the death-penalty statute in Georgia was crafted in a way to avoid the arbitrary and capricious imposition of death sentences, statistics presented to the Court in a subsequent case revealed that there is racial disparity in the implementation of that statute. In *McCleskey v. Kemp* (1987), the Supreme Court considered the constitutional implications of a study that found that black defendants convicted of murder in Georgia were more likely to receive the death penalty than defendants who were white. The study also found that the race of the victim had a bearing on the likelihood of receiving a death sentence; defendants whose victims were white were much more likely to receive the death penalty than defendants whose victims were black. The death penalty was imposed in 22% of the murder cases involving a black defendant and a white victim, 8% of the cases involving a white defendant and a white victim, 3% of the cases involving a white defendant and a black victim, and only 1% of the cases in which both the defendant and the victim were black.

The defendant in *McCleskey*, a black man sentenced to death for killing a white police officer, argued that the above statistics confirmed that racial discrimination permeated the capital punishment system in Georgia in violation of the fourteenth amendment's guarantee of equal protection of the law and the eighth amendment's prohibition of cruel and unusual punishments. The Supreme Court, however, in a 5–4 decision, concluded that the defendant's right to be accorded the equal protection of the law had not been violated, since there was no evidence that the jury in this particular case had imposed the death penalty because of the defendant's race or the race of his victim. Nor was there any evidence that the Georgia legislature had acted with the intent to discriminate against blacks when enacting the death-penalty statute.

The absence of proof that race had been a factor in the jury's decision in this particular case to return a death sentence was also cited by the Court in rejecting the defendant's cruel and unusual punishment claim. The Court furthermore rejected the argument that there was unconstitutional arbitrariness in the imposition of death sentences in Georgia because of the demonstrated risk that racial bias plays a role in juries' decisions whether or not to sentence a defendant to death. After noting that there were many procedural safeguards within

Georgia's capital punishment system whose purpose was to avert arbitrariness in the imposition of the death penalty, the Court summarily concluded that the statistical risk that the death penalty was imposed because of the defendant's or the victim's race was not "constitutionally significant."

This observation of the Court prompted a sharp rebuke from Justice Brennan. In his dissenting opinion, Justice Brennan noted that for every eleven defendants in Georgia sentenced to death for killing a white person, only five would have received the death penalty if their victims had been black. He argued, "Surely we would not be willing to take a person's life if the risk that his death was irrationally imposed is *more* likely than not."

Concerns about the arbitrary imposition of the death penalty have prompted the Supreme Court to strike down death-penalty statutes whose language is unconstitutionally vague. *See, e.g., Maynard v. Cartwright* (1988) (statute treating murder that was "especially heinous, atrocious, or cruel" as an aggravating factor was unconstitutionally vague). Similar concerns have led the Court to hold unconstitutional death-penalty statutes that mandate the imposition of the death penalty for certain crimes. In *Woodson v. North Carolina* (1976), the Supreme Court cited three reasons why a mandatory death-penalty statute for first-degree murder was unconstitutional under the eighth amendment. First, the mandatory death-penalty statute, according to the Court, conflicted with societal standards of decency. Although the Court acknowledged that at common law, the mandatory penalty for murder was death, the Court basically said that times have changed. As an indicator of current societal values, the Court pointed to the frequent decisions of juries in jurisdictions with mandatory death-penalty statutes to acquit murderers to avoid having them subjected to a penalty which, under the circumstances, is too extreme. The Court furthermore underscored that in jurisdictions with discretionary death-penalty statutes, juries decide that the death-penalty is not appropriate in the vast majority of capital-murder cases.

The Supreme Court also cited the movement away from mandatory death-penalty statutes as an indicator of societal standards of decency. By 1963, no state mandated death for the crime of murder. While it was true that some states had resurrected the practice of mandating death for certain crimes after the Supreme Court decided *Furman v. Georgia* in 1972, the Supreme Court viewed these legislative enactments as rather frantic attempts by the states to comport with the dictates of Furman rather than as a newfound endorsement of mandatory death sentences.

The Supreme Court's second reason for holding that the mandatory death-penalty statute in *Woodson* violated the eighth amendment was that the statute, despite its mandatory character, as a practical matter left the decision whether or not to impose the death penalty within the unbridled discretion of the jury. This problem of unchanneled jury discretion stemmed from the phenomenon mentioned earlier of juries acquitting some defendants, but not others, to avoid imposition of the death penalty. The end result was arbitrariness in the selection of those defendants who would be put to death for their crimes.

The third constitutional defect identified in the mandatory death-penalty statute in *Woodson* was that it abridged the right of defendants, under the eighth amendment, to an individualized sentencing determination in a capital case. The mandatory death-penalty statute lumped all first-degree murderers into an amorphous mass, treating all of them as deserving of death. The Supreme Court said in *Woodson* that the "fundamental respect for humanity" that undergirds the eighth amendment instead requires that juries be permitted to consider the individuality of defendants in capital cases—their personal attributes, their backgrounds, and the circumstances of their crimes that counsel against imposing the death penalty.

Since *Woodson*, the Supreme Court has struck down other mandatory death-penalty statutes. *See, e.g., Sumner v. Shuman* (1987) (mandatory death sentence for a murder committed when serving a life sentence without possibility of parole is unconstitutional); *Roberts v. Louisiana* (1977) (mandatory death sentence for murdering a police officer violates the eighth amendment). Having some type of mandatory component in a death-penalty statute does not always, however, give rise to the constitutional problems flagged by the Court in Woodson and its progeny. For example, in *Blystone v. Penn-*

sylvania (1990), the Supreme Court upheld a death-penalty statute that required the imposition of the death penalty when a sentencing jury found that aggravating circumstances in a case outweighed any mitigating circumstances.

In each of the cases in which the Supreme Court has held a mandatory death-penalty statute unconstitutional, the Court has emphasized the right of defendants to bring to the attention of the sentencer any mitigating circumstances that might demonstrate that imposition of a death sentence is unwarranted. *See also Hitchcock v. Dugger* (1987) (defendant has the right to introduce evidence of mitigating circumstances not listed in the death-penalty statute). Some Justices on the Supreme Court have contended that there is an irreconcilable conflict between the eighth amendment requirement that sentencing discretion in capital cases be circumscribed to prevent the arbitrary imposition of the death penalty and the requirement that sentencing be individualized, with expansive consideration by the sentencer of mitigating circumstances, to ensure that only those individuals who deserve to die for their crimes receive the death penalty. The Justices, however, have varied in their views on how the Court should respond to this conflict. After many years of supporting the death penalty, Justice Blackmun, shortly before retiring from the Court, called on the Court to declare the death penalty *per se* unconstitutional and end its futile quest to reconcile the competing goals of avoiding arbitrariness while at the same time providing for individual fairness in the imposition of the death penalty. *Callins v. Collins* (1994) (Blackmun, J., dissenting). Justice Scalia, on the other hand, has urged the Court to simply abandon the requirement that sentencers be permitted to consider an unlimited array of mitigating circumstances in capital cases. *Walton v. Arizona* (1990) (Scalia, J., concurring).

While the Supreme Court has held that the eighth amendment prohibits legislatures from defining certain types of crimes for which the death penalty must be imposed, the Court has identified certain instances when the death penalty can never be imposed. One of those instances is when an individual has been convicted of raping, but not murdering, an adult. In *Coker v. Georgia* (1977), the Supreme Court held that no matter how vicious and injurious a rape, the death penalty for rape is disproportionate to the severity of the crime since it does not involve the taking of a human life. The Court added that its conclusion that the death penalty was an unconstitutionally disproportionate penalty for raping an adult was buttressed by the fact that only one state authorized the death penalty for raping an adult (two others authorized the death penalty for raping a child), that juries in the state of Georgia rarely sentenced rapists to death, and that very few countries in the world authorized the death penalty for rape.

Although the Supreme Court has ruled that the death penalty for rape, at least for rape of an adult, is unconstitutional because the victim is not killed, according to the Supreme Court, a defendant need not actually be the person who killed a victim in order for imposition of the death penalty to be constitutional. In *Tison v. Arizona* (1987), the Supreme Court considered the constitutionality of the death sentences of two brothers who had smuggled guns into a prison and then used them to help their father and another prisoner escape. The father and the other prisoner later shot and killed four people who had stopped to help them when their car broke down. The two brothers were convicted of capital murder under the state's felony-murder statute as well as a statute which held certain felons responsible for crimes committed by their accomplices.

The Supreme Court, in a 5–4 decision, upheld these death sentences, noting that the brothers' participation in "the felony" was "major" and that they had acted with "reckless indifference to human life" by helping to effectuate a prison escape that they knew posed "a grave risk of death." The Court distinguished the case before it from *Enmund v. Florida* (1982), a case where the Court had struck down the death sentence imposed on a defendant who had driven the getaway car in an armed robbery, but had not killed the two murder victims. The defendant in *Enmund*, according to the Court, had played only a minor role in the armed robbery and murders, and there was no finding that he had acted with the intent that the victims be killed or with reckless disregard that such loss of life might ensue.

The Supreme Court has addressed the constitutional significance of a number of other factors in the death-penalty context. In *Penry v. Lynaugh* (1989), for example, the Court considered the constitutionality of putting to death a man, with the mental capacity of a six-year-old, who had raped and murdered a woman. The Court held, in a 5–4 decision, that just because the defendant was mentally retarded did not necessarily mean that imposition of the death penalty constituted cruel and unusual punishment. The defendant's mental capacity was rather simply one mitigating factor that could and should be considered by the sentencer when deciding whether imposition of the death penalty was warranted.

The Supreme Court has, however, treated the chronological age of a defendant somewhat differently than the defendant's mental capacity. In *Thompson v. Oklahoma* (1988), the Court considered whether defendants who were fifteen or younger when they committed their crimes could constitutionally be sentenced to death. Four Justices on the Court concluded that they could not. They explained first that the death penalty for fifteen-year-olds violated societal standards of decency, since no state which specified the age below which the death penalty could not be imposed authorized the death penalty for defendants who were that young at the time of their crimes. In addition, these four Justices opined that imposing the death penalty on such youthful defendants would constitute the constitutionally proscribed unnecessary and wanton infliction of pain. In their opinion, the prospect of death does not deter such young people from committing crimes since people, at that age, are prone to acting impulsively and rashly. The goal of retribution also does not, in the opinion of these Justices, justify the imposition of the death penalty because juveniles, due to their immaturity, are not as culpable for their crimes as adults.

Whether the death penalty is always unconstitutional when imposed on a defendant who was fifteen or younger at the time of a crime's commission is still a bit in doubt because of the qualifying points inserted by Justice O'Connor in her concurring opinion, which provided the fifth vote for invalidating the defendant's death sentence in *Thompson*. Justice O'Connor was actually not sure that there was a national consensus against imposing the death penalty on defendants who were fifteen or younger when they committed their crimes. In the face of such uncertainty, she believed that the death penalty was unconstitutional when a state's death-penalty statute, like the one in Oklahoma, did not specifically authorize imposing death sentences on defendants of such a young age.

Just a year after its decision in *Thompson*, the Supreme Court held that the death penalty can constitutionally be imposed on defendants who were sixteen or seventeen when they committed their crimes. *Stanford v. Kentucky* (1989). The Court acknowledged the infrequency with which defendants of that age are sentenced to death, just as it had pointed in *Coker v. Georgia* to the infrequency with which rapists were sentenced to death. But unlike in *Coker*, the Court in *Stanford* dismissed the significance of the infrequency with which the death sentences were imposed, saying that the very reasons why the defendants argued that the death penalty could never constitutionally be imposed on sixteen and seventeen-year-olds explained why prosecutors rarely sought, and juries infrequently imposed, the death penalty on such defendants.

Even when it is constitutional to impose the death penalty on a defendant, circumstances may develop that preclude, for constitutional reasons, the execution of that sentence. In *Ford v. Wainwright* (1986), the Supreme Court held that executing an insane person would constitute cruel and unusual punishment. In discussing why the execution of insane prisoners has not garnered support in the states, the Court noted that there are doubts about whether the death penalty can serve its retributive aim when the individuals being executed are so mentally deranged that they cannot understand why they are being killed. In addition, the Court acknowledged the religious roots of the opposition to the execution of the insane—the belief that people should only be executed after they have had a chance to ask God to forgive them for their sins.

CHAPTER 7

CRUEL AND UNUSUAL PUNISHMENT AND NONCAPITAL CASES

In the noncapital context, cruel and unusual punishment claims have generally focused on the alleged gross disproportionality of a penalty to the severity of the crime of which a defendant was convicted. In *Rummel v. Estelle* (1980), the Supreme Court confronted such a claim. The defendant in that case was sentenced to life in prison under a Texas recidivist statute that mandated a life sentence upon conviction of a third felony. The defendant's first felony conviction was for obtaining $80 worth of goods or services through the fraudulent use of a credit card. His second felony conviction was for forging a check worth $28.36, and his third was for obtaining $120.75 by false pretenses.

Rebuffing the defendant's claim that his life sentence constituted cruel and unusual punishment, the Supreme Court, in a 5–4 decision, dismissed the significance of an array of factors to which the defendant pointed in support of his claim. First, the defendant underscored that all of his crimes were nonviolent. The Court, however, responded that society can have a strong interest in deterring or punishing crimes that are nonviolent in nature. As examples of serious, but nonviolent crimes, the Court cited bribery, antitrust violations, and the violation of clean air or water standards by the head of a large corporation.

Second, the defendant reminded the Court that his crimes had involved only a "small" amount of money. The Supreme Court responded though that what is a small or a large amount of money is a question which is best remitted to the legislature. In addition, the Court noted that there was another state interest at stake here other than the interest in punishing those who unlawfully acquire the property of others—the interest in punishing more severely those individuals who repeatedly flout the law.

Third, the defendant pointed to the unusual severity of his penalty compared to the way in which other states punish three-time felons. The Supreme Court did not consider this factor of any import either though. The Court noted that many states only varied slightly from Texas in the way in which they punished repeat offenders. The Court also cited the difficulty of comparing sentencing statutes in different states because the states vary widely in their parole practices and the granting of good-time credits. In other words, comparing the sentences imposed in different jurisdictions can be misleading because there are often substantial differences between the sentences imposed on individuals and the sentences actually served. For example, while the defendant in this case had received a life sentence, he would become eligible for parole after serving twelve years in prison.

The Supreme Court's central response to the defendant's citation to the sentencing practices of other states, however, was that even if a state punishes a crime more severely than any other state, that fact does not mean that the punishment is cruel and unusual. A state has the prerogative, observed the Court, to view the severity of a crime differently than other states. In the Court's words, "[a]bsent a constitutionally imposed uniformity inimical to traditional notions of federalism," there will almost always be one state which punishes a particular crime more severely than any other state.

The Supreme Court also dismissed the defendant's argument that a comparison of how Texas punished criminals who have committed other crimes is relevant to the question of whether a grossly disproportionate penalty had been imposed on the defendant. The Court said that comparing the penalties for different crimes is a meaningless exercise, since different crimes can implicate quite different societal interests.

In *Hutto v. Davis* (1982), the Supreme Court followed *Rummel's* lead and cursorily rejected the defendant's eighth amendment disproportionality claim. The defendant in *Hutto* had been sentenced to prison for a total of forty years for the possession and distribution of about nine ounces of marijuana. The Supreme Court, however, reiterated that it was reluctant, except in an "exceedingly rare" case, to usurp the legislative prerogative to define the penal sanction to be imposed for a crime.

The Supreme Court's handling of the disproportionality claims in *Rummel v. Estelle* and *Hutto v. Davis* is to be contrasted with the result and analysis in *Solem v. Helm* (1983). The defendant in *Solem* had also, like the defendant in *Rummel*, received a life sentence under a recidivist statute, although the life sentence was without the possibility of parole. The defendant in *Solem*, however, had been convicted of many more felonies than the defendant in *Rummel*—seven, and his convictions were for seemingly more serious crimes—three third-degree burglaries, a third-offense drunk driving, grand larceny, obtaining money under false pretenses, and writing a bad check for $100. The Supreme Court in *Solem* nonetheless concluded, in another 5–4 decision, that the defendant's life sentence constituted cruel and unusual punishment.

Solem and *Rummel* can be reconciled on their facts, since, as mentioned earlier, the life sentence in *Solem*, unlike the life sentence in *Rummel*, was without the possibility of parole. What is more difficult to square is the Supreme Court's analysis in *Solem* of the factors that the Court said bear on the resolution of an eighth amendment disproportionality claim and its dismissal of these same factors in *Rummel* as irrelevant.

In *Solem*, the Supreme Court set forth a three-part analysis to be undertaken by courts considering eighth amendment disproportionality claims. First, a court should consider the severity of the crime and the harshness of the penalty that was imposed for the crime. In assessing the severity of the crime, the Supreme Court in *Solem*, in seeming contradiction with what it had said earlier in *Rummel*, counselled courts to consider the "absolute magnitude" of the crime—how much money, for example, a defendant had stolen—and whether the crime involved violence or the threat of violence. The Court mentioned other factors that bear either on the harm caused or threatened by the defendant or the defendant's culpability, including: whether a crime was a lesser-included offense or the greater offense, whether the defendant had attempted or completed the crime, what the defendant's state of mind was when committing the crime—whether negligent, reckless, knowing, intentional, or malicious, and what the defendant's motive was.

The second and third components identified by the Supreme Court in *Solem* as relevant to an eighth amendment disproportionality analysis had likewise been discounted by the Court in *Rummel*— the sentences imposed within the state for other crimes and the sentences imposed in other jurisdictions for the crime of which the defendant had been convicted. Yet despite the conflict between the Court's analysis in *Solem* and its analysis in *Rummel v. Estelle*, the Court rejected the opportunity in Solem to overrule its decision in *Rummel*.

In *Harmelin v. Michigan* (1991), the Supreme Court was presented with the opportunity to eliminate the confusion engendered by its opinions in *Rummel* and *Solem*. Instead, the Court rendered, once again, another 5–4 decision, with no view on what is the appropriate eighth amendment disproportionality analysis commanding majority support on the Court.

The defendant in *Harmelin* had received a life sentence after being convicted of possessing 672 grams of cocaine. The defendant's conviction was his first, but the statute under which he was sentenced mandated life imprisonment without parole for possession of more than 650 grams of cocaine.

A majority of the Court rejected the defendant's claim that his sentence was unconstitutionally disproportionate to the severity of the crime of which he was found guilty, but the Justices split as to their reasoning. Two of the Justices—Justice Scalia, joined by Chief Justice Rehnquist—insisted that there is not even a proportionality principle in the eighth amendment that governs prison sentences. Based on Justice Scalia's interpretation of the history of the eighth amendment, he argued that the eighth amendment is concerned with the kinds of penalties imposed for crimes rather than with the extent to which those penalties, or at least prison sentences, have been calibrated with the crimes for which they are imposed. In addition, Justice Scalia cited the text of the eighth amendment as support for his position that there is no disproportionality principle subsumed within it that encompasses prison sentences. The eighth amendment, he pointed out, specifically proscribes "excessive fines," but says nothing about excessive prison sentences. Justice Scalia, however, conceded that despite this silence, there is still a proportionality requirement in the eighth amendment that has to be met in a capital case because "death is different."

In a dissenting opinion joined by Justices Blackmun, Stevens, and Marshall, Justice White chastised Justice Scalia for what Justice White considered his skewed reading of the eighth amendment. Justice White wondered how the same words, "cruel and unusual," could mean one thing in the capital context and another thing in the noncapital context; grossly disproportionate sentences, he argued, were either unconstitutional or they were not.

Justice White also ridiculed the notion that the proscription in the eighth amendment of "excessive" fines somehow implied that excessive prison sentences were constitutional. Not only was this reading of the Constitution, in Justice White's opinion, illogical, but in his opinion, it demanded clarity and specificity in the language of the Constitution that were not the norm. As examples of the obfuscatory language that is to be found in much of the Constitution, Justice White cited the requirements of "due process of law" and the fourth amendment's prohibition of "unreasonable searches and seizures."

Justice Kennedy, joined by Justices O'Connor and Souter, upheld the defendant's sentence in *Solem* for another reason. Unlike Justice Scalia, Justice Kennedy believed that there is a proportionality principle in the eighth amendment, although a "narrow" one, that governs prison sentences. Justice Kennedy simply felt though that in this case, that principle had been adhered to; in other words, the defendant's sentence was not "grossly disproportionate" to the crime of which he was found guilty.

What was most significant about Justice Kennedy's opinion was the way in which he suggested the *Solem* balancing test should be applied. In his opinion, the second and third factors of that test— the intra- and interjurisdictional sentencing practices—should be examined by a court only in the unusual case when the first factor supports an inference of "gross disproportionality." And in this case, Justice Kennedy opined, a comparison of the gravity of the crime with the harshness of the penalty imposed did not create such an inference because of the tremendous harm to society caused by drug use, including drug-related violence.

In his dissenting opinion, Justice White strongly objected to Justice Kennedy's description of the severity of the defendant's crime in this case. Justice White argued that the defendant was no more responsible for all of the adverse consequences that stem from drug use than those who sell alcohol are responsible for all of the adverse effects that attend the abuse of alcohol. Justice White furthermore underscored that the defendant had only been convicted of possession of the cocaine, not possession with the intent to distribute, and that he was a first-time offender.

More fundamentally, Justice White disagreed with the twist given by Justice Kennedy to the *Solem* balancing test. How, Justice White queried, is a court supposed to objectively assess how grave a crime is compared to the harshness of the penalty imposed without looking at sentencing practices both within and without the jurisdiction?

When Justice White then applied the full *Solem* balancing test to the facts of the case before the Court, he concluded that the defendant's life sentence without the possibility of parole was unconstitutionally disproportionate. In addition to his observation mentioned earlier about the gravity of the defendant's crime, Justice White also cited the following factors as support for his conclusion: the fact that the defendant's sentence was the harshest that could be imposed in the state, since Michigan has no death penalty; the fact that not even second-degree murderers, rapists, or armed robbers had to be sent to prison for life in Michigan; and the fact that no other state punished a crime like the defendant's as harshly.

Interestingly, while the defendant in *Harmelin* failed to prevail in the Supreme Court on his federal constitutional claim based on the alleged disproportionality of his sentence, the statute under which he was convicted was later struck down by the Michigan Supreme Court as violative of the state constitution. *People v. Bullock* (1992). The Michigan Supreme Court explained that the ban under the state constitution of "cruel or unusual" punishments was broader than the proscription of "cruel and unusual" punishments in the eighth amendment.

There was another issue before the Supreme Court in *Harmelin v. Michigan* that managed to command a majority view on the Court. The defendant in *Harmelin* had argued that the mandatory nature of his sentence made his sentence unconstitutional. He contended that, as in the death-penalty context, he had the right to individualized sentencing. The issue raised by the defendant had significant national implications because of the large number of mandatory-minimum sentencing statutes that have been enacted in recent years as part of the drive to "get tough" on crime.

A majority of the Court—Justice Scalia and Chief Justice Rehnquist in one opinion, and Justices Kennedy, O'Connor, and Souter in another—noted, however, that death is different from other criminal sanctions and that therefore a mandatory prison sentence is not inherently unconstitutional. Justice Kennedy specifically left open the possibility, however, of a prison sentence violating the eighth amendment because of its mandatory nature, but he cautioned that this would occur "only in the most extreme circumstance."

*

PART TWO

THE LAW OF CORRECTIONS AND PRISONERS' RIGHTS

CHAPTER 8

PRISONERS' RIGHTS: AN INTRODUCTION

In 1974, the Supreme Court announced in *Wolff v. McDonnell* (1974) that "[t]here is no iron curtain drawn between the Constitution and the prisons of this country." To some people, this statement is heretical. "Prisoners should have no rights," they argue. Yet when pressed, these individuals will generally acknowledge that inmates should be afforded some rights. They should, for example, be fed, be provided with medical care, and be permitted to engage in certain religious practices, such as reading the Bible or the Koran. So the real question is not whether inmates do or should have constitutional rights, but rather what is the scope of those rights.

A. HISTORY OF PRISONERS' RIGHTS— A GENERAL OVERVIEW

It is helpful when discussing the subject of the scope of prisoners' rights to explore the evolution of courts' views on this subject. The opinion of the Court of Appeals of Virginia in *Ruffin v. Commonwealth* (1871) typifies the view about prisoners' rights that first prevailed in this country. In that case, the court described prisoners as "slaves of the State." The Court observed that prisoners had no rights; any rights that they once had were forfeited while they were incarcerated as part of the price they had to pay for their crimes.

The early to mid–1900s marked a subtle shift in courts' views about inmates' rights. Most courts no longer insisted that inmates had no rights. Instead, the courts said that while inmates might have rights, it was not within the courts' province to enforce those rights. Rather, the enforcement of prisoners' rights was the responsibility of the legislative and executive branches of the government.

The courts gave several reasons for embracing what is commonly known as the "hands-off doctrine." First, the courts relied on the notion of separation of powers, arguing that judicial enforcement of inmates' rights would interfere with the operation of prisons by the legislative and executive branches of the government. Second, the courts pointed to the principle of federalism entrenched in the Constitution, expressing the concern that federal courts' commands to state officials to respect the constitutional rights of prisoners would unduly encroach on the authority of the states to run their prisons.

Third, the courts observed that judicial involvement in the operation of prisons might jeopardize institutional security and frustrate the goals of incarceration. The judges recognized that they lacked correctional expertise, and they were also concerned that the prospect of liability might sometimes dissuade prison officials from taking the steps needed to protect institutional security, with resultant harm to people and property within the prisons. The courts furthermore recognized the security problems that would accompany prisoners' lawsuits, as prisoners, who were parties or witnesses in those lawsuits, were shuffled to and from court.

A final reason for the courts' adoption of the hands-off doctrine was the concern that opening the litigation spigot would result in the courts being flooded with prisoners' complaints, many of which would, no doubt, be frivolous. Not only would these lawsuits be a hassle for the courts to deal with, but they would clog up the court system, impeding the adjudication of other legitimate claims.

During the 1960s and '70s, the courts retreated from the view that prisoners' lawsuits are to be shunned and began to acknowledge that courts not only have the power, but the duty to resolve the constitutional claims of prisoners. Several developments contributed to this shift in the courts' perspective.

First, the '60s were a time of turmoil in this country—a time of war protests, ghetto riots, and assassinations. Prisons were not insulated from this turmoil. As prisoners, particularly black Muslim prisoners, became more militant and assertive, their claims became harder for the courts to ignore.

Second, as a cadre of lawyers committed to civil rights doggedly pursued the goals of improving conditions in the nation's prisons and vindicating inmates' constitutional rights, the horrendous conditions in many prisons came to light, making it difficult for the courts to adhere to the view that they could trust the executive and legislative branches of the government to respect the constitutional rights of prisoners. It became even more difficult to rely on this assumption when riots swept through some of the nation's prisons during this time, particularly the riot in 1971 at the Attica State Prison in Attica, New York that resulted in the deaths of forty-three people.

Another significant development was the change in the composition of the Supreme Court. Compared to the Court in earlier years, the "Warren Court," named after the Chief Justice who headed the Court during this time, was an activist Court. The "Warren Court" was prone to broadly interpreting the Constitution and committed to extending the protection of the Constitution to disfavored minorities, including persons accused of crimes and prisoners. It was during this era that the Supreme Court rendered such landmark decisions as *Miranda v. Arizona* (1966) (*Miranda* warnings must precede custodial interrogation) and *Mapp v. Ohio* (1961) (fourth amendment exclusionary rule applies to the states).

Some developments in the law also contributed to the disintegration of the hands-off doctrine. First, in *Monroe v. Pape* (1961), the Supreme Court removed a legal roadblock that had stood in the way of prisoners wanting to file civil rights suits under 42 U.S.C.A. § 1983. In *Monroe*, the Supreme Court clarified the meaning of the requirement in 42 U.S.C.A. § 1983 that government officials must have acted "under color of" a state statute, ordinance, regulation, custom, or usage for a constitutional claim to be cognizable under § 1983. *Monroe v. Pape* involved a § 1983 suit brought by several individuals whose home was searched by police officers without a warrant. The state constitution as well as several state statutes prohibited the actions undertaken by the police officers. Nonetheless, the Supreme Court held that the under-color-of-state-law requirement of § 1983 could be met even if a state law actually prohibited the actions of the government officials that had allegedly violated the Constitution. The Court noted that § 1983 was enacted to provide a federal remedy for the violation of constitutional rights in large part because the states, in the post-Civil War era, often looked the other way when confronted with violations of the law. The Court therefore concluded that the under-color-of-state-law requirement is met as long as a constitutional violation stems from the " '[m]isuse of power, possessed by virtue of state law and made possible only because the wrongdoer is clothed with the authority of state law.' "

The second significant legal development that opened the courts to prisoners' civil rights suits occurred in a series of cases in which the Supreme Court held that certain constitutional provisions that apply to the federal government also apply to the states via the due process clause of the fourteenth amendment. A particularly important case for prisoners was *Robinson v. California* (1962), which held that the eighth amendment prohibition against cruel and unusual punishments extends to the states.

The Supreme Court has now recognized that prisoners have an array of constitutional rights. These rights include the right to freedom of speech, the right to religious freedom, the right to marry, the right to have access to the courts, the right to equal protection of the law, due process rights, and the right not to be subjected to cruel and unusual punishments. At the same time, however, vestiges of the hands-off doctrine remain. In a number of cases, the Supreme Court has emphasized the deference due the assessments of correctional officials as to what is needed to protect institutional security and further correctional goals. This deference, in turn, has led to decisions narrowly interpreting the scope of prisoners' constitutional rights.

B. THE PURPOSES OF INCARCERATION

Since the scope of prisoners' constitutional rights is not only dependent on the demands of institutional security but also on the purposes of incarceration, it is important to define what those purposes are. Traditionally, correctional policymakers and experts have referred to four principal purposes of incarceration—incapacitation, deterrence, rehabilitation, and retribution. These four goals, which are briefly defined below, are discussed in greater depth in Chapter 1 on pages 2 through 8.

One purpose of incarceration is incapacitation. Certain criminal offenders are incarcerated simply to prevent them, while they are incarcerated, from being able to commit further crimes against the public.

The second touted purpose of incarceration is deterrence—dissuading the future commission of crimes. This deterrent objective has two facets to it—specific and general deterrence. The aim of specific deterrence is to discourage the individual who is incarcerated from committing additional crimes, while the focus of general deterrence is on the public. The premise of the theory of general deterrence is that members of the public will refrain from criminal conduct when they see how others are punished for their misdeeds.

The third reason sometimes cited for incarceration is rehabilitation. The rehabilitative rationale for incarceration is premised on the assumption that by participating in treatment and other programs while in prison, the mores of prisoners will be changed and the underlying problems that contributed to their criminal conduct will be resolved. It is thought that prisoners will then desist from committing further crimes upon their release from prison. Critics, however, argue that the notion that incarceration can be rehabilitative is naive. They point out that the isolation and stigma that attend incarceration, as well as the criminogenic influences to which inmates are exposed while incarcerated, will counteract any beneficial effects of prison programs, assuming that such programs are even made available to the inmates in the first place.

The fourth purpose commonly cited for incarceration is retribution; people are incarcerated simply because they deserve to be incarcerated as punishment for the crimes they have committed. Many of those who subscribe to the retributive aim of criminal justice, however, also embrace the notion of "just deserts." This limiting principle calls for the imposition of punishment that is no greater than warranted by the severity of the crime of which a person has been convicted.

The chapters that follow discuss the courts' views about the scope of prisoners' constitutional rights. In reading these materials, readers are encouraged to give some thought as to what the purposes of incarceration should be and how those identified purposes should affect the scope of prisoners' constitutional rights. Just as important, thought should also be given to the policy question of the rights that should be afforded prisoners separate and apart from their rights under the United States Constitution, since states have the prerogative to extend rights to prisoners under their own constitutions, statutes, and regulations that go beyond the federal constitutional minima.

CHAPTER 9

FIRST AMENDMENT RIGHTS

A. FREEDOM OF SPEECH

The first amendment to the United States Constitution provides in part that "Congress shall make no law ... abridging the freedom of speech." The first amendment directly applies to federal officials. State and local officials, however, are also subject to the dictates of the first amendment, since it is applicable to the states via the due process clause found in the fourteenth amendment.

Perhaps no other area of law confirms more clearly the constricted scope of prisoners' rights than the first amendment area. The threshold question that had to be resolved when courts were first presented with prisoners' claims alleging abridgements of their free speech rights was whether the first amendment provides any protection at all to the communications of prisoners. The Supreme Court had the opportunity to, but ultimately did not resolve this question in *Procunier v. Martinez* (1974).

In *Procunier*, a group of prisoners challenged the constitutionality of a set of state regulations that governed the censorship of prisoner mail. One of these regulations prohibited letters in which inmates "unduly complain" or "magnify grievances."

Another prohibited writings that expressed "inflammatory political, racial, religious, or other views." And still another proscribed "otherwise inappropriate" letters.

The Supreme Court first noted the confusion that had reigned in the lower courts about the extent to which, if at all, the first amendment affords protection to the speech of prisoners. Yet the Court declined to immediately alleviate this confusion. Instead, the Court focused upon the fact that the regulations implicated the free speech interests of nonprisoners, the individuals outside prison with whom the prisoners corresponded. Under these circumstances, the Court noted, the regulations had to meet the requirements of a somewhat stringent two-part test to pass constitutional muster.

First, the regulations had to further an "important" or "substantial" governmental interest not related to the suppression of expression. In other words, the restrictions on speech had to be prompted by something other than the simple desire to suppress views with which certain government officials disagreed. The Court cited the government's interests in maintaining institutional security and order and in rehabilitating prisoners as interests that were sufficiently weighty to support restrictions on prisoners' correspondence.

Second, the regulations could not restrict the interest in unimpeded communications more than was "generally necessary" to protect any of the substantial government interests outlined above.

In discussing this least-drastic-alternative requirement, the Court noted that prison officials needed
some leeway in assessing the "probable consequences" of allowing certain speech within the volatile confines of a prison.   Therefore, they did not
have to show absolute certainty that a particular
letter would, for example, imperil institutional security to justify restrictions placed on the transmis-
sion or receipt of that letter.   A showing of a
general necessity for the restriction would suffice.
The Court furthermore noted that when assessing
the need for a particular restriction on inmate mail,
the policies of other prisons would be relevant,
though not controlling.

The Supreme Court then proceeded to apply this
two-part test to the censorship regulations before it
and concluded, for several reasons, that they were
unconstitutional.   First, the Court was not persuad-
ed that some of the regulations actually furthered
the interests invoked by the prison officials in their
defense.   For example, although the officials had
argued that limitations needed to be placed on
inmate complaints in order to prevent riots and
promote the rehabilitation of inmates, they had not,
according to the Court, explained how complaints
contained in letters sent to individuals outside a
prison could cause riots or impede the rehabilitation
of inmates.   What is significant about this portion
of the Court's opinion is that it showed that there
were limits to the deference that the Court would
accord the judgments of prison officials about what

was needed to protect institutional security or to further other important correctional goals.

The regulations also failed to pass muster under the second prong of the two-part test. The Court observed that there were other ways of achieving the objectives of the censorship regulations, ways that did not so drastically impinge on first amendment freedoms. For example, the regulation prohibiting writings containing "inflammatory" views was not, as it should be, confined to communications that would provoke violence. Nor was the regulation confined to just incoming mail.

Procunier demonstrates that the censorship of inmate mail may run afoul of other constitutional provisions as well. In *Procunier* itself, the Supreme Court held that the inmates and the individuals with whom they corresponded had not been afforded procedural due process when their mail was censored. To avoid errors and arbitrariness in censorship decisions, the Court said that the following procedural safeguards have to attend the censorship process: (1) notice to an inmate when a letter written to or by the inmate is censored; (2) an opportunity afforded the letter's author to protest the censorship decision; and (3) review of the censorship decision by someone other than the individual who made the initial decision.

In *Pell v. Procunier* (1974), the Supreme Court answered the question left open in *Procunier v. Martinez* and held that prisoners do indeed have some first amendment rights. Specifically, the

Court held that inmates retain first amendment rights that do not conflict with their "status" as prisoners or "legitimate penological objectives." The Court expounded upon the list of correctional objectives set forth in *Procunier* that would support curbs on first amendment freedoms in the prison context, citing not only the interests in maintaining institutional security and rehabilitating prisoners but also the interests in deterring crime and incapacitating individuals posing a threat to the public's safety.

At issue in *Pell* was the constitutionality of a state regulation that prohibited members of the media from conducting face-to-face interviews with selected inmates. In finding this regulation to be constitutional, the Supreme Court emphasized several points. First, the Court noted the conflict between permitting such interviews and maintaining institutional security. For security reasons, the Court observed, prison officials needed to keep the number of prison visitors to a "manageable level." In addition, prison officials had legitimate security reasons for wanting to avert what was known as the "big-wheel phenomenon," where inmates who have garnered attention through media interviews wield more influence over other inmates that can be used towards disruptive ends.

The Court also emphasized in *Pell* though that the inmates had other viable means of communicating with the media, both through letters and by sending messages with family members, friends, attorneys, and clergy. *Pell* then was the first of a succession of cases in which the Court, in assessing the constitutionality of prison regulations under the first amendment, has balanced the governmental interests furthered by a restriction on first amendment freedoms against the burden on inmates caused by the restriction. *Pell* is also noteworthy because the Court in that case did not adopt a least-drastic-alternative requirement as it had in *Procunier v. Martinez* when addressing the first amendment rights of nonprisoners. In other words, prison regulations that impinged on inmates' first amendment interests could still be constitutional, even if there were less restrictive means by which prison officials could accomplish their correctional objectives. The Court in *Pell* did not, in fact, even bother discussing the less drastic alternatives that were discussed by Justice Powell in his dissenting opinion in the companion case of *Saxbe v. Washington Post Company* (1974). One of the suggested alternatives was to limit the number of interviews that could be conducted with any one inmate during a specified time period.

The Supreme Court in *Pell v. Procunier*, incidentally, rebuffed another first amendment challenge to the regulation restricting media interviews of inmates. Certain media members contended that the regulation abridged the freedom of the press protected by the first amendment, but the Court simply responded that members of the press have no greater right to have access to prisons than do members of the general public.

In cases decided since *Pell*, the Supreme Court has continued to focus on institutional security concerns and the availability of alternative means of expression when evaluating the free speech claims of prisoners. In *Jones v. North Carolina Prisoners' Labor Union* (1977), for example, the Court upheld three state regulations that curbed inmate involvement in a prisoner labor union. The first regulation barred inmates from soliciting other inmates to join the union; the second prohibited union meetings in the state's prisons; and the third prohibited bulk mailings of union materials for redistribution to inmates. Prison officials argued that these restrictions were needed to protect institutional security. They contended, for example, that a prisoner union might encourage work slowdowns or stoppages that might in turn culminate in riots.

In responding to the prisoners' argument that these predictions about the disruptive effects of prisoner unions were not supported by any evidence of actual disruptions in the past, the Supreme Court showed great deference towards correctional officials' opinions about what was needed to protect institutional security. The Court simply noted that the prison officials' concerns were "reasonable" and that they had not been "conclusively shown to be wrong." Prison officials, according to the Court, did not have to wait until a prison was on the verge of a riot before they could take steps to thwart a prison disruption.

The Court in *Jones*, however, also noted the alternative outlets available for the expression impaired by the prison regulations. For example, inmates had other ways to communicate their complaints to prison officials, including inmate grievance procedures. In addition, although union materials could not be mailed in bulk to prisoners because of the ease with which contraband can be hidden in bulk mailings, the mailing of union materials to individual inmates was permitted.

In *Bell v. Wolfish* (1979), the Supreme Court again found a correctional regulation constitutional in the face of a first amendment challenge. The regulation at issue prohibited inmates and pretrial detainees, who are individuals incarcerated while awaiting trial, from receiving hardbound books mailed from a source other than a bookstore, a book publisher, or a book club. Noting the difficulty of detecting contraband hidden in the bindings of hardbound books, the Court observed that the restriction was a "rational response" to "an obvious security problem." The Court also underscored, however, that the burden caused by the restriction was dissipated by several factors. First, the inmates and detainees were still permitted to receive magazines and softbound books from any source. Second, they had access to a well-stocked library. And third, the pretrial detainees were affected by the regulation for a relatively short period of time, since the vast majority of them were released within sixty days.

In a dissenting opinion, Justice Marshall objected to applying the same watered-down first amendment test that was applied to convicted criminals to pretrial detainees, who are presumed innocent of any criminal wrongdoing. The majority of the Court, however, in defending its decision not to differentiate between the first amendment claims of inmates and those of pretrial detainees, noted that pretrial detainees often pose the same, and sometimes greater threats to institutional security as individuals incarcerated for crimes of which they have been convicted.

Pell, Jones, and *Bell* were the prelude to *Turner v. Safley* (1987), a pivotal Supreme Court case that fleshed out the contours of the test to be applied to prisoners' first amendment claims. One of the regulations whose constitutionality was at issue in *Turner* generally prohibited inmates from writing to each other unless they were close relatives or were corresponding about legal matters. In enunciating the test to be applied in determining whether this regulation was constitutional, the Supreme Court stated that "when a prison regulation impinges on inmates' constitutional rights, the regulation is valid if it is reasonably related to legitimate penological interests."

The Court then discussed four factors to be considered under this reasonable-relationship test. First, there must be a "valid, rational connection" between the regulation and the interest it is designed to further. In other words, the connection between the regulation and its purpose must not be so attenuated as to produce arbitrary or irrational results. In addition, the interest that a regulation purportedly furthers must be both "legitimate" and "neutral," meaning that its application is not contingent on the content of the expression being regulated.

Second, a court must examine the extent to which inmates have other ways of exercising the right in question. This factor, as mentioned earlier, bears on the burden on inmates caused by a particular restriction.

The third factor to be considered is the effect that recognizing the claimed right will have on other inmates, correctional officers, and prison resources. And the fourth factor looks at the extent to which there are less drastic means of achieving the legitimate objectives of the regulation—means that do not so greatly impinge upon the asserted rights of prisoners. The existence of less drastic alternatives is a relevant factor to be weighed under the *Turner* test, but in contrast to the test applied by the Court in *Procunier v. Martinez*, there is no least-drastic-alternative requirement that must be met under the *Turner* test.

The factors outlined in *Turner* as relevant to the reasonableness inquiry simply represented a more detailed exposition of a balancing process that had begun years earlier in *Pell v. Procunier*. What was noteworthy about *Turner* though was the way in which the Court construed some of these factors so as to almost foreordain a finding in favor of the constitutionality of most prison regulations and practices. For example, when applying the second factor to the facts of the case before it, the Court broadly construed what constitutes an available alternative to a claimed right. Noting that the inmates had not been deprived of "all means of expression," the Court seemed unconcerned that the ban on inmate-to-inmate correspondence totally prevented inmates from communicating with certain individuals with whom they wanted to correspond.

The Court similarly construed the fourth factor in a way that makes it exceedingly difficult for inmates to prevail on their first amendment claims. The Court said that if an alternative means of achieving the government's objectives entails more than "*de minimis* costs" to legitimate penological objectives, it is not to be considered a viable option and consequently is not an indicator of a regulation's unconstitutionality. It is unlikely then that this factor will often weigh in favor of inmates' constitutional claims, since extending almost any right to prisoners will have security implications. As the United States District Court for the District of New Jersey observed in *Valentine v. Englehardt* (D.N.J.1979), "A naked man in chains poses no risk. From that point on, every increase in freedom brings at least some decrease in security."

Not surprisingly, the Supreme Court found in *Turner* that the regulation prohibiting inmate-to-inmate correspondence did not unconstitutionally abridge inmates' first amendment free speech rights. The Court first observed that there was the requisite rational connection between this regulation and legitimate security interests since inmates at different prisons could, through the mail, coordinate gang activity and plan assaults, murders, and other activities inimical to the safety and security of individuals within the state's prisons. The second factor, according to the Court, weighed in favor of the regulation's constitutionality since, as mentioned earlier, the inmates had other means of expression available to them, even though they were forbidden from communicating with some of the individuals with whom they perhaps most wanted to communicate. Third, permitting inmates to correspond with each other would have harmful effects on the inmates and staff whose safety would be jeopardized by such correspondence. And finally, the Court noted that there were no "obvious, easy alternatives" to the ban on inmate-to-inmate correspondence. Screening inmates' mail would consume valuable staff resources, and risks to institutional security would remain because of encoded messages that might be missed during the screening process.

Although it will now be an uphill battle for an inmate to prevail on a constitutional claim to which the *Turner* test is applied, *Turner* itself reveals that it is not impossible for an inmate to do so. While the Court in *Turner* upheld the ban on inmate-to-inmate correspondence, the Court also struck down another regulation which prohibited inmates from getting married without the warden's consent. Under this regulation, the warden was not supposed to approve such marriages unless there was a "compelling" reason for the marriage, such as pregnancy or the birth of a child.

The Supreme Court found that there was no reasonable relationship between the marriage prohibition and the interests invoked in its defense—security and rehabilitation. The threshold requirement of a logical connection between the prohibition and security interests was absent since the "love triangles" that prison officials argued might lead to violence could develop whether or not inmates were married. The Court also felt that there were less drastic means of achieving the security objectives of the marriage prohibition. Prison officials could, for example, just prohibit marriages that posed a distinct threat to institutional security rather than institute a general across-the-board ban on inmate marriages.

The Court also noted that the prohibition on inmate marriages was broader than necessary to achieve the rehabilitation goals asserted by the prison officials. The prison officials had argued that female inmates, many of whom have been victims of abuse in the past, needed to learn to become self-reliant while in prison, a task made more difficult if they were married. The paternalistic regulation adopted by the officials, however, seems at odds with the very goal of developing self-reliance that it was purportedly designed to further. The Court's principal focus in striking down the regulation, however, was on its overbreadth, since it encompassed marriages about which the prison officials had expressed little concern—marriages of male inmates and inmate marriages to civilians.

The progression of Supreme Court cases in which inmates' free speech rights were narrowly construed culminated in *Thornburgh v. Abbott* (1989). In *Thornburgh*, the Supreme Court considered the constitutionality of some prison regulations that governed the censorship of publications that were sent to prisoners. Like the censorship regulations that were at issue in *Procunier v. Martinez*, these regulations had an impact on the free speech interests of nonprisoners as well as prisoners. The Court, however, refused to apply the two-part *Procunier* test to the regulations, narrowly construing *Procunier* in the process.

Despite the breadth of the language in *Procunier* discussing when the two-part test enunciated in that case would apply in the prison context and the fact that the regulations at issue in *Procunier* had applied to both incoming and outgoing correspondence, the Court in *Thornburgh* claimed that *Procunier* had primarily concerned just outgoing personal correspondence. Such outgoing correspondence, the Court said, was to be distinguished from incoming publications, which tend to circulate widely within a prison and whose contents pose a much greater potential threat to institutional security. Accordingly, the Court held that the *Turner* test should apply to incoming publications and overruled *Procunier* to the extent that it suggested otherwise. Although the only issue actually before the Court was the standard to be applied to incoming publications and not the standard to be applied to incoming personal correspondence, the Court sweepingly announced that application of the *Procunier* test was to be confined to outgoing correspondence.

While the Court in *Thornburgh* insisted that the *Turner* test is not a "toothless" one, *Thornburgh* itself confirmed the ease with which prison regulations can survive that test. The Court, for example, took pains to note that there was no need to demonstrate that a particular publication was "likely" to cause violence to justify banning it from a prison; all that was necessary was that the publication pose "an intolerable risk of disorder."

The Court also qualified what it had said earlier in *Procunier v. Martinez* regarding the relevance of other prisons' policies to the constitutionality of prison regulations. The Court noted that just because a publication was admitted into some prisons, and not others, did not mean that prison officials were necessarily acting irrationally or arbitrarily. The Court observed that prisons can differ greatly from one another and even the same prison can vary greatly over time as far as the steps needed to preserve its security.

The Court also expounded upon what it had meant in *Turner* when it had referred to a "neutral" interest to which a restriction on prisoners' rights must be rationally connected. The Court in *Turner* had said that this neutrality requirement meant that application of a regulation could not hinge upon a communication's content. That definition obviously posed a problem in *Thornburgh*, where incoming publications might or might not be admitted into a prison, depending on their content. Because the regulations in *Thornburgh*, however, only allowed censorship for security reasons and perhaps also because they specifically disallowed censorship for other reasons, the Court said that that the regulations were "neutral" in the technical sense required by *Turner*.

Perhaps the most revealing portion of the Court's opinion in *Thornburgh* was its discussion of whether there were viable, less drastic alternatives to the way in which publications were censored under the regulations. Under the regulations, if a passage or article in a publication was censorable, the entire publication could be withheld from prisoners. Justice Stevens, in dissent, described this "all-or-nothing rule" as "a meat-ax abridgement" of the first amendment rights of both free citizens and prisoners. The Court, however, responded that the regulations were still constitutional because the belief of prison officials that inmates would get upset if they received publications with parts missing was "reasonably founded." The Court in addition noted that it would be "inconvenient" for prison officials to have to take the time to remove censorable materials out of incoming publications.

B.   FREEDOM OF ASSOCIATION

Another right protected by the first amendment and applicable to the states through the due process clause of the fourteenth amendment is known as the freedom of association. A threshold question concerning this first amendment right is whether it even extends to prisoners. In *Jones v. North Carolina Prisoners' Labor Union* (1977), the Supreme Court seemed to assume that inmates retain some associational rights, although the Court in that case ultimately concluded that certain restrictions on the activities of a prisoner labor union did not unconstitutionally abridge inmates' freedom of association.

Assuming that prisoners retain some degree of freedom of association despite their incarceration, the next question concerns the scope of prisoners' associational rights. At least some answers to this question were provided by the Supreme Court in *Block v. Rutherford* (1984), a case involving the rights, not of prisoners, but of pretrial detainees. In *Block*, a group of pretrial detainees challenged the constitutionality of a jail policy that prohibited contact visits between pretrial detainees and their visitors, including family members. A contact visit is one in which there is no physical barrier, such as a plexiglas wall, between inmates or detainees and their visitors.

The Supreme Court analyzed the constitutionality of this ban on contact visits under the due process clause of the fourteenth amendment. The pivotal question, according to the Court, was whether this ban was tantamount to punishment, since the due process clause prohibits the punishment of individuals who have not been convicted of any crime. Such proscribed punishment will be found

when a policy or practice is des
pretrial detainees. Even in the ab
an intent to punish, however, pur
found to exist when a policy or pr
negative effect on pretrial detainees is not reasonably related to a legitimate governmental objective."

The latter way in which *Block* said punishment
can be established seems to mirror the reasonable-
relationship test that the Court later said in *Turner
v. Safley* should be applied to the first amendment
claims of prisoners. Yet the way in which the
Court applied the reasonable relationship test in
Block stands in marked contrast to the way in
which it was subsequently applied in *Turner*.

In *Block*, the Court noted that contact visits can
cause a lot of security problems in correctional
facilities. Visitors can smuggle drugs, weapons, and
other contraband that pose a direct threat to the
security of an institution to the detainees with
whom they are visiting. There is also always the
risk that detainees might harm visitors, using them,
for example, as hostages in an escape attempt.

The district court had readily conceded the legitimacy of the security concerns caused by contact
visits, but the court believed that the ban on contact visits was an excessive response to those concerns. The district court therefore crafted an order
that it felt addressed the security risks posed by
contact visits without so drastically impinging upon
the interest of pretrial detainees in maintaining,

rough contact visits, ties with their family members and friends. Because the impact of the contact-visitation ban fell most heavily on detainees incarcerated for lengthy periods of time, the district court generally lifted the ban for detainees incarcerated for a month or more. Mindful of the security risks posed by contact visits, however, the district court authorized continuing the ban for long-term detainees who had drug or escape propensities. In addition, the court placed a cap on the total number of contact visits that the jail officials had to allow each month.

The Supreme Court lambasted the lower court for its balancing of the security interests that prompted the contact-visitation ban against the burden to detainees caused by that ban. The Court brusquely said that once the district court found that contact visits actually threaten institutional security, its analysis should have ended. By instead balancing these interests against the interests of the detainees, the district court had, according to the Supreme Court, impermissibly supplanted the judgment of jail administrators about what was needed to maintain jail security with its own view.

This rejection of a balancing of interests is completely at odds with a long line of cases in which the Supreme Court has done exactly what it said the lower court should not have done. And in most of those cases, such as *Pell v. Procunier* (1974) and *Turner v. Safley* (1987), the Court was analyzing the rights of prisoners, not detainees who are presumed innocent of any criminal wrongdoing.

Block therefore seems to be an aberration in correctional-law jurisprudence. Even if the Court in *Block*, however, had applied a balancing test, the end result of the case might very well have been the same, particularly if the Court had applied a test as tilted in favor of correctional officials as the *Turner* test. The Court in *Block*, for example, had noted that the detainees, although not allowed contact visits, were still permitted unmonitored noncontact visits during most of the day. This fact would weigh in favor of the contact-visitation ban's constitutionality under the second factor of the *Turner* test which examines the alternative means available to inmates to exercise the right in question. In addition, since the Court had expressed concerns in *Block* about the risks of allowing even detainees classified as low-security risks to have contact visits, the other *Turner* factors would support the constitutionality of the contact-visitation ban. The Court had observed that even detainees who are classified as low-security risks might be induced or coerced by other detainees to smuggle contraband into the jail. In addition, the Court had stated that allowing contact visits for some detainees and not others might fuel tensions between them. Finally, the Court had noted the fallibility of the classification systems through which detainees are assigned a risk level.

C. FREEDOM OF RELIGION

Another first amendment right upon which much prisoners' rights litigation has focused is the right to religious freedom. The Supreme Court confirmed that inmates have the right to freedom of religion in *Cruz v. Beto* (1972). In that case, a Buddhist inmate claimed that prison officials violated his right to religious freedom by making accommodations for inmates of other faiths that they did not make for him. He charged, for example, that other inmates were permitted to use the prison chapel, while he was not, and that the state only paid for Catholic, Jewish, and Protestant clergy and Jewish and Christian Bibles.

In holding that the district court had erred in dismissing the plaintiff's complaint, the Supreme Court noted that inmates must be afforded "reasonable opportunities" to practice their religious faith and that these opportunities must be comparable to those afforded prisoners of other religions. At the same time, however, the Court emphasized that prison officials need not provide different religious sects with identical facilities and personnel to facilitate the exercise of inmates' religious freedom; the number of inmate adherents to a particular religion can rather be taken into account when making personnel decisions and decisions regarding the use of facilities.

In *O'Lone v. Shabazz* (1987), the Supreme Court embellished upon the scope of inmates' right to religious freedom. In that case, a group of Muslim inmates challenged the constitutionality of some prison regulations, one of which required inmates assigned to work details outside the prison to remain with those details throughout the day. The effect of these regulations was to prevent the Muslim inmates from being able to attend Jumu'ah, a group worship service that, according to the Koran, must be held at a certain time on Friday afternoons.

The Supreme Court applied the *Turner* test in assessing the constitutionality of these regulations. The Court first found a logical connection between the prohibition on returns to the prison during the day and legitimate penological interests. Inmates returning to the prison posed security risks at the main gate through which they returned because of the heavy amount of traffic that also traveled through the gate during the day. Letting inmates leave work early, according to the Court, also interfered with the rehabilitative purpose of the work details.

Turning to the second *Turner* factor, the Court acknowledged that the Muslim inmates had no alternative way of attending Jumu'ah. Nonetheless, this fact, in the opinion of the Court, did not weigh against the regulations' constitutionality because the Muslim inmates were not deprived of "all forms of religious exercise." They could meet together at other times to worship; they were provided special pork-free meals; and they were permitted to eat at different times than other inmates during the holy month of Ramadan. The state also paid for an imam, a Muslim prayer leader, to provide religious services to the Muslim inmates.

This portion of the Court's opinion drew a sharp rebuke from Justice Brennan, who objected to treat-

ing religious practices as though they are inter-
changeable. Justice Brennan insisted that the deprivation in this case was total and that this fact
therefore weighed heavily against the regulations'
constitutionality.

Justice Brennan also disagreed with the way in
which the majority spurned the less drastic alternatives proffered by the Muslim inmates as ways to
eliminate the security concerns caused by inmates
leaving their work details while preserving the Muslim inmates' ability to attend Jumu'ah. One of the
suggestions of the plaintiffs was to have the Muslim
inmates not work on Fridays so that they could
remain in the prison to attend Jumu'ah and then
work on weekends to compensate for the work
missed on Fridays. The majority of the Court,
however, did not consider weekend work details to
be a viable option. The Court cited three concerns
expressed by the prison officials to support this
conclusion—that it would be difficult to supervise
work details on weekends when staffing is already
sparse; that work details comprised of Muslim inmates only would be "affinity groups" that would
be more likely to challenge the authority of prison
officials; and that other inmates would resent what
they perceive as the special treatment of Muslim
inmates.

One of Justice Brennan's objections to these reasons for opposing weekend work details of Muslim
inmates was that they seemed to reflect an anti-
Muslim bias. He noted that the prison officials did
not seem at all concerned about the staff needed on

weekends to accommodate the religious needs of Christian and Jewish inmates who wanted to attend group worship services. Nor did they seem at all concerned about affinity groups when the inmates working together were Christians. Finally, the prison officials seemed to give no thought to the resentment ensuing when Muslim inmates, denied the opportunity of participating in Jumu'ah, saw prison officials making arrangements to enable Christian and Jewish inmates to attend their own group worship services.

With some frequency, inmates continue to seek accommodations of their religious needs and practices. Some of the more common claims are brought by inmates who, for religious reasons, want to wear their hair long or grow a beard, want to eat only certain foods, or want to change their names. *See, e.g., Ward v. Walsh* (9th Cir.1993) (kosher diet); *Powell v. Estelle* (5th Cir.1992) (long hair and beards); *Ali v. Dixon* (4th Cir.1990) (name change).

The Supreme Court has never acknowledged the apparent tension between the admonition in *Cruz v. Beto* that inmates must be afforded "reasonable opportunities" to practice their religion and the begrudging approach to inmates' religious rights taken by the Court in *O'Lone v. Shabazz*. But with the lower courts generally following the Supreme Court's lead in *O'Lone*, it has been the exception rather than the rule for inmates to prevail on their freedom-of-religion claims.

This trend in the caselaw may change, however, with the enactment of the Religious Freedom Restoration Act of 1993. That Act, which currently includes prisoners within the scope of its protection, provides that actions taken by government officials that place a "substantial burden" on a person's exercise of religion are illegal unless those actions further a "compelling" governmental interest and are the "least restrictive means" of furthering that interest. 42 U.S.C.A. § 2000bb–1. In the years to come, the courts will have to flesh out the implications of this Act in the prison context. It is clear, however, that since the Religious Freedom Restoration Act contains a least-drastic-alternative requirement, the Act places obligations on prison officials to accommodate inmates' religious practices that go beyond the requirements of the first amendment, as that amendment has been construed by the Supreme Court.

CHAPTER 10

RIGHT OF ACCESS TO
THE COURTS

While the protection that the Constitution affords inmates is not as broad as the protection afforded the citizenry at large, prisoners still, as mentioned earlier, have a number of constitutional rights. These rights mean nothing as a practical matter though if inmates have no means of enforcing them.

The primary vehicle for enforcing inmates' constitutional rights has been civil rights suits filed in federal or state courts, primarily under 42 U.S.C.A. § 1983. Prisoners have, however, sought and continue to seek access to courts for reasons other than to simply challenge the conditions of their confinement or their treatment while confined. They also contest the legality of their convictions through habeas corpus petitions and other postconviction complaints, and, like other individuals, they turn to the courts to resolve such civil matters as divorces or parental-rights disputes.

Since inmates, who are insulated from public view, are so dependent on the courts to enforce their rights, the question of the extent to which inmates have a right of access to the courts is an important one. It is clear from the decisions of the

Supreme Court that a right of access to the courts is embedded within the Constitution, finding its source in the due process clauses of the fifth and fourteenth amendments. It is also clear that the litmus test for determining whether the right has been violated is whether inmates have been provided with "meaningful access" to the courts. *Bounds v. Smith* (1977). But what exactly does this mean?

The Supreme Court has provided us with some definitive answers to this question, although many questions still remain. It is clear, for example, that prison officials cannot refuse to mail to a court legal papers that an inmate has prepared because the officials believe that the papers are not in proper form. It is rather for the courts, and the courts alone, to decide whether the documents that an inmate wants to file meet procedural and substantive requirements. *Ex parte Hull* (1941). Preventing inmates from filing legal documents can also violate their right to the equal protection of the law, since individuals outside of prison who wish to file similar documents enjoy relatively unencumbered access to the courts. *See Cochran v. Kansas* (1942) (equal protection violated when prison officials prevented prisoner from filing papers needed to appeal his conviction).

The Supreme Court has also held that the constitutional rights of inmates are not violated when mail sent to them by an attorney is opened and inspected for contraband, at least when the inspection occurs in the inmate's presence. In *Wolff v. McDonnell* (1974), the Court noted that there was no risk of censorship, since under the inspection scheme in question, inmates' mail was not read. Nor was there any risk that communications between inmates and attorneys would be chilled because of the fear that prison officials might read their correspondence, since that risk was obviated by the inmate's presence.

While the Court added in *Wolff* that the prison officials might even have gone beyond the requirements of the Constitution by allowing inmates to be present when attorney-inmate mail was inspected, most of the lower courts have held that such presence is constitutionally required. *See, e.g., Jensen v. Klecker* (8th Cir.1981). Most have also held that correctional officials cannot, at least usually, read attorney-inmate mail. *See, e.g., Lemon v. Dugger* (11th Cir.1991) (exception when there is "probable cause" to believe letter poses a threat to institutional security). If correctional officials do read correspondence between inmates and their attorneys, they may violate not only the due process right of access to the courts but also, in the case of inmates awaiting trial or sentencing, their sixth amendment right to receive the assistance of counsel at trial, sentencing, and other "critical stages" of a criminal prosecution.

In *Procunier v. Martinez* (1974), the Supreme Court fleshed out the analysis to be undertaken when resolving inmates' due process right-of-access claims. In *Procunier*, the issue before the Court concerned the constitutionality of an across-the-board ban on interviews of inmates by law students and paralegals who were working for attorneys. The Court first noted the "substantial burden" that this ban placed on inmates' right of access to the courts. The Court observed that travelling to a prison to interview a prisoner is time-consuming and expensive for an attorney, particularly since so many prisons are located far away from urban areas. To preclude attorneys from defraying the expenses of assisting an inmate by using law students or paralegals to conduct inmate interviews would therefore discourage many attorneys from providing any legal assistance to inmates.

The Court noted though that just because inmates' right of access to the courts was substantially burdened by the regulation restricting who could interview inmates did not necessarily mean that that regulation violated the right of access to the courts. To complete the analysis, the burden that the regulation imposed on inmates had to be weighed against any "legitimate interest in penal administration" that it furthered. In other words, the burden caused by the regulation had to be weighed against the need for it. If the need for the regulation outweighed the burden that it caused, the regulation would be constitutional despite the "substantial burden" on inmates' access to the courts.

In this case, however, the Supreme Court concluded that the legitimate penological interest in maintaining institutional security that was invoked in the regulation's defense did not warrant the across-the-board ban on interviews of inmates by law students and paralegals working for attorneys. Noting that the ban was not limited to law students and paralegals who posed a "colorable threat" to security or to interviews of "especially dangerous" inmates, the Court concluded that the prison officials had not demonstrated that a more narrow restriction would "unduly burden" or impede their task of screening and monitoring visitors to maintain institutional security.

It is interesting to note the difference between the Court's discussion in *Procunier v. Martinez* of the significance of the existence of less drastic alternatives to right-of-access claims and its discussion of less drastic alternatives in the first amendment context. In *Procunier*, the Court seemed to be placing the burden on prison officials of proving that there were no viable less restrictive means of achieving the objectives of a regulation that impinged on inmates' access to the courts. By contrast, the Court in *Turner v. Safley*, a first amendment case, seemed to suggest that it was incumbent on inmates asserting first amendment claims to demonstrate the viability of less restrictive alternatives when it said:

[P]rison officials do not have to set up and then shoot down every conceivable alternative method of accommodating the claimant's constitutional complaint. But if an inmate claimant can point to an alternative that fully accommodates the prisoner's rights at *de minimis* cost to valid penological interests, a court may consider that as evidence that the regulation does not satisfy the reasonable relationship standard.

The Supreme Court's decision in *Johnson v. Avery* (1969) is further confirmation of the fact that the Court, at least thus far, has treated prisoners' right-of-access claims differently than their first amendment claims. *Johnson* involved the constitutionality of a regulation that prohibited inmates from providing legal assistance to other inmates. The Supreme Court recognized that there were sound reasons for this regulation. Jailhouse lawyers, as they are popularly known, can endanger institutional security. They sometimes, for example, extract an extortionate price for their services, even demanding sexual favors from the inmates they are assisting. In addition, because of the legal knowledge they have and their willingness to challenge the authority of prison officials in court, they can become power figures within a prison, exerting a disproportionate, and often negative influence on other prisoners. The Court also noted the burden on courts caused by the complaints and other legal documents that are ineptly drafted by some jailhouse lawyers.

Nonetheless, the Supreme Court struck down the ban on jailhouse lawyers because of the burden that it placed on inmates' right of access to the courts. The Court noted that the effect of the ban was to prevent illiterate and poorly educated inmates from seeking and obtaining habeas corpus relief when they were unconstitutionally confined. The rigor with which the Court appeared to apply the balancing test it had enunciated is to be contrasted with the more perfunctory balancing that has occurred in cases where the Court has applied the *Turner* test, under which the existence of more than *de minimis* costs of accommodating an inmate's constitutional rights weigh heavily against the inmate's constitutional claim.

The Supreme Court in *Johnson v. Avery* did say that prison officials can place "reasonable restrictions" on the activities of jailhouse lawyers. Prison officials can, for example, limit the times and places that jailhouse lawyers can render assistance to other inmates, and they can bar jailhouse lawyers from receiving any form of compensation for their labors.

In addition, the Court observed that prison officials can avoid the hassles and risks caused by jailhouse lawyers and ban them altogether if they instead provide some "reasonable alternative" assistance to inmates. The Court dropped some clues as to what might constitute "reasonable alternative" assistance in its discussion of some programs that already existed in some of the states. Some of these programs used public defenders to provide legal assistance to inmates; one used senior law students for this purpose; and still another utilized lawyer volunteers to consult with the prisoners. Whatever the alternative devised, the Court made it clear that it must enable inmates to prepare their habeas corpus petitions with "reasonable adequacy."

In *Wolff v. McDonnell* (1974), the Supreme Court held that the right to receive assistance from a jailhouse lawyer or some "reasonable alternative" is not confined to inmates in need of assistance when preparing habeas corpus petitions. The right also extends to inmates who wish to bring civil rights suits challenging the conditions of their confinement or their treatment while incarcerated.

One of the questions which remains after *Johnson v. Avery* and *Wolff v. McDonnell* is whether permitting jailhouse lawyers to operate within a prison is enough to ensure that inmates' access to the courts is indeed "meaningful." Even if prison officials permit jailhouse lawyers to provide legal assistance to other inmates, there is a concern that some inmates, so many of whom are illiterate or poorly educated and some of whom cannot even speak English, will still be unable to prepare their legal documents with "reasonable adequacy." Some jailhouse lawyers may, for example, be incompetent, and even those who are competent, may refuse to help some inmates who need assistance.

The due process right to assistance discussed in *Johnson v. Avery* and *Wolff v. McDonnel* does not, however, mean that inmates generally have the right to the assistance of an attorney when litigating a civil rights claim or even when seeking habeas corpus relief. In *Pennsylvania v. Finley* (1987), the Supreme Court specifically rejected the claim that an indigent inmate challenging the validity of a conviction in a state postconviction proceeding has the right to the assistance of an appointed attorney.

And in *Murray v. Giarratano* (1989), the Court even rejected the claim that an inmate facing the death penalty has the right to such assistance.   In *Murray*, however, Justice Kennedy, who wrote the concurring opinion that provided the fifth vote needed to reject the prisoner's claim, emphasized the special circumstances of the case before the Court. Justice Kennedy noted, for example, that there was no evidence that any inmate on death row in the state in question had actually been unable to find a lawyer willing to assist the inmate in a postconviction proceeding.   It is unclear whether in a case with different facts, the Court might find that an indigent inmate on whom the death penalty has been imposed has a constitutional right to the assistance of an attorney when challenging the validity of his or her conviction in a postconviction proceeding.

While inmates do not, at least generally, have the constitutional right to the assistance of counsel when litigating civil rights claims or claims raised in postconviction proceedings, they may, by statute, be accorded such a right.   For example, as is discussed more fully in Chapter 18 on page 290, federal courts have the discretion under 28 U.S.C.A. § 1915(d) to appoint counsel to represent indigent inmates who have filed suit under § 1983.

If jurisdictions do choose to appoint attorneys to assist inmates in litigating civil rights and habeas corpus actions, they will have clearly satisfied, and even exceeded, other constitutional requirements stemming from the right of access to the courts that were described by the Supreme Court in *Bounds v. Smith* (1977). In *Bounds*, the Court held that inmates must either be afforded access to "adequate" law libraries or be provided with "adequate" assistance from persons "trained in the law." The Court recognized that without such access or assistance, the opportunity of inmates to litigate their constitutional claims would not be, as the Constitution requires, "reasonably adequate". Inmates would often not know such basics, for example, as where their lawsuits should be filed, against whom their lawsuits can and should be brought, and the information that should be included in their complaints to state an actionable claim.

The Court in *Bounds* did not define what constitutes an "adequate" law library, but it is clear that the failure of a library to stock the books needed for inmates to meaningfully pursue their constitutional claims in court will violate the due process right to have "meaningful" access to the courts. *See, e.g., Gilmore v. Lynch* (N.D.Cal.1970), *aff'd sub nom. Younger v. Gilmore*, 404 U.S. 15 (1971) (omission of U.S. Supreme Court Reports, other federal reporters, the United States Code, annotated copies of the state's code, many local federal district rules, and U.S. Law Week violates right of access to the courts). Placing undue limits on the time that inmates can spend in the law library to do their legal research can also violate their constitutional right of access to the courts. *See, e.g., Ramos v. Lamm* (10th Cir.1980) (striking down regulation which resulted in inmates having access to law library only three hours every thirteen weeks).

Questions also still remain concerning when the alternative assistance provided to an inmate will be considered constitutionally "adequate" and what kind of background and training the person rendering assistance to an inmate must have to be considered "trained in the law" within the meaning of *Bounds*. It is clear, however, that if prison officials opt to provide inmates with "adequate" assistance from persons "trained in the law," they will have satisfied their obligations under both *Bounds* and *Johnson v. Avery*, which permits prison officials to provide inmates with "reasonable alternative" assistance in lieu of permitting jailhouse lawyers to operate within the confines of a prison.

When inmates have exercised their right of access to the courts and filed lawsuits against correctional officials, some correctional officials have responded by retaliating against the inmates. This retaliation has come in a variety of forms, including transferring the inmates to other prisons or parts of the same prison with worse conditions of confinement, firing the inmates from their prison jobs, and taking other measures to generally make the inmates' lives more miserable. Such retaliation for pursuing litigation is, however, itself an abridgement of the right of access to the courts for which the inmate can seek redress in a civil rights suit. *See, e.g., Goff v. Burton* (8th Cir.1993).

CHAPTER 11

PRISON DISCIPLINARY PROCEEDINGS

A. PROCEDURAL DUE PROCESS

Both prison officials and inmates have a critical stake in the proper functioning of the disciplinary process in a prison. For prison officials, what is at stake is their ability to maintain order in a prison by disciplining inmates who violate prison rules. For inmates, what is at stake in a disciplinary proceeding will depend on the nature of an inmate's alleged misconduct and the penalties authorized for such misconduct. Often, inmates face the prospect of losing good-time credits if they are found guilty of violating prison rules, which means that the length of time that they will be incarcerated will be prolonged. Alternatively, or in addition, inmates may be placed in segregation for their disciplinary infractions, where they will have to remain in their cells almost all of the time and will lose many of the privileges afforded inmates in the general population unit of the prison. For less serious violations of prison rules, prisoners may remain in the general population unit but lose one or more privileges for a period of time, such as television or commissary privileges.

Because of the sanctions that may ensue from a finding of guilt of disciplinary misconduct, inmates obviously have an interest in ensuring that they are only punished for a disciplinary violation of which they are actually guilty. The Supreme Court has held that at least in some circumstances, this interest gives rise to constitutional protection. In *Wolff v. McDonnell* (1974), the Court held that when inmates may lose good-time credits if they are found guilty of violating prison rules, due process requires that certain procedural safeguards attend the disciplinary process to protect the inmates from arbitrary deprivation of those credits. In a footnote, the Court added, in *dictum*, that the same procedural protections must be extended to inmates who may be placed in segregation if found guilty of disciplinary misconduct. The Court did not resolve the question of what, if any, procedural safeguards must attend disciplinary proceedings that will result only in a loss of privileges.

In *Wolff*, the Court outlined five procedural safeguards to which inmates are constitutionally entitled during disciplinary proceedings that may result in a loss of good-time credits. First, the inmates must receive written notice of the infractions with which they have been charged at least twenty-four hours before their disciplinary hearings. The purpose of this notice is to both make sure that the inmates are aware of the actual charges confronting them and to enable them to collect evidence and otherwise prepare their defense.

Second, inmates have the right to call witnesses to testify at their disciplinary hearings and the right to present documentary evidence at the hearings, except when the exercise of those rights would be "unduly hazardous to institutional safety or correctional goals." The Court gave some examples of when it would be permissible to restrict inmates' general right to call witnesses at disciplinary hearings—when the witness's testimony would be irrelevant, when the witness's testimony would be unnecessary, when calling the witness would create a risk of retaliation against the witness, and when calling the witness would "undermine authority." The Court did not, however, fully flesh out the contours of some of these exceptions, failing to explain, for example, when calling a witness might "undermine authority" or be unnecessary. Justice Marshall, in his opinion partially concurring in and partially dissenting from the majority's opinion, however, provided an example of when a witness's testimony would be unnecessary, noting that a disciplinary decisionmaker is not required to hear the duplicative testimony of numerous witnesses.

While the Supreme Court in *Wolff* held that inmates have a general right to call witnesses at disciplinary hearings, the Court at the same time said that a disciplinary decisionmaker need not explain at a disciplinary hearing why a request to call a witness was denied. In the subsequent case of *Ponte v. Real* (1985), however, the Court held that if such a contemporaneous explanation is not provided and an inmate later brings suit challenging the denial of a request to call a witness, then due process requires that the reason or reasons for the denial be tendered in a "limited manner" to the court. The Court added though that when disclosure of the reasons in open court might cause security problems, the reasons can be presented to the court *in camera*.

The third right to which inmates are entitled during disciplinary hearings is the right to assistance in preparing and presenting a defense to a disciplinary charge. This right to assistance is a limited one. In *Wolff*, the Supreme Court said that illiterate inmates and those facing disciplinary charges that raise complex issues are entitled to assistance. The Court did not, however, purport to be enunciating an all-inclusive list of the instances when an inmate might have a constitutional right to assistance at a disciplinary hearing. Mentally ill inmates and inmates who do not speak English would, for example, seem to be in similar need of such assistance.

While some inmates have the right to assistance during disciplinary proceedings, that right does not include the right to the assistance of an attorney. The Court in *Wolff* observed that injecting attorneys into the disciplinary process would make the process adversarial in nature, contrary to its rehabilitative objectives. The Court also noted the delay that would ensue if attorneys were involved in disciplinary proceedings and the cost of providing counsel to inmates charged with disciplinary infractions. The Court therefore held that the right to assistance means only that an inmate either be permitted to obtain the assistance of another inmate or, alternatively, be provided with "adequate substitute aid" from a staff member or a "sufficiently competent" inmate selected by the correctional officials.

The fourth procedural due process right identified in *Wolff* is the right of inmates found guilty of a disciplinary violation to receive a written statement recounting the evidence relied on by the disciplinary decisionmaker and the reasons for the disciplinary action taken. The purposes of this procedural safeguard are multifold—to protect an inmate from adverse "collateral consequences," such as the denial of parole or transfer to a prison with a higher security level, that might follow from a misunderstanding of the import of the guilty finding; to enable an inmate who has the grounds to do so to challenge, in court or elsewhere, what occurred in a disciplinary proceeding; and to induce disciplinary decisionmakers to render their decisions with care by reminding them that their actions may be reviewed by others. The Court recognized that sometimes, for security reasons, the disciplinary decisionmaker might appropriately omit reference to a particular piece of evidence upon which the disciplinary decision was founded, such as the identity of a confidential informant. The Court added though that the fact of this omission must then be denoted in the written statement.

The final right outlined in *Wolff*, though somewhat sketchily, is the right to have a "sufficiently impartial" decisionmaker adjudicate a disciplinary charge. While not much was said by the Court about this right, it is clear that the fellow employees of a correctional official who has brought a disciplinary charge against an inmate can adjudicate that charge without necessarily impinging upon the inmate's due process rights. In *Wolff* itself, the disciplinary committee which survived the Court's constitutional scrutiny was comprised of an associate warden, the director of the reception center, and the director of the prison industries program. While one might expect that correctional officials might feel some pressure to give credence to the allegations of coworkers over the conflicting statements of an inmate, the Court observed that the record before it did not reveal that this disciplinary committee posed a sufficient risk of "arbitrary decisionmaking" to give rise to due process concerns. Even Justice Marshall, who dissented from other portions of the Court's opinion, saw no inherent constitutional problem in having correctional officials employed at the facility where a disciplinary charge was filed adjudicate the charge. He noted, however, that a due process violation would occur if any of these officials had investigated or prosecuted the charge or had some other "personal involvement" in the case.

One of the rights that due process does not accord to inmates during disciplinary proceedings, according to the Supreme Court, is the right to confront and cross-examine adverse witnesses. The primary impetus for this conclusion was the Court's concern that the tension that ensues when an inmate confronts and cross-examines an adverse witness might culminate in violence in the volatile confines of a prison. Over the long run, this threat of violence would impede the functioning of the disciplinary process by dissuading witnesses from bringing disciplinary charges or testifying about the misconduct of inmates against whom disciplinary charges have been filed. The Court also noted that extending the right of confrontation and cross-examination to inmates during disciplinary proceedings would prolong those proceedings in a way that the Court believed might interfere with the rehabilitative effects of swiftly disciplining inmates for their misconduct.

Justice Marshall sharply disagreed with this conclusion of the Court, noting that greater procedural fairness during a disciplinary proceeding would enhance rather than detract from the proceeding's rehabilitative aims. Justice Marshall underscored the value of cross-examination in uncovering bias, malice, mistakes about identity, and memory and perception problems. While Justice Marshall acknowledged that sometimes, for security reasons, the right of confrontation and cross-examination would have to be curtailed, he accused the majority of letting "the tail ... wag the constitutional dog" by condoning across-the-board restrictions on what he believed to be a constitutional right. Even when it would be constitutionally permissible to prohibit an inmate from personally confronting and cross-examining an adverse witness, Justice Marshall said that due process requires the disciplinary decision-maker to question the witness *in camera* to assess the credibility of the witness.

The Court in *Wolff* took pains to emphasize several times in its opinion that its decision was not "graven in stone." The Court seemed to be suggesting that it might be willing at some point in the future to revisit such questions as the extent to which, if at all, inmates have a right to confront and cross-examine adverse witnesses.

There was also no suggestion in the Court's opinion that the list of procedural rights that it was enunciating was necessarily all-inclusive. In fact, in the later case of *Superintendent, Massachusetts Correctional Institution, Walpole v. Hill* (1985), the Court identified another right, though a watered-down one, that inmates have during disciplinary proceedings. In that case, the Court held that the decision to revoke an inmate's good-time credits must be supported by "some evidence" in the record that the prisoner violated prison rules, a standard of proof that is lower than a preponderance of the evidence.

An interesting question which remains after *Wolff* and *Hill* is the extent to which inmates have other procedural rights during prison disciplinary proceedings. Several lower courts have, for example, held that inmates have the right to be apprised of the rules for whose violation they may be disciplined. *See, e.g., Noren v. Straw* (D.Mont.1982). Examples of some other possible due process rights include the right to be apprised of the procedural safeguards, such as the right to assistance in some circumstances, to which the inmate is entitled during the disciplinary process (*cf. Vitek v. Jones* (1980) (inmates facing possible transfer to a mental hospital must be apprised of the rights they have during transfer proceedings); the right to have disciplinary reports submitted under oath; and the right to a reasonably prompt disciplinary hearing. Even if due process does not encompass certain rights, it must also be remembered that statutes and correctional regulations may accord inmates rights that go beyond the constitutional minima. *See, e.g.*, Mich. Comp. Laws § 791.251(4) (hearings officer must be an attorney); 28 C.F.R. § 541.15(i) (all inmates have the right to receive assistance from a staff member during disciplinary hearings).

B. MIRANDA AND THE PRIVILEGE AGAINST SELF–INCRIMINATION IN THE CORRECTIONAL CONTEXT

In *Miranda v. Arizona* (1966), the Supreme Court held that for statements obtained from a person subjected to custodial interrogation to be admissible in a criminal prosecution, the custodial interrogation must have been preceded by the giving of what are known as the *Miranda* warnings and the obtaining of a valid waiver of the rights to which the warnings refer, such as the right to remain silent. Two general questions arise concerning the applicability of *Miranda* in the prison context. First, must inmates questioned by correctional or other government officials first be given *Miranda* warnings in order for any statements that they make to be admissible in a disciplinary hearing? And second, must inmates, since they are always in a literal sense in custody, be given *Miranda* warnings in order for any statements that they make in response to questioning to be admissible in a criminal prosecution?

The Supreme Court has provided a clear answer to the first question, holding that *Miranda* does not apply to prison disciplinary proceedings. *Baxter v. Palmigiano* (1976). In other words, statements obtained without first apprising inmates of their rights under *Miranda* are admissible in a prison disciplinary proceeding.

The answer to the second question is not, however, at this point altogether clear. In *Mathis v. United States* (1968), the Supreme Court held that an inmate incarcerated for a state crime should have been given *Miranda* warnings before being questioned by an IRS agent about a suspected federal tax crime. Since he was not, the Court held that his incriminating statements should not have been admitted at his trial.

On the other hand, in *Illinois v. Perkins* (1990), the Court held that a defendant's Miranda rights were not violated when he was questioned about a murder by an undercover police officer with whom he was incarcerated in the same jail cell while awaiting trial for another crime. The Court observed that since the defendant was unaware that his cellmate was an undercover officer, he was not subjected to the kind of overbearing pressures, with which *Miranda* was concerned, that threaten a person's fifth amendment privilege against self-incrimination.

Perkins is significant because it tells us that there will be times when *Miranda* does not apply even though, in a technical sense, a person is both in custody and subjected to interrogation. The intriguing question which remains after *Perkins* is whether correctional officials who wish to question an inmate about suspected misconduct that constitutes both a disciplinary infraction and a crime must first give the inmate *Miranda* warnings in order for any statements of the inmate to be admissible in a subsequent criminal prosecution. Some lower courts have held that *Miranda* does not apply in this context unless the inmate is subject to constraints on his or her freedom above and beyond those that normally attend day-to-day confinement. *See, e.g., Garcia v. Singletary* (11th Cir.1994). The Supreme Court in *Perkins* added fuel to the speculation that statements made without the giving of *Miranda* warnings during some or all of the steps of the prison disciplinary process might still be admissible in a criminal prosecution when the Court volunteered that "[t]he bare fact of custody may not in every instance require a warning even when the suspect is aware that he is speaking to an official."

While inmates have no right to be given *Miranda* warnings at a disciplinary hearing in order for their incriminating statements to be considered as evidence of guilt by the disciplinary decisionmaker and while they may or may not have such a right in order for their statements to be admissible in a subsequent criminal prosecution, they can still invoke their privilege against self-incrimination during a disciplinary hearing. In *Baxter v. Palmigiano* (1976), however, the Supreme Court held that a disciplinary decisionmaker can draw an adverse inference if an inmate invokes that privilege.   In other words, the inmate's silence can constitutionally be treated as evidence of his or her guilt of the disciplinary infraction.   The Court emphasized though that under the state disciplinary procedures whose constitutionality the Court was upholding, a guilty finding could not be based solely on an inmate's silence.

The effect of *Baxter* is that it may put some inmates in a damned-if-you-do, damned-if-you-don't situation. If the inmates do not speak during their disciplinary hearings to refute the charges against them, their silence may provide the quantum of evidence needed to tilt the balance of the evidence towards a finding of guilt. On the other hand, if they testify during the hearings, they may say things that are incriminating that will lead the disciplinary decisionmaker to find them guilty of misconduct and that, in addition, may later be used against them in a criminal prosecution.

CHAPTER 12

CLASSIFICATION, TRANSFERS, AND WITHHOLDING OF PRIVILEGES

A. PROCEDURAL DUE PROCESS

In addition to the steps taken by prison officials to discipline inmates found guilty of violating prison rules or regulations, prison officials, on a daily basis, make decisions that have adverse, and sometimes substantially adverse, effects on prisoners. Prison officials often, for example, transfer prisoners to prisons where they have fewer privileges and the conditions of confinement are much worse. Other transfers occur within the confines of the prison itself—from, for example, a general population unit to an administrative segregation unit where privileges are sparse and inmates' freedom of movement is substantially curtailed. Prisoners also often lose prison jobs and other privileges for a variety of reasons, including the concern that an inmate will, in the future, abuse the privilege in question.

The question which arises is whether prison officials must take any steps to ensure that the actions they take against an individual inmate are well-founded—that they are not based on misinformation or personal animosity towards the inmate. The question, in short, is whether due process requires the emplacement of certain procedural safeguards in the decisionmaking processes to avoid unfounded decisions that can have such negative effects on prisoners.

In order for a prisoner, like any other individual, to be entitled to the protections of due process, the prisoner must be deprived of an interest falling within the rubric of the due process clause—life, liberty, or property. Much litigation has centered on the question of what constitutes "liberty," the deprivation of which triggers due process protections. According to the Supreme Court, there are two kinds of liberty interests—those that stem from the Constitution itself and those that are created by state law. In a series of cases, the Court has attempted to flesh out when either type of liberty interest exists in the prison context.

In *Meachum v. Fano* (1976), the Supreme Court held that the transfer of a prisoner from one prison to another does not implicate a constitutionally-derived liberty interest. The Court explained that when a person is convicted of a crime through a process that is replete with due process protections, the person loses his or her liberty to the extent that the person can be confined or transferred to any prison that correctional officials deem most suitable. The Court noted that confinement in any prison is "within the normal limits or range of custody which the conviction has authorized the State to impose." It does not matter that a prisoner is being transferred to a prison with substantially more onerous conditions of confinement or is being transferred because the prisoner violated prison rules. *Montanye v. Haymes* (1976). Even the transfer of a prisoner out of state, to a prison thousands of miles from his or her family, does not implicate a constitutionally-derived liberty interest. *Olim v. Wakinekona* (1983) (prisoner transferred from Hawaii to prison 2500 miles away in California).

The same rationale underlying the Supreme Court's conclusion in *Meachum* that interprison transfers do not deprive prisoners of any constitutionally-derived liberty interest led the Court to conclude in *Hewitt v. Helms* (1983) that inmates are not deprived of any liberty that stems from the Constitution itself when they are transferred from the general population unit of a prison into the administrative segregation unit. The Court observed that the transfer of an inmate from one part of a prison to another with less palatable conditions is "well within the terms of confinement ordinarily contemplated by a prison sentence" and that prisoners should "reasonably anticipate" undergoing such a transfer sometime during the period of their incarceration.

Meachum v. Fano and *Hewitt v. Helms* are to be contrasted with the Supreme Court's decision in *Vitek v. Jones* (1980). In *Vitek*, the Court considered whether an inmate transferred from a prison to a mental hospital had been deprived of liberty without due process of law. In addressing the threshold question of whether such a transfer deprives a prisoner of liberty within the meaning of the due process clause, the Court once again applied the "within-the-sentence test." This time, however, the Court concluded that confinement in a mental hospital is not within the range of conditions implicitly authorized by a conviction. The Court cited two reasons for this conclusion—one, the stigma that attends confinement in a mental hospital and two, the behavioral modification programs that an inmate may be forced to participate in while confined in a mental hospital.

The within-the-sentence test applied by the Supreme Court when determining whether a prisoner has been deprived of a constitutionally-derived liberty interest has been criticized by some members of the Court as knowing "few rivals for vagueness and pliability." *See, e.g., Kentucky Department of Corrections v. Thompson* (1989) (Marshall, J., dissenting). The way in which the Court has said states can create liberty interests has also engendered controversy.

In *Meachum v. Fano*, the Court held that prisoners who were transferred from one prison to another were not deprived of any state-created liberty interest, since a state statute left the decision whether or not to transfer a prisoner within the unconfined discretion of correctional officials. By contrast, the transfer of the prisoner from the general population unit to the administrative segregation unit that was at issue in *Hewitt v. Helms*, according to the Supreme Court, did deprive the prisoner of a state-created liberty interest because of the limits placed by state law on the discretion of prison officials when ordering such transfers. A state statute authorized such transfers only in certain delineated situations, such as when an inmate's continued presence in the general population unit posed a serious threat of harm to the inmate or others. Similarly, the prisoner who brought suit in *Vitek v. Jones* was deprived of a state-created liberty interest when he was transferred from a prison to a mental hospital because a state statute made such a transfer contingent on a finding that the prisoner was suffering from a mental disease or defect that could not adequately be treated in the prison.

In *Kentucky Department of Corrections v. Thompson* (1989), however, the Supreme Court clarified that it requires more than what it called "substantive predicates" that govern the exercise of official discretion for state statutes or regulations to create a liberty interest. The Court noted that at least the most common means of creating a liberty interest requires not only substantive criteria that limit officials' discretion when making a decision that has negative repercussions on the liberty of an inmate, but also a mandated result, such as a transfer, when those criteria are met.

The Court held in *Thompson* that the plaintiffs, inmates who had lost the privilege of visiting with certain friends and family members whom prison officials thought had abused their visiting privileges, had not been deprived of any state-created liberty interest. One of the points emphasized by the Court was that while the pertinent prison regulations spelled out reasons why visiting privileges might be curtailed, the list did not purport to be all-inclusive. Visitors might be excluded, according to the regulations, for reasons not set forth on the list. In addition, the Court noted that the prison regulations only said that a visitor "may" be barred from visiting a prisoner for any of the reasons listed, as well as others. According to the Court, the requisite mandatory language was absent.

The problem with this portion of the Court's analysis is that this mandatory language was also missing from the statutes and regulations that the Court in *Hewitt v. Helms* and *Vitek v. Jones* held created liberty interests. In both cases, the relevant statutes and regulations said that an inmate "may" be transferred—in one case, to administrative segregation, and in the other, to a mental hospital—in certain defined circumstances. In *Hewitt* and *Vitek*, however, all of the circumstances that could lead to the deprivations—the transfers—were described in the statutes. Such an all-inclusive list, it can be argued, does implicitly mandate an outcome in the sense that no deprivation, such as a transfer to administrative segregation, can occur if none of the prescribed conditions for a transfer exist. The statutes and regulations at issue in *Hewitt* and *Vitek* did not, on the other hand, as *Thompson* arguably seemed to suggest was necessary, "mandat[e] the outcome to be reached upon a finding that the relevant criteria have been met." Instead, the statutes and regulations only implicitly mandated the outcome to be reached upon a finding that the relevant criteria have not been met.

Some of the Justices on the Supreme Court have belittled the majority of the Court for making the existence of a liberty interest, which triggers the important protections of due process, hinge on the presence or absence of a few words in a state statute or regulation. Justice Stevens, for example, has pointed out that predicating due process protection on the language that happens to be found in a state statute or regulation gives individuals only ephemeral constitutional protection, since the liberty that the government grants today can as quickly be taken away tomorrow by changing the language of a statute or regulation. *Hewitt v. Helms* (1983) (Stevens, J., dissenting). Another concern is that finding that states have created liberty interests when they constrain official discretion through "substantive predicates" and mandated outcomes may discourage states from making laudable attempts to control the exercise of government officials' discretion. The end result may be more arbitrary decisionmaking, a result that seems distinctly at odds with one of the very core purposes of the due process clause. See *Wolff v. McDonnell* (1974) ("The touchstone of due process is protection of the individual against arbitrary action of government.").

Once it has been determined that an action contemplated by prison officials, if taken, would deprive a prisoner of a liberty interest falling within the scope of the protection of due process, the next question concerns the procedural safeguards which must attend the process leading to the deprivation. In *Hewitt v. Helms* (1983), the Supreme Court's answer to the question of what "process" is "due" an inmate deprived of a liberty interest through a transfer from general population to administrative segregation was, "Not much." First, the inmate must be afforded "some notice" of the reason for the transfer. The Court did not, however, say that this notice must be in writing. Second, the inmate must be given the chance to communicate his or her views about the transfer to the person who will decide whether the inmate's confinement in administrative segregation is warranted. However, in most instances, an inmate has no right to appear in person to explain why his or her confinement in administrative segregation is unjustified or not needed. The Court said that "ordinarily," permitting the inmate to submit a written statement will suffice.

Third, the inmate has the right to have the transfer decision and the evidence upon which it was founded reviewed by a prison official within a "reasonable time" after the transfer. This informal review does not, however, have to occur in the course of a hearing, because, as mentioned earlier, an inmate generally has no right to be present when the transfer decision is being reviewed.

Finally, if the inmate remains confined in the administrative segregation unit, the need for continued confinement must be periodically reviewed

by prison officials. According to the Supreme
Court, however, an inmate does not "necessarily"
have the right to submit any evidence or even a
written statement to be considered during this peri-
odic-review process. The Court explained that any
facts about the prisoner needed to make the decision whether or not to keep the prisoner in the
administrative segregation unit will already have
been obtained during the initial review process. In
addition, the retention decision will often be based
on predictions about the future behavior of the
prisoner and other inmates that would not be aided
by the formal introduction of evidence.

In a dissenting opinion, Justice Stevens disagreed
with the majority's assessment of the value of the
contribution that a prisoner might make to the
decision whether or not to continue the prisoner's
confinement in the administrative segregation unit.
Justice Stevens argued that a prisoner has a right
to appear in person to state his or her views as to
why continued confinement in administrative segregation is unwarranted.

In addition, Justice Stevens insisted that if the
decision is made to continue to keep a prisoner in
segregation, the decisionmaker has to provide the
prisoner with at least a brief written statement
recounting the reasons for this decision. According
to Justice Stevens, this statement will provide guidance to the prisoner as to the steps that he or she
can take to procure release from segregation. The
statement will also enable the inmate to bring any
errors upon which the segregation decision has been

founded to the attention of prison authorities and will prompt those conducting the review to make their decision with greater care. Finally, such a written statement will facilitate the administrative and judicial review of segregation decisions.

The dearth of procedural safeguards that, according to the Supreme Court, must attend transfers to administrative segregation when state law creates a liberty interest in remaining in the general population unit is to be contrasted with the many procedural safeguards that must surround transfers of a prisoner from a prison to a mental hospital. In *Vitek v. Jones* (1980), the Supreme Court agreed with the district court that the following procedures are constitutionally mandated when transferring prisoners to mental hospitals: (1) written notice of the contemplated transfer far enough in advance of the hearing to permit the prisoner to adequately prepare for it; (2) a hearing that the inmate has a right to attend; (3) the right to make an oral statement at the hearing; (4) the right to be apprised of the information upon which the transfer recommendation is predicated; (5) the right to present documentary evidence in opposition to the transfer; (6) the right to call witnesses to testify on the prisoner's behalf unless there is "good cause" for not permitting the prisoner to call a particular witness to testify; (7) the right to confront and cross-examine adverse witnesses unless there is "good cause" for prohibiting the exercise of these rights; (8) the right to have an "independent decisionmaker" make the transfer decision, although this decisionmaker might work within the prison or mental hospital and still be considered sufficiently "independent"; (9) the right to receive a written statement outlining the evidence relied on and the reasons for the transfer; and (10) "effective" and "timely" notice of all of the above rights.

The district court in *Vitek* had also held that an inmate facing a possible transfer to a mental hospital is entitled to be represented by an attorney at the transfer hearing, a conclusion with which four Justices on the Supreme Court agreed. Justice Powell, however, wrote a separate concurring opinion in which he set forth his view that due process is satisfied as long as the prisoner receives assistance from someone who is both "qualified" and "independent" when contesting the recommended transfer to a mental hospital. He explained that a prisoner can be adequately, and perhaps even better assisted by a licensed psychiatrist or other mental-health professional during a transfer proceeding, since the focus of the hearing is on a medical issue. An inmate confronted with a possible transfer to a mental hospital must therefore receive assistance from someone who is "qualified" and "independent," but not necessarily an attorney, as the eleventh procedural safeguard mandated by due process.

The vast difference between the paltry amount of procedural safeguards that must attend certain transfers to administrative segregation and the breadth of procedural protection that surrounds transfers of prisoners to mental hospitals is due to the balancing test discussed earlier in this book that the Court customarily applies when determining what "process" is "due" in a particular situation involving a deprivation of life, liberty, or property. *See* pages 39–40 in Chapter 3.   Under this test, first enunciated in *Mathews v. Eldridge* (1976), the following three factors are balanced: (1) the private interest that is at stake; (2) the effect on any governmental interests if a particular procedural safeguard were incorporated into the decisionmaking process; and (3) the safeguard's value and the risk of an erroneous deprivation of the private interest in question if the safeguard is not put in place.

When the Supreme Court applied the *Mathews* balancing test in *Hewitt v. Helms* and *Vitek v. Jones*, one of the chief differences in the Court's analysis in the two cases was in its discussion of the private interest at stake in each case.   In *Hewitt*, the Court asserted that an inmate's interest in remaining in the general population unit and not being transferred to administrative segregation is "not of great consequence."   The Court noted that no great stigma attaches to such a transfer, since a prisoner can be transferred to administrative segregation for so many different reasons.   In addition, there was no evidence in the record that confinement in administrative segregation might reduce a prisoner's chances of being released on parole.   By contrast, the Court in *Vitek v. Jones* emphasized the opprobrium that accompanies the label, "mentally ill," as well as the intrusiveness of the unwanted medical treatment to which individuals in mental hospitals are subjected.

When balancing the remaining two factors under the *Mathews* balancing test in *Hewitt v. Helms*, the Supreme Court seemed to deviate from the way in which it normally analyzes those two factors. The second factor, as mentioned earlier, generally focuses on the extent to which inserting a particular procedural safeguard into a process will advance or detrimentally affect a governmental interest or interests. To the extent that an important governmental interest will be adversely affected by inclusion of the procedural safeguard in the process, it is less likely that the safeguard is constitutionally mandated. On the other hand, to the extent that the safeguard will promote a significant governmental interest, it is more likely that the procedural safeguard will be considered part of due process.

In *Hewitt v. Helms*, however, the Supreme Court narrowed its traditional focus when it examined the second factor under the *Mathews* balancing test. The Court simply looked at "the governmental interests involved" in the prisoner's transfer to administrative segregation whose constitutionality was at issue in the case and assessed how important those interests were. According to the Court, two interests were implicated in this case when the prisoner was transferred to administrative segregation after a prison riot in which he was suspected of participating. One was the interest in isolating a prisoner who posed a risk of harm to other prisoners or correctional staff. The other was the interest in confining the prisoner away from other prisoners while his involvement in the riot was investigated, to prevent him from hurting or coercing witnesses who might attest to his involvement.

The Court basically underscored the centrality of each of these interests, and that was the end of its analysis. Had the Court gone on, however, and analyzed the extent to which each of these interests would have been affected by a particular procedural safeguard, such as having the inmate be present when the need for his confinement in the administrative segregation unit was reviewed, the Court might have concluded that the governmental interests implicated by the transfer would not have been adversely affected by affording the inmate this safeguard.

The Supreme Court skewed its application of the *Mathews* balancing test in another way that may have contributed to the dearth of procedural protection that the Court concluded must be afforded an inmate transferred to administrative segregation. When examining the third factor under the *Mathews* balancing test—the value of the claimed safeguard and the risk of an erroneous deprivation of the private interest at stake if the safeguard is not provided—the Court discussed the value that a "detailed adversary proceeding" would have on the reliability of the decision to transfer an inmate to administrative segregation. The Court ultimately concluded that such an adversary process would not be overly helpful because of the complexity and subjectivity of the assessments made by prison officials when deciding whether an inmate needs to be confined in administrative segregation. Such a decision may not even be grounded on specific facts about what an inmate has done, since even untrue rumors about an inmate might justify the isolation of the inmate to protect the inmate from retaliation from those who believe the rumors to be true. In addition, transfers are often based on predictions about what an inmate or others might do in the future.

The problem with the Court's analysis is that by lumping all procedural safeguards into one amorphous category—"detailed adversary proceeding"— the Court failed to examine the potential value of individual safeguards subsumed within that general category. For example, while it might be true that there would not be any great benefit in turning a transfer review into a "detailed adversary proceeding," that does not necessarily mean that the reliability of the process might not be enhanced by, for example, permitting an inmate, as Justice Stevens proposed, to appear in person before those individuals charged with periodically reviewing the need for the inmates's continued confinement in administrative segregation. In sum, the way in which the Supreme Court applied the *Mathews* balancing test in *Hewitt v. Helms* tilted the Court towards its finding that transfers to administrative segregation need be accompanied by few procedural safeguards.

In *Washington v. Harper* (1990), the Supreme Court addressed some of the procedural due process requirements that must be met when psychotropic drugs are involuntarily administered to a mentally ill inmate. The Court first concluded that such involuntary administration of antipsychotic medication deprives an inmate of a constitutionally-derived liberty interest. The Court also noted that the inmate who had brought suit in *Harper* had been deprived of a state-created liberty interest as well, since the involuntary administration of psychotropic drugs to inmates in the state of Washington was contingent on certain factual findings, such as that an inmate had a "mental disorder" that created a "likelihood of serious harm" to the inmate, others, or their property.

Turning to the question of what "process" is "due" an inmate to whom government officials wish to compulsorily administer antipsychotic medication, the Court first rejected the inmate's claim that the decision about whether such involuntary medication is warranted has to be made by a judge. The Court recognized the substantiality of the private interest at stake; antipsychotic drugs can cause severe side effects—even death. The Court nonetheless believed that inmates' interest in avoiding unwanted medical treatment can be protected, and perhaps even better protected, by having independent mental health professionals make the medication decision. The Court, however, also emphasized in *Harper* that in Washington, an inmate could obtain judicial review of the determination that the involuntary administration of psychotropic drugs was justified.

The Court in *Harper* also gave short shrift to the inmate's claim that he was entitled to be represented by an attorney at the hearing where it would be determined whether to administer antipsychotic drugs to him over his objection. The requirements of due process would be satisfied, the Court observed, as long as the inmate was represented by a person who was "independent" and understood the psychiatric issues in the case.

The Court furthermore rejected the inmate's claim that the need to administer antipsychotic drugs over his objection had to be proven by "clear, cogent, and convincing evidence" before such forced drugging could occur. The Court gave no reason for this conclusion other than that this standard of proof was "neither required nor helpful" when this type of medical determination is being made.

There are a number of questions that remain after *Harper* about the procedural safeguards that must surround the involuntary administration of psychotropic drugs to inmates. The state of Washington, on its own, afforded inmates a broad measure of procedural protection in this situation, including periodic review of the advisability of continuing the involuntary medication seven days after the treatment had begun and every fourteen days thereafter. The Supreme Court therefore had no opportunity to consider in *Harper* whether these safeguards are constitutionally mandated. In determining what procedural safeguards are required by due process, courts will apply the *Mathews* balancing test. In addition, they will turn to other relevant Supreme Court cases, such as *Vitek v. Jones*, for guidance.

B. EQUAL PROTECTION OF THE LAW

In prisons, racial tensions abound. The discord between races that often simmers in the free world can explode when combined with the anger, frustration, loneliness, and resentment that permeates the lives of prisoners.

Some prison officials have attempted to respond to the reality of racial hatred in prisons and the threat of violence that it creates by separating prisoners of different races. In *Washington v. Lee* (M.D.Ala.1966), the United States District Court for the Middle District of Alabama struck down such a segregation scheme as violative of the equal protection clause found in the fourteenth amendment. The court did, however, recognize that in some "isolated instances," segregation by race might be constitutionally permissible for a "limited period" of time.

In its summary affirmance of the district court's judgment, the Supreme Court seemed to agree that the interest in maintaining institutional security can sometimes override the interest in averting the racial discrimination that inheres in attempts to keep prisoners of different races apart. *Lee v. Washington* (1968). In a concurring opinion, Justice Black clarified what he felt was implicit in the majority's opinion: that prison officials must have acted in good faith and in response to "particularized circumstances" to trigger the limited exception to the general rule that the Constitution will not countenance racial discrimination—even in a prison.

While the Supreme Court in *Lee v. Washington* left open a loophole that might, in some limited instances, permit correctional officials to separate inmates on the basis of their race, the lower courts have generally been hostile to even limited segregation schemes. *See, e.g., Stewart v. Rhodes* (S.D. Ohio 1979) (striking down a policy of double celling only inmates of the same race together during the eight-week period they were processed upon entry into the corrections system). Even when the concerns of prison officials about racial conflict are well-founded, the courts have generally required prison officials to take steps other than segregating prisoners to preserve institutional security. *See, e.g., Blevins v. Brew* (W.D.Wis.1984). Some of the alternative steps mentioned by the courts have included increasing the supervision of inmates, disciplining and isolating assaultive inmates, and decreasing the prison population to enhance officials' ability to supervise and control the prisoners.

The way in which the courts have brushed aside very real security concerns when striking down segregation schemes on equal protection grounds stands in marked contrast to the deference they show prison officials' assessments of what is needed to protect institutional security in cases involving constitutional claims of inmates to which the *Turner* test is applied. *See* pages 144–146 in Chapter

9). If the *Turner* test were applied in cases like *Lee v. Washington*, the outcome in many of these cases might very well be different. Under the *Turner* test, for example, the alternatives to segregation cited by the lower courts would not even be considered viable because they entail more than *de minimis* costs. But under a standard of review that is less deferential than the *Turner* test to the security assessments of prison officials, these segregation schemes can be and have been stricken down, in part due to the recognition that over the long term, segregation can actually aggravate racial tensions. *See, e.g., Stewart v. Rhodes* (S.D. Ohio 1979).

Thus far, most courts have also not applied the *Turner* test to inmate claims alleging gender-based discrimination. Many of these claims have centered on the diminished work and educational opportunities afforded female inmates compared to their male counterparts. In reviewing these claims, most of the lower courts have required that female inmates receive "parity of treatment." *See, e.g., McCoy v. Nevada Dept. of Prisons* (D.Nev.1991). Parity of treatment does not mean identical treatment. A class offered, for example, at a men's prison does not automatically have to be included in course offerings at a women's prison. The facilities, programs, and privileges of female inmates must, however, be "substantially equivalent ... in substance if not form" to those of male inmates. *Glover v. Johnson* (E.D.Mich.1979). Male inmates cannot, for example, be trained for high-paying jobs, while female inmates are consigned to training programs that will enable them to perform only low-paying, menial work.

If the facilities, programs, and privileges offered female inmates are not substantially equivalent to those offered male inmates, the government has the burden of proving that the differences are "substantially related to the achievement of important government objectives." *Pitts v. Thornburgh* (D.C.Cir. 1989). When this burden is not met, a finding that the female inmates' equal protection rights have been violated will follow.

Even though there are some equal protection claims asserted in the correctional context, such as claims alleging racial or gender discrimination, that will trigger, at least at present, more stringent review by the courts, most equal protection claims will be analyzed under a rational-basis test. In *Jones v. North Carolina Prisoners' Labor Union* (1977), a case discussed earlier in this book (*see* page 142 in Chapter 9), some prisoners contended that some regulations that prohibited the bulk mailing of prisoner union materials and prisoner union meetings violated their right to the equal protection of the law. The basis for their equal protection claim was the fact that inmates in two other organizations, the Jaycees and Alcoholics Anonymous, were permitted to send such group mailings and hold group meetings.

The Supreme Court, however, rejected the prisoners' claim, noting that there was a "rational basis" for the differential treatment of inmates in the

Jaycees and Alcoholics Anonymous. Those two organizations, the Court noted, had rehabilitative objectives, while the principal goal of the prisoners' union was to require prison officials to engage in collective bargaining with the union, a practice that was actually illegal under state law.

CHAPTER 13

SEARCHES, SEIZURES, AND PRIVACY RIGHTS

In prisons, privacy is a rare commodity. Often, prisoners' letters to and from family members and friends are opened and read by prison officials. Prisoners' movements throughout the prison are observed, monitored, and regulated, and there is no place where they can go for refuge. Most inmates share a cell with one or more other inmates or live in dormitories filled with many other prisoners. Even for those fortunate few inmates who have their own cells, privacy is nonexistent. They can be observed in their cells or rooms through cellbars or windows at any moment, even when defecating or urinating in a toilet within the cell. And every inch of their cells and every piece of property that they own can and often will be inspected as correctional officials attempt to fulfill their responsibility of ferreting contraband out of the institution.

Because of the demands of maintaining institutional security, inmates' privacy must necessarily be curtailed. The question that remains is whether inmates have any residual privacy rights that are protected by the Constitution.

A. THE FOURTH AMENDMENT

One of the primary purposes of the fourth amendment is to protect individuals' privacy from being intruded upon by the government. The fourth amendment protects our "persons, houses, papers, and effects" from "unreasonable searches and seizures" and also sets forth the requirements that must be met in order for a warrant to be valid. But does the fourth amendment extend any protection to prisoners?

In *Hudson v. Palmer* (1984), the Supreme Court provided a partial answer to this question. In that case, a prisoner had brought a lawsuit in which he contended that his fourth amendment rights were violated when his cell was searched and personal property destroyed for no other reason than to harass him. The Supreme Court disagreed, holding that the predicate for a finding of a violation of the fourth amendment did not exist in this case; according to the Court, no search or seizure had occurred that would even trigger further analysis under the fourth amendment.

The Supreme Court first held that the inspection of the prisoner's cell was not a "search" within the meaning of the fourth amendment. In arriving at this conclusion, the Court, as it has in other contexts, departed from the literal meaning of the word "search." Instead, the Court said that for a search in the fourth amendment sense to occur, there must be an incursion by the government into an area where a person has a "legitimate" or "reasonable" expectation of privacy. In order for an expectation of privacy to be considered legitimate or reasonable, the Court explained, it must be one that "society is prepared to recognize as 'reasonable.' " The Court then stated that any expectation that inmates have that they will have some measure of privacy in their cells is not reasonable because of the obvious need for correctional officials to have uninhibited access to cells to locate weapons, drugs, and other contraband, to find evidence of impending escapes, and to ensure that the cells are sanitary.

In addition to rejecting the plaintiff's claim that the search of his cell violated his fourth amendment rights, the Supreme Court in *Hudson* also gave short shrift to the plaintiff's claim that the destruction of his property constituted an "unreasonable seizure" proscribed by the fourth amendment. In a footnote, the Court cursorily addressed this claim, simply noting that prisoners cannot contest seizures of their property under the fourth amendment for the same reasons that they cannot contest searches of their cells. In analogizing searches of cells and seizures of property, the Court nowhere acknowledged, much less responded to, the argument of Justice Stevens in dissent that seizures of property are different from searches of property because they implicate not just privacy, but also possessory interests.

Instead, the Court summarily announced that prison officials need the freedom to confiscate items that, in their opinion, threaten "legitimate institutional interests." In the same breath, however, the

Court assured prisoners that they are not remediless when their property is unjustifiably destroyed by correctional officials.   They can, for example, seek redress under state law.   In addition, the destruction of property sometimes violates the eight amendment's prohibition of cruel and unusual punishments (for example, eyeglasses of an almost blind inmate) or other constitutional provisions, such as the first amendment (for example, a Bible) or the due process right of access to the courts (legal papers).   The irony of this portion of the Court's discussion is that the Court was saying that the fourth amendment provides no protection to inmates whose property has been destroyed because prison officials must be free to seize items which, under other portions of the Constitution, they are forbidden from seizing.

In other cases, the Supreme Court has held that inmates and pretrial detainees do not even have a right to observe searches of their cells to avert the theft or the unnecessary confiscation or destruction of their property.   *See Block v. Rutherford (1984)*; *Bell v. Wolfish* (1979).   The Court's rationale is that the presence of inmates while their cells are being searched might spark confrontations between the inmates and the correctional officers searching through their personal belongings.   In addition, inmates might frustrate the purposes of cell searches by passing contraband from one cell to another as the searches are being conducted.

While the claims before the Supreme Court in *Hudson v. Palmer* concerned only the search of a cell and the destruction of personal property, the Court, in rejecting those claims, used broad language that suggested that prisoners might have no rights at all under the fourth amendment. At one point in its opinion, the Court said, "We are satisfied that society would insist that the prisoner's expectation of privacy *always* yield to what must be considered the paramount interest in institutional security." (emphasis added).

The question that remains after *Hudson* then is to what extent, if at all, inmates retain any rights under the fourth amendment. In particular, does the fourth amendment place any constraints on the observation or touching of inmates' bodies?

Many of the lower courts that have addressed this question have held that the fourth amendment does place some limits on searches of inmates' bodies. *See, e.g., Cornwell v. Dahlberg* (6th Cir.1992). It is clear, however, from the Supreme Court's decision in *Bell v. Wolfish* (1979) that if the fourth amendment extends to inmates when their bodies are being searched, the protection afforded by that amendment is quite limited.

Bell involved a challenge by convicted inmates, as well as pretrial detainees, to visual body-cavity inspections to which they were subjected after contact visits, which, as mentioned earlier in this book, are visits where there is no physical barrier between inmates and their visitors. During these inspections, male inmates had to bend over and lift their genitals to permit correctional officials to visually inspect their rectums, while female inmates had their vaginal and anal cavities visually inspected.

The Supreme Court began its analysis of the constitutionality of these inspections by assuming, without deciding, that inmates and pretrial detainees retain some fourth amendment rights. The Court, however, went on to conclude that visual body-cavity inspections can be conducted after contact visits even if correctional officials do not have any particular reason to believe an inmate is attempting to smuggle contraband into the institution.

In arriving at this conclusion, the Court applied the balancing test that it typically applies when assessing the constitutionality of what it deems to be administrative searches, searches whose primary purpose is something other than the detection of evidence of a crime or the apprehension of a criminal. Under this balancing test, the Court weighs the intrusiveness of a search against the need for the search.

In *Bell*, the Court acknowledged that visual body-cavity inspection are grossly invasive. Yet the Court upheld such inspections, even in the absence of any suspicion of wrongdoing on the part of an inmate, because of the need to not only detect, but deter the inflow of contraband, such as weapons and drugs, into an institution.

In the course of assessing the need for visual body-cavity searches after contact visits, the Court rejected the argument that the existence of less intrusive means of achieving the objectives of the searches would necessarily mean that the searches are unreasonable and hence unconstitutional.   In subsequent cases, the Court has explained that the question under the fourth amendment is not simply whether an alternative was available, but whether an official was unreasonable in failing to recognize or implement the alternative. *See United States v. Sharpe* (1985).   Consequently, in *Bell v. Wolfish*, the Court rebuffed the suggestion that the correctional officials had acted unreasonably in conducting visual body-cavity inspections because they could, alternatively, have used metal detectors to thwart the smuggling of contraband into the facility or more closely observed inmates and their visitors during contact visits.   The Court noted the drawbacks of these alternatives.   Metal detectors cannot detect nonmetallic contraband, such as drugs, while closer monitoring of contact visits would interfere with their purpose of fostering and maintaining family and other ties by enabling inmates to converse with loved ones in a somewhat private setting.

Bell was a close case, with the Court splitting 5–4 on the issue of the constitutionality of visual body-cavity inspections.   Three of the dissenting Justices—Justices Marshall, Stevens, and Brennan—would have required probable cause to believe an inmate was attempting to smuggle contraband into a facility before permitting such a search.   Justice Powell, on the other hand, insisted that such searches be predicated on at least "reasonable suspicion," a more lax standard than probable cause.

While the majority of the Court concluded that there is no individualized-suspicion requirement when visual body-cavity inspections are conducted after contact visits, the Court hastened to add that such inspections must be conducted in a "reasonable manner." This caveat raises the possibility of successful fourth amendment challenges to visual body-cavity inspections because of where they were conducted, who conducted them, or who else observed them. In addition, *Bell* leaves unanswered questions about the circumstances under which manual body-cavity inspections, those involving physical touching of body cavities, are constitutional. In answering these questions, the need for a particular type of manual inspection would, under the fourth amendment balancing test, have to be weighed against its intrusiveness.

B. RIGHT OF PRIVACY

In addition to the protection afforded privacy interests by the fourth amendment, there is, according to the Supreme Court, a general right of privacy subsumed within the Constitution. The Supreme Court has vacillated as to the source of this right. In some cases, the Court has said that the right springs from the "penumbras" of several constitutional provisions—the first amendment right to freedom of association; the third amendment, which prohibits the government from requiring that private homes be used to shelter soldiers during times of peace; the fourth amendment; the fifth amendment privilege against self-incrimination; and the ninth amendment, which states that individual rights are not limited to those listed in the Constitution. *See, e.g., Griswold v. Connecticut* (1965). In other cases though, the Court has simply said that the right of privacy is subsumed within the "liberty" protected by the due process clauses of the fifth and fourteenth amendments. *See, e.g., Zablocki v. Redhail* (1978).

The Supreme Court has never explicitly held that the right of privacy extends to inmates, but the Court seemed to implicitly acknowledge as much in *Turner v. Safley* (1987). In that case, which was discussed earlier in Chapter 9 on pages 144–149, the Court struck down a regulation, which restricted inmate marriages, because it unconstitutionally impinged upon the right to marry, a right which is encompassed within the more general constitutional right of privacy.

Most of the lower courts have assumed or held that inmates retain some privacy rights under the Constitution. Their energies have instead been directed towards defining the scope of inmates' right of privacy.

Much of the litigation in this area has centered on questions concerning the extent to which correctional officers of a different gender can search inmates or observe them in the nude while they are bathing, dressing, sleeping, or using the toilet. The courts have really struggled with these questions because of the clash between several competing interests that are at stake—inmates' interest in their privacy; the interest of correctional officers, both male and female, in having equal employment opportunities; and the institutional interest in maintaining security.

Another interest is also arguably implicated by the question of the work to be performed by correctional officers of the opposite sex—that of rehabilitation. Some courts have argued that the presence of, for example, female correctional officers in a men's prison is rehabilitative. *See, e.g., Bagley v. Watson* (D.Or.1983). These courts contend that with women working in prisons, the prisons will be more like "the real world," facilitating inmates' ability to adjust and their ability to relate positively to women upon their release from prison. Detractors of this rehabilitation argument, however, maintain that the presence of female correctional officers in men's prisons is dehumanizing and therefore actually anti-rehabilitative. They point out that in the "real world," persons of one sex do not normally watch strangers of the other sex undress, bathe, urinate, and defecate. *See, e.g., Bowling v. Enomoto* (N.D.Cal.1981).

The state of the law in this area is in flux, but some areas of general consensus have emerged. First, the courts generally concur that the right of privacy is not violated by the inadvertent or infrequent observation of a nude inmate by a correctional officer of a different gender. *See, e.g., Smith v. Chrans* (C.D.Ill.1986). Second, the courts agree that inmates' right of privacy is not abridged when a person of the opposite sex is in the area where inmates live for a short, but designated period of time, because the inmates can take steps during these predetermined times to avoid being seen in the nude or using the toilet. *See, e.g., Avery v. Perrin* (D.N.H.1979). Finally, the courts agree that whatever limitations the Constitution places on the observation or touching of inmates by correctional officers of the opposite sex, those limitations can be overridden in an emergency situation. *See, e.g., Lee v. Downs* (4th Cir.1981) (no abridgement of the right to privacy when two male correctional officers restrained the arms and legs of a female inmate, a very big and strong woman, while a female nurse searched her vagina for matches after the inmate had set fire to her paper dress).

Rather than holding that inmates' interest in their privacy must always give way to the interest in providing equal employment opportunities to men and women or, conversely, that inmates' privacy interests always supersede the interest of others in equal employment opportunities, the courts have generally sought to accommodate both interests without undermining institutional security. Where the courts have differed is on how far correctional officials must go to accommodate inmates' interest in their privacy.

The different responses of the trial court and the Eighth Circuit Court of Appeals to the inmates' right-to-privacy claims asserted in *Timm v. Gunter* (8th Cir.1990) exemplify the variation in views about the degree to which accommodations must be made. In that case, male inmates at a maximum-security prison contended that patdown searches conducted by female correctional officers and visual surveillance by these officers of inmates when they were dressing, showering, using the toilet, and sleeping violated their constitutional right of privacy. The district court agreed and ordered the prison officials to take a number of steps to avoid impinging on the inmates' privacy interests. One of those steps was to permit an inmate to request that a male correctional officer search him when both a male and a female correctional officer were working at the same post. Another was to limit the extent to which female correctional officers could observe inmates, who were undressed or using the toilet, by modifying work schedules, by making modifications to the facility, such as the addition of toilet doors in one unit, and by admonishing female correctional officers to avoid looking at unclothed inmates or those who were using the toilet.

The Eighth Circuit Court of Appeals, however, reversed the lower court's order, holding that none of these accommodating measures were constitutionally required. In arriving at this conclusion, the court emphasized the adverse effects on security of some of the accommodations, as well as their costs, both financial and administrative. The prescribed modifications in the facility's physical plant, for example, would be quite costly and would impede the observation of inmates needed to preserve institutional security. Modifying female correctional officers' work schedules, on the other hand, would create scheduling problems. And permitting inmates to request that they be searched by a male, instead of a female correctional officer, would diminish the perceived authority of female correctional officers, to the detriment of the institution's overall security.

The court of appeals in *Timm v. Gunter* also expressed concern about the impact of some of the accommodations on employment opportunities for women. The court noted the resentment felt by male correctional officers when they see female correctional officers assigned to different, and generally less dangerous, posts because of their gender. The court also observed that limiting the job opportunities and responsibilities of female correctional officers would make them less knowledgeable, and therefore less effective, if they were later promoted to supervisory positions.

Finally, the court of appeals stated that the incursions on inmates' privacy were, in its opinion, really quite minimal. The court noted that there were already some physical obstructions that limited the viewing of inmates in the nude, such as the three-sided wall surrounding the urinal in the prison yard. In addition, the prisoners could take steps to further protect their privacy, such as covering themselves with a towel when using the toilet.

While there is certainly no uniformity in the decisions of the lower courts as to the scope of inmates' right to privacy, most of the courts seem to be moving in the direction taken by the court of appeals in *Timm v. Gunter*—towards countenancing incursions on inmates' privacy by correctional officers of the opposite sex. This trend is most apparent in cases contesting patdown searches and visual surveillance of living and bathing areas by such officers. One of the themes repeated in many of these cases is that as long as the correctional officers act professionally when performing patdown searches or monitoring living and bathing areas, the intrusion on inmates' privacy will be limited, just as it is limited when a doctor examines a patient of a different gender.

While the courts are increasingly permitting correctional officers of the opposite sex to perform tasks that may intrude upon inmates' privacy, some of them are drawing the line at strip searches, holding that these searches cannot generally be performed or observed by correctional officers of a different gender. *See, e.g., Lee v. Downs* (4th Cir. 1981). *See also Canedy v. Boardman* (7th Cir. 1994). In addition, many courts have required or permitted greater restrictions on searches and surveillance of female inmates by male correctional officers than those imposed on searches and surveillance of male inmates by female correctional officers. In rejecting the argument that this differential treatment of male and female inmates violates the equal protection rights of male inmates, the courts have asserted an assortment of justifications for the differential treatment. Some, such as the court of appeals in *Timm v. Gunter*, have cited the greater risks to security posed by male inmates because of their more serious criminal backgrounds and their greater propensity to use violence while they are incarcerated. Others have pointed to the large number of female inmates who have been sexually or otherwise physically abused by men and who would suffer severe emotional trauma if male officers patted down their bodies, including their breasts and genital areas, in a search for contraband. *See, e.g., Jordan v. Gardner* (9th Cir.1993). Finally, at least one court has concluded that maximizing the number of tasks that female correctional officers can perform in men's prisons, while not permitting male correctional officers to perform similar functions in women's prisons, is a defensible means of ensuring that women have adequate employment opportunities in prisons, which still predominantly house male inmates. *Madyun v. Franzen* (7th Cir.1983).

In addition to the restrictions placed on the work to be performed by women in men's prisons in order to accommodate what is believed to be inmates' right to privacy, security interests may, at least in some circumstances, justify such restrictions. In *Dothard v. Rawlinson* (1977), the Supreme Court upheld a regulation that prohibited women from working in positions in maximum-security prisons for men in Alabama where they would frequently be physically near the inmates. The Court rejected the argument that this regulation violated Title VII of the Civil Rights Act of 1964, 42 U.S.C.A. § 2000e, which prohibits gender-based employment discrimination. Instead, the

Court found that the ban on the employment of women was permissible under the statutory exemption which permits sex-based discrimination when gender is "a bona fide occupational qualification reasonably necessary to the normal operation of that particular business or enterprise."   42 U.S.C.A. § 2000e–2(e).

The Court acknowledged that the "bfoq exception" was "an extremely narrow" one. Nonetheless, the Court held that the ban on the employment of women in contact positions in Alabama's maximum-security prisons fell within this exception because there was such a risk that prisoners would sexually assault female correctional officers.

Justice Marshall was incensed by what he described as the Court's paternalistic attitude towards women. He noted that "[o]nce again, '[t]he pedestal upon which women have been placed has . . ., upon closer inspection, been revealed as a cage.' " Let women decide for themselves, he argued, whether they were willing to undergo the risk of being sexually assaulted. The Court, however, responded that more than the safety of prospective female correctional officers was at stake, since an increase in assaults in a prison would undercut the officials' control of prisoners and thereby undermine the safety and security of other correctional officers and the inmates.

By underscoring in *Dothard* that Alabama's maximum-security prisons for men, with their "jungle atmosphere," were "not typical," the Supreme

Court seemed to be intimating that the case before it was an exceptional one and that normally women cannot be barred from working in contact positions in prisons for security reasons. Many of the conditions in the Alabama prisons that the Court cited as distinguishing characteristics, however, exist in other correctional facilities as well—rampant violence, understaffing, dormitory living arrangements, and the commingling of sex offenders within the general prison population.

It seems clear though from the Court's resolution of another Title VII claim in *Dothard v. Rawlinson* that while women may sometimes be barred from working in contact positions in some men's prisons because of their "very womanhood," they cannot be excluded because they are assumed to be less strong than men. In *Dothard*, the Court struck down some height and weight requirements that an individual had to meet in order to be hired as a correctional officer in Alabama. These requirements had led to a disproportionate number of women being disqualified from employment as correctional officers. The defendants had argued that the height and weight standards were needed to ensure that persons hired as correctional officers were strong enough to perform their duties. The Supreme Court, however, responded that if a certain amount of strength is needed to perform the duties of a correctional officer, then an applicant's strength should be measured directly, instead of employing surrogate indicators of strength.

CHAPTER 14

DUE PROCESS CLAIMS FOR PERSONAL INJURIES AND PROPERTY DEPRIVATIONS

As was discussed in the previous chapter, the Supreme Court in *Hudson v. Palmer* (1984) observed that the destruction of a prisoner's property, while not actionable under the fourth amendment, might give rise to a claim cognizable under other provisions of the Constitution. One question is whether the destruction or loss of an inmate's property by prison officials violates the inmate's right to due process of law, a right, as mentioned earlier, accorded federal inmates by the fifth amendment and state and local inmates by the fourteenth amendment. In order for a due process violation to have occurred, the inmate must have been "deprived" of that property within the meaning of the due process clause, and the deprivation must have occurred "without due process of law."

In *Daniels v. Williams* (1986), the Supreme Court addressed the question of what constitutes a "deprivation" within the meaning of the fourteenth amendment's due process clause. In that case, a jail inmate brought a § 1983 suit against a deputy sheriff when he was injured after slipping on a pillow negligently left on the stairs in the jail. The issue before the Supreme Court was whether negligence can effect a "deprivation" that triggers due process requirements.

In resolving that issue, the Court noted that the purpose of the due process clause is to avert and redress the " 'affirmative abuse of power' " by government officials. The Court then concluded that the negligence of government officials—their simple failure to act with reasonable care—does not involve the abuse of power with which the due process clause is concerned. Accordingly, while the plaintiff in *Daniels* may have been deprived in a literal sense of his liberty interest in not being injured, according to the Court, he suffered no deprivation in the constitutional sense. The Court emphasized that its conclusion did not mean that claims grounded on the negligence of government officials are unimportant; it simply meant that these claims are more suitable for consideration in a different forum—in a tort action filed in a state court.

While the Supreme Court in *Daniels v. Williams* said that the negligence of government officials would not support a due process claim, but that the intentional actions of the officials would, the Court left unresolved whether officials acting with a state of mind falling somewhere in between negligence and intent can effect a deprivation in the constitutional sense. Specifically, the question left open after *Daniels* is whether gross negligence or recklessness, which generally requires some subjective appreciation of the substantial risk that harm will ensue, will suffice to support a due process claim. When considering how this issue should be resolved, it is interesting to note that the Supreme Court has held, in another context, that reckless conduct can be sufficiently serious to make imposition of the death penalty constitutional in some cases involving such conduct. *See Tison v. Arizona* (1987) (death penalty constitutional even though defendants, who were convicted under a felony-murder rule, did not kill victims and had no intent to kill them; defendants had acted with "reckless indifference to human life").

In *Davidson v. Cannon* (1986), a case decided on the same day as *Daniels v. Williams*, the Supreme Court reaffirmed that the negligence of prison officials will not give rise to a due process claim. *Davidson* involved a lawsuit brought by an inmate who, after being threatened by another inmate, apprised certain prison officials of the threats. The officials, however, took no steps to protect the plaintiff, and he was eventually seriously injured when he was assaulted by the inmate who had previously threatened him.

The Supreme Court rejected the plaintiff's argument that the defendants' failure to protect him violated his right to due process of law, invoking the rationale and holding of *Daniels v. Williams* that negligence alone will not give rise to a violation of due process. In a dissenting opinion though, Justice Blackmun distinguished the facts of the case in *Davidson* from those in *Daniels*. Justice Blackmun conceded that negligence alone will not ordinarily effect a due process deprivation, but noted that in this case, the plaintiff had been deprived by the state of all means of protecting himself. He could not possess or use weapons, he could not fight back, and he could not escape. Being deprived of all means of self-protection, the plaintiff was totally dependent on the prison officials to protect him. Justice Blackmun concluded that under these circumstances, the prison officials' negligence in ignoring the probable risk of harm to the plaintiff did constitute the requisite abuse of governmental authority needed to trigger the protections of due process.

When an inmate has suffered a deprivation of liberty or property within the meaning of the due process clause, the next question is whether the inmate was afforded due process. The Supreme Court discussed the requirements of due process in *Parratt v. Taylor* (1981). In that case, the plaintiff, a prisoner, filed a § 1983 suit after his hobby kit worth $23.50 was lost due to the negligence of some prison officials. The Court first concluded that the negligence of the defendants had effected a constitutional deprivation, a conclusion that was later overruled in *Daniels v. Williams*. The Court then turned to the question of whether the deprivation of the plaintiff's property had occurred without due process.

The Supreme Court began by acknowledging that normally, due process requires a predeprivation hearing, in other words, a hearing where a person can raise objections to a contemplated deprivation before the deprivation occurs. The Court recognized, however, that sometimes a predeprivation hearing will not be feasible, such as when property must be immediately seized because of an emergency. The Court then found that a predeprivation hearing is not feasible and therefore not constitutionally required when a prisoner is deprived of property through the random and unauthorized act of a government official. The Court observed that in such a situation, the government cannot realistically be expected to provide the prisoner with a predeprivation hearing because the government does not know when the deprivation will occur. Under these circumstances, due process is satisfied as long as the prisoner is afforded a "meaningful" postdeprivation hearing.

In *Parratt*, the Supreme Court provided some guidance as to what constitutes a meaningful postdeprivation hearing. The plaintiff in that case had the option of filing a tort suit in the state court to obtain redress for the loss of his property. The plaintiff, however, contended that this tort remedy did not satisfy the dictates of due process because it did not provide the plaintiff with some of the benefits that attend the filing of a civil rights suit under 42 U.S.C.A. § 1983. In the state action, the plaintiff could not recover punitive damages and could only sue the state and not employees of the state. The plaintiff also had no right to a jury trial.

The Supreme Court, however, concluded that the tort remedy provided the plaintiff with the due process to which he was constitutionally entitled since he could be fully compensated for the loss of his property. It is not entirely clear from the Court's opinion whether the Court was saying that a state remedy must always offer an individual who suffered a deprivation the prospect of receiving full compensation for the loss suffered or whether the Court was simply saying that whatever the requirements of due process, those requirements are clearly met when the remedy available can lead to full compensation for a loss.

In *Hudson v. Palmer* (1984), the Supreme Court held that postdeprivation hearings can satisfy due process even when a prisoner has been intentionally deprived of property through the random and unauthorized action of a government employee. In such a situation, although the offending employee may know when a deprivation is about to occur, the state cannot know when an employee will intentionally disregard the rules and consequently cannot provide a prisoner with a predeprivation hearing.

Just because the actions of a government employee that cause a deprivation of liberty or property are unauthorized does not, however, mean that the existence of a tort remedy will always satisfy the requirements of due process. In *Zinermon v. Burch* (1990), the Supreme Court narrowly construed *Parratt* and *Hudson* and held that a due process violation will still exist if safeguards could have been put in place that would have prevented the deprivation from occurring in the first place. Thus, if procedures could be put in place that would, for example, avert the erroneous deprivation of inmates' property through the intentional actions of some prison officials, the failure to put these procedures in place would constitute a violation of due process.

In addition, a postdeprivation hearing will not satisfy due process when the deprivation of a prisoner's property or liberty occurs, not through the random and unauthorized actions of a prison official, but through some "established state procedure." *Logan v. Zimmerman Brush Co.* (1982). When a deprivation occurs through such an "established state procedure," affording a prisoner a predeprivation hearing is feasible.

CHAPTER 15

CRUEL AND UNUSUAL PUNISHMENT

The eighth amendment to the United States Constitution prohibits the imposition of "cruel and unusual punishments." This amendment is applicable to the states via the due process clause of the fourteenth amendment.

An eighth amendment claim can be raised in a number of different contexts. We have already discussed constraints placed by the eighth amendment on the imposition of the death penalty and, in unusual cases, on noncapital sentences. See Chapters 6 and 7 on pages 100–125. The way in which an inmate who has been convicted of a crime is treated while in prison or jail can also violate the eighth amendment. Eighth amendment claims in this context generally concern alleged deficiencies in medical care, the use of force by correctional officers, the failure to afford protection from attacks by other inmates, and the conditions of the inmates' confinement. Because the eighth amendment applies only to individuals convicted of a crime, when pretrial detainees assert similar claims, their claims are analyzed under other constitutional provisions, usually the due process clause.

A. MEDICAL, DENTAL, AND PSYCHIATRIC CARE

1. The Right to Be Treated

Inmates are dependent on correctional officials to get the medical care which they need. As the Supreme Court has recognized, the failure to provide inmates with that care can, in some circumstances, transgress societal standards of decency or result in the "unnecessary and wanton infliction of pain," thereby violating the eighth amendment.

It is clear, however, that not every inadequacy in the medical care afforded inmates gives rise to an eighth amendment claim. Negligence alone will not suffice. A government official must have acted with "deliberate indifference" to an inmate's "serious medical needs" for that official's actions or inaction to be considered cruel and unusual punishment. *Estelle v. Gamble* (1976). If the official's actions constituted mere negligence—the failure to act reasonably—an inmate will be remitted to pursuing a tort remedy in the state courts.

The Supreme Court provided some feedback as to what constitutes deliberate indifference in its analysis of the inmate's claim that was before the Court. The inmate in *Estelle* hurt his back and then saw three different doctors and a medical assistant seventeen times over a three-month period. The medical personnel responded to his complaints of pain in a number of different ways—by prescribing bed rest, muscle relaxants, and pain relievers. Nonetheless, the inmate claimed that his back pain persisted and that the failure to adequately diagnose the source of his pain and treat it constituted cruel and unusual punishment. Specifically, the inmate claimed that the doctors were remiss for failing to order an X-ray of his back. The Supreme Court, however, held that this failure was, at most, medical malpractice for which the eighth amendment provides no redress.

In *Farmer v. Brennan* (1994), the Supreme Court identified three requirements which must be met before it can be said that a correctional official acted with deliberate indifference. First, the official must have been aware of the facts revealing that an inmate faced a substantial risk of serious harm. Second, the official must have actually deduced from these facts that the inmate was at significant risk of being seriously harmed. Finally, the official must have failed to take reasonable steps to prevent the harm from occurring. In other words, even if a correctional official was actually aware of a significant risk of serious harm to an inmate, the official did not act with deliberate indifference if the official acted reasonably, though unsuccessfully, to protect the inmate from harm.

While the Supreme Court in *Farmer v. Brennan* held that deliberate indifference requires an official's subjective awareness of the significant threat of serious harm posed to an inmate, the Court noted that the official's awareness of the risk of harm could often be deduced from the obviousness of the risk. The Court added, however, that if an official was actually unaware of the risk of harm, despite its obviousness and despite the fact that a reasonable person would have recognized the risk, then the deliberate-indifference requirement is not met.

Deliberate indifference to the serious medical needs of an inmate can be manifested in a number of different ways. Correctional officers, for example, may act with the requisite deliberate indifference when they prevent an inmate from getting needed medical treatment or delay the obtaining of such treatment. Doctors, on the other hand, may act with deliberate indifference when they take no steps or only superficial steps in response to an inmate's medical complaints.

Alternatively, the existence of deliberate indifference can sometimes be inferred by looking beyond the facts surrounding the rendition of medical care to a particular inmate. For example, a recurring failure to adequately attend to a particular type of medical problem may reveal the presence of deliberate indifference on the part of officials when a review of just one of the incidents involving such a failure might suggest that only negligence has occurred. In addition, the risks posed by systemic problems in a correctional facility's medical-care system might be so substantial and the need to rectify those problems so apparent that the failure to do so supports an inference of deliberate indifference. Examples of areas where such systemic problems often arise include medical staffing, facilities, equipment, and recordkeeping. *See, e.g., Bass v. Wallenstein* (7th Cir.1985) (sick-call procedures failed to ensure prompt access to medical care);

Wellman v. Faulkner (7th Cir.1983) (two of three prison doctors could barely speak English; failure to stock necessary medical supplies, such as colostomy bags).

When pretrial detainees complain that the medical care they have received does not meet constitutional requirements, their claims are not analyzed under the eighth amendment because, as mentioned earlier, that amendment only applies to individuals convicted of crimes. The claims of pretrial detainees are instead analyzed under the due process clauses of either the fifth or the fourteenth amendment. According to the Supreme Court, however, pretrial detainees have at least as much protection from the Constitution, in terms of the medical care with which they must be provided, as do inmates serving criminal sentences. *City of Revere v. Massachusetts General Hospital* (1983). Consequently, the deliberate indifference of correctional officials to the serious medical needs of a pretrial detainee clearly constitutes a violation of due process.

Even if correctional officials act with deliberate indifference to an inmate's medical needs, no violation of the eighth amendment ensues unless the inmate's medical need is "serious." The Supreme Court has not defined what it meant in *Estelle v. Gamble* by a "serious" medical need, but the lower courts have attempted to flesh out the meaning of this requirement. Most have agreed that a medical need should be considered serious if either a doctor has determined that medical treatment is required or the need for treatment is so obvious that even a layperson would recognize the need for treatment. *See, e.g., Gaudreault v. Municipality of Salem, Massachusetts* (1st Cir.1990). Whether or not the need for medical treatment would be considered obvious to a layperson depends on a number of different factors, including the following: the type of medical problem; the likelihood that pain or injury would result if the medical problem is not attended to; the severity of that pain or injury; and the extent to which pain or injury has already occurred.

The courts have recognized that mental problems can cause suffering that is as unbearable as that caused by physical ailments. Accordingly, a mental affliction may constitute a serious medical need that, in conjunction with the deliberate indifference of government officials, will trigger liability under the eighth amendment. In order for a mental or emotional problem to be considered "serious" within the meaning of *Estelle v. Gamble*, however, an inmate must allege more than that he or she has felt depressed, because almost every inmate feels depressed sometime during the period of incarceration.

Some lower courts have applied a three-part test that must be met in order for a psychiatric or psychological problem to rise to the level of a "serious" medical need. Under that test, a doctor or other health-care provider must have concluded that: (1) the prisoner's symptoms stem from a serious disease or injury; (2) the disease or injury can be cured or the symptoms substantially alleviated; and (3) the risk of harm to the prisoner is great if treatment is delayed or denied. *See, e.g., Bowring v. Godwin* (4th Cir.1977).

In addition to the protection that the Constitution affords sick and disabled inmates to care and treatment, statutes may provide a separate source of protection to such inmates. Perhaps the most significant example of the breadth of protection that may be afforded by a statute is the Americans with Disabilities Act, codified at 42 U.S.C.A. §§ 12101–12213. That Act prohibits state and local governments and other public entities from discriminating against any "qualified individuals with a disability" and from excluding individuals from programs, services, or activities because of their disability. 42 U.S.C.A. § 12132. A "qualified individual with a disability" is defined as "an individual with a disability who, with or without reasonable modifications to rules, policies, or practices, the removal of architectural, communication, or transportation barriers, or the provision of auxiliary aids and services, meets the essential eligibility requirements for the receipt of services or the participation in programs or activities provided by a public entity." 42 U.S.C.A. § 12131(2). Because of this Act, state and local correctional officials must take a number of steps, including sometimes physical-plant modifications, to accommodate the needs of disabled inmates and to extend correctional programs and services to such inmates. Another federal statute, the Rehabilitation Act of 1973, also prohibits federal agencies and state or local agencies that receive federal financial assistance from discriminating against individuals because of their disabilities. *See* 29 U.S.C.A. § 794.

2. The Right Not to Be Treated

Some prisoners assert claims, not to receive medical treatment, but to not be subjected to certain forms of treatment. Generally, these claims of a right to refuse medical treatment arise when mentally ill inmates resist the administration of medication to temper the effects of their illnesses.

In *Washington v. Harper* (1990), the Supreme Court addressed several constitutional questions concerning the involuntary administration of antipsychotic medication to a mentally ill inmate. The questions concerning the procedural safeguards that must attend the involuntary administration of such medication were discussed in Chapter 12 on pages 198–201. Another question before the Court was a substantive due process one—when can antipsychotic medication be administered to an inmate over the inmate's objection?

The prison policy whose constitutionality the Supreme Court was analyzing permitted antipsychotic drugs to be involuntarily administered when an inmate "suffers from a mental disorder and as a result of that disorder constitutes a likelihood of serious harm to himself or others and/or is gravely disabled." The plaintiff in *Harper* contended that this policy abridged his substantive due process rights. He underscored the invasiveness of such unwanted medical treatment—not only the physical intrusion that results from such treatment but also the degradation of having someone else decide what to do with his body. In addition, he noted the serious and sometimes lethal side effects that can be caused by antipsychotic drugs, including catatonia, swelling of the brain, drowsiness, restlessness, high blood pressure, nausea, vomiting, headaches, constipation, blurred vision, impotency, eczema, tremors, muscle spasms, and involuntary movements so disabling that a person cannot perform such basic tasks as driving a car. Antipsychotic drugs can also cause neuroleptic malignant syndrome, which is fatal in 30% of the cases in which people suffer from this affliction.

Because of the indignity of being forced to take drugs that one does not want to take as well as the negative effects of those drugs, the plaintiff in *Harper* contended that medication could not be forced on him unless he was incompetent to make decisions concerning his medical welfare. He further argued that even if he was incompetent, the medication could still not be administered to him over his objection unless a finding was made that he would have consented to such treatment if he were competent.

The Supreme Court, however, refused to put so many roadblocks in the path of officials trying to prevent mentally ill inmates from harming themselves or other. Applying the *Turner* test discussed earlier in Chapter 9 on pages 144–146, the Court instead observed that the prison policy governing the involuntary administration of antipsychotic drugs would be constitutional as long as it was "reasonably related to legitimate penological interests."

The Supreme Court ultimately concluded that this test was met in this case. The Court noted the obligation of prison officials to not only protect others from prisoners, but also to protect prisoners from themselves. In addition, the Court emphasized the absence of any viable alternatives that could accommodate inmates' desire not to be forcibly drugged at only *de minimis* cost to legitimate penological objectives. The Court, for example, had doubts about the medical efficacy of either secluding or physically restraining mentally ill inmates who posed a risk of harm to themselves or others. The Court also noted the harm that inmates could inflict on themselves, even when physically restrained, and the injuries they could inflict on others attempting to place restraints on them. Of course, such injuries, it would seem, could also be inflicted by inmates to whom antipsychotic medication is being involuntarily administered.

The Supreme Court concluded by holding in *Washington v. Harper* that if inmates have a "serious mental illness," antipsychotic drugs can be involuntarily administered to them as long as two requirements are met: one, the inmates pose a danger to themselves or others, and two, the treatment is in their "medical interest." One of the ironies of the Supreme Court's opinion in *Harper* though is that the prison policy upheld by the Court in that case did not, on its face, actually meet the substantive due process requirements described by the Court. Nowhere in that policy was there a requirement that the medication decision be made with the medical interests of the inmate in mind. The Court, however, was apparently operating under the assumption that doctors would prescribe medication only to meet the medical needs of their patients. In fact, the Court referred in its opinion to the ethical duty of doctors to do so. The dissenters, on the other hand, emphasized what they considered to be the very real risk that antipsychotic drugs would be prescribed, not to advance inmates' medical interests, but to make it easier for officials to control unruly inmates.

B. USE OF FORCE AND THE PROTECTION OF INMATES

Correctional officials may use force in their dealings with inmates for a number of different reasons. Force may be used, for example, to end a prison riot, to stop a fight between two inmates, and to get a resisting inmate into his or her cell. At some point, the use of force becomes excessive and violates constitutional strictures. The question is: how do we identify that point?

In *Whitley v. Albers* (1986), the Supreme Court was confronted with the question of when force employed to quell a prison riot or disturbance constitutes cruel and unusual punishment in violation of the eighth amendment. The plaintiff in *Whitley*, a prisoner, filed a § 1983 suit against several correctional officials after he was shot in the knee in the midst of a prison disturbance. The disturbance had begun after a number of inmates became upset by what they considered the too forceful treatment of several of their fellow inmates whom some correctional officers had discovered to be drunk. Led by their ringleader, an inmate by the name of Klenk, the defiant prisoners refused orders to return to their cells, broke furniture, and seized a correctional officer as a hostage. This hostage was eventually placed in a cell on the second tier of the cellblock.

Captain Harol Whitley, the prison security manager, visited the cellblock several times to confirm that the hostage was safe. The inmates in the cell in which the hostage was confined assured Whitley that they would protect the hostage, but Klenk, who had a knife, warned Whitley that he would kill the hostage if a riot squad entered the cellblock. Klenk also told Whitley that one inmate had already been killed. This latter statement, unbeknownst to Whitley, was not true, although one inmate had in fact been beaten by other inmates.

Whitley and his superiors eventually decided that they needed to storm the cellblock to save the hostage's life and protect other inmates. They ruled out tear gas as a means of disabling the inmates upon their entry into the cellblock, since they believed it would not work fast enough to prevent some inmates from harming other inmates or the hostage. Instead, the officials settled on the following plan: Whitley was to go into the cellblock first and attempt to reach the cell where the hostage was confined before Klenk. Three other correctional officers, armed with shotguns, were to immediately follow Whitley, and they in turn were to be followed by a group of unarmed correctional officers. One of the armed correctional officers, Officer Kennicott, was directed to fire a warning shot upon entering the cellblock and to then shoot low at any prisoner who tried to run up the stairs to the second tier.

When Whitley later entered the cellblock in accordance with this plan, Klenk saw him and immediately ran up the stairs, followed by Whitley. After Officer Kennicott fired the warning shot, the plaintiff also began to run up the stairs in an attempt to get to the relative safety of his cell on an upper tier. According to the plaintiff, he locked eyes with Officer Kennicott, and then Officer Kennicot shot him in the knee, severely injuring him.

At the trial, there was conflicting testimony of expert witnesses as to whether there was a need to use the force that had resulted in the plaintiff's injuries. Nonetheless, the trial court directed a verdict for the defendants, which meant, of course, that the question of the constitutionality of the defendants' actions was not submitted to the jury.

The technical question before the Supreme Court was the propriety of entering this directed verdict, but to answer this question, the Court first had to clarify when the use of force would constitute cruel and unusual punishment under these circumstances. As in earlier cases, the Court noted that the "unnecessary and wanton infliction of pain" abridges the eighth amendment. It is clear from *Whitley*, however, that what constitutes the "unnecessary and wanton infliction of pain" depends upon the context in which a cruel and unusual punishment claim is asserted.

In *Estelle v. Gamble* (1976), the Supreme Court had held that "deliberate indifference" to an inmate's "serious medical needs" represents the unnecessary and wanton infliction of pain which violates the eighth amendment. In *Whitley v. Albers*, however, the Supreme Court refused to apply a deliberate-indifference standard when examining correctional officials' use of force during a prison disturbance. The Court explained that the provision of needed medical care to inmates does not conflict with other important governmental responsibilities, so a standard of review which is less deferential to government officials is appropriate in the medical-care context. By contrast, when officials are deciding whether or not to use force to quell a disturbance, they are often faced with a Hobson's choice: use force, which may lead to some inmates and/or hostages being harmed, or refrain from using force, leaving hostages and some inmates vulnerable to injuries and even death at the hands of other inmates.

The Court in *Whitley* ultimately concluded that to prevail on an eighth amendment claim based on the force used to end a prison disturbance, a prisoner would have to prove that the force was used " 'mali-

ciously and sadistically for the very purpose of causing harm.' " Such unconstitutionally excessive
force was to be contrasted with force used in " 'a
good faith effort to maintain or restore discipline.' "
The Court listed several factors to be examined
when determining whether a correctional official
had acted with the malicious intent needed for the
use of force to be considered cruel and unusual
punishment: (1) the need to use force; (2) the
relationship between that need and the amount of
force that was used; (3) the gravity of the ensuing
injuries caused by the use of force; (4) the extent to
which, based on the facts known by the correctional
officials at the time, inmates and staff faced harm if
force was not employed; and (5) the steps taken by
the correctional officials, if any, to limit the force
employed. Some of these factors, however, seem to
overlap. For example, the fourth factor (the risks
posed to inmates and staff) seems subsumed within
the first factor (need for the force), while the second
factor (the extent to which the amount of force was
calibrated to the need for the force) seems to encompass the fifth factor, which focuses on efforts to
dissipate the forcefulness of the response.

Having enunciated the applicable eighth amendment standard, the Supreme Court then turned to
the task of applying that standard to the facts of the
case before it. The Court acknowledged that there
was some evidence that the inmates had quieted
down somewhat by the time that the riot squad
entered the cellblock and that the expert witnesses
differed in their views as to whether the force

employed in regaining control of the cellblock was necessary. The Court concluded, however, that this evidence suggested, at most, that the defendants had acted negligently in constructing their rescue plan. The Court observed that in order for this case to have been submitted to the jury, the evidence adduced at trial would have to have supported an inference that the defendants acted wantonly—either in the development of the plan for taking back the cellblock and rescuing the hostage or in the execution of that plan. The Court, however, found the evidence of wantonness simply lacking in this case. The Court underscored how volatile and dangerous the situation remained—a correctional officer was still held hostage, the most outspoken inmate was armed with a knife, and the inmates retained control of the cellblock. Under these circumstances, according to the Court, it could not be said that there was "no plausible basis" for believing that the use of force, as planned, was necessary to rescue the hostage and retake control of the cellblock.

The plaintiff in *Whitley v. Albers* also contended that when he was shot, his right to substantive due process was violated. The Supreme Court, however, summarily rejected this claim, simply noting that the due process clause affords inmates no greater protection than the eighth amendment when they are contesting the constitutionality of the force used against them.

The Supreme Court has now clarified that the eighth amendment standard enunciated in *Whitley v. Albers* is to be applied whenever inmates claim that excessive force was used against them in violation of the eighth amendment. *Hudson v. McMillian* (1992). The Court in *Hudson* also rejected the notion that an inmate must have suffered a "significant injury" in order for the force used to be considered cruel and unusual punishment. The Court was concerned that to rule otherwise would leave prisoners vulnerable to forms of torture that cause no physical injuries or leave any lasting physical imprints. At the same time, however, the Court emphasized in *Hudson* that not every "malevolent touch" by a correctional officer is a constitutional grievance. The Court explained that certain *de minimis* uses of force do not offend the "conscience of mankind" and therefore do not rise to the level of cruel and unusual punishments.

At times, inmates will sue correctional officials, not because the officials have hurt them, but because the officials have failed to protect them from being hurt by other inmates. The failure to protect an inmate from being harmed by other inmates can, in some circumstances, constitute cruel and unusual punishment. To violate the eighth amendment, however, the officials must have been more than just negligent in their failure to protect an inmate. The officials must have acted with deliberate indifference to a substantial risk that an inmate would be seriously harmed by another inmate. In other words, the officials must have been subjectively aware of the significant risk of serious harm and then failed to act reasonably to prevent the harm from occurring. *Farmer v. Brennan* (1994).

The failure to protect inmates, not from others, but from themselves may also, in some circumstances, violate the eighth amendment and, in the case of pretrial detainees, due process of law. Just because an inmate commits suicide, however, does not mean that correctional officials will be held legally responsible for the death. As the courts have recognized, persons bent on killing themselves will usually eventually succeed. When officials act with deliberate indifference to the substantial risk that an inmate will commit suicide, however, then a violation of the eighth amendment ensues. *Tittle v. Jefferson County Commission* (11th Cir.1994).

C. CONDITIONS OF CONFINEMENT

The conditions of inmates' confinement can, unquestionably, in some circumstances inflict cruel and unusual punishment on them. Inmates have asserted a variety of claims contesting the constitutionality of the conditions of their confinement. They have, for example, complained about inadequate food, poor ventilation, rodent and insect infestation, fire hazards, inoperable toilets, and rampant violence. One of the most common complaints, however, has concerned the crowded conditions to which inmates are subjected in so many of the nation's prisons and jails.

As was mentioned in Chapter 1, the United States reportedly has the highest incarceration rate of any country in the world. To house the ever increasing number of inmates, prisons and jails are being built around the clock across the country, at a cost of billions of dollars to American taxpayers. Even with the enormous diversion of resources from other government programs for the construction and operation of these new correctional facilities, however, construction has not been able to keep pace with the demand for prison and jail space. With too many inmates and not enough space for them, correctional officials have been forced to respond by setting up beds for inmates in gymnasiums, dayrooms, hallways, and many other places throughout their correctional facilities. They have also responded by housing two and sometimes more inmates in cells, many of which were constructed with the idea that they would house only one inmate.

It is clear that the double celling of prisoners is not *per se* unconstitutional. In *Bell v. Wolfish* (1979), the Supreme Court considered the constitutionality, under the due process clause of the fifth amendment, of housing federal pretrial detainees, two to a cell, in cells that were designed to hold only one person. Each cell had seventy-five square feet of cell space.

In rejecting the plaintiffs' argument that double celling them in effect punished them in violation of their right to due process of law, the Supreme Court emphatically declared that there is no "one man, one cell" principle subsumed within the Constitution. At the same time, however, the Court emphasized two factors that supported the Court's conclusion that the double celling in this case did not abridge any constitutional rights. First, most of the detainees were not confined in the detention center for very long. Almost all of them were released within sixty days. And second, even while in the correctional center, the detainees had a great deal of freedom of movement. They only had to stay in their cells seven to eight hours a day, during which time they slept, thereby mitigating any hardships ensuing from the double celling.

In *Rhodes v. Chapman* (1981), the Supreme Court confirmed that just because inmates are double-celled does not mean that their constitutional rights have been violated. The inmates who brought suit in *Rhodes* were double-celled because the prison, built with 1620 cells, housed 2300 inmates. Each cell was sixty-three square feet in size, but much of this space was consumed by a bunk bed, sink, toilet, and cabinets. Since the prison in question was a maximum-security facility, most of the inmates within it were more serious offenders with long prison sentences who could expect to be subjected to the conditions about which they complained for many years.

The Supreme Court, however, balked at the suggestion that the double celling of the inmates, under the circumstances, constituted cruel and unusual punishment. The Court underscored that the trial judge had toured the prison and had found the prison to be "unquestionably a top-flight, first-class facility." The food was adequate, the ventilation system worked reasonably well, the noise level was not too high in the cellblocks, and the temperature within the prison was neither too hot nor too cold. Although it was true that violence had increased within the prison in recent years, the Court considered it significant that there was no evidence that this increase was attributable to the double bunking of inmates.

A particularly significant fact to the Court was that most inmates did not have to remain within their cells during the day. They could go to a dayroom next to their cellblock from 6:30 in the morning until 9:30 at night. Each dayroom had a television, card tables, and chairs and was, according to the Court, the equivalent of a living room or den.

The Supreme Court concluded that these conditions did not either conflict with the "evolving standards of decency that mark the progress of a maturing society" or constitute the "unnecessary and wanton infliction of pain." The Court conceded that the amount of living space accorded each inmate was much less than the amount prescribed by the standards of numerous professional organizations at the time, such as the American Correctional Association (60–80 square feet per inmate) and the National Sheriffs' Association (70–80 square feet). The Supreme Court observed, however, that while the opinions of experts are relevant to the question of whether conditions of confinement constitute cruel and unusual punishment, they are not conclusive. Far more important, in the Court's opinion, are the views of the general public as to the acceptability of a particular punishment, and the Court could find no evidence of public opposition to the double celling of inmates. To the extent that the conditions of the inmates' confinement were unpleasant and even harsh, that, according to the Court, was part of the price that they had to pay for the crimes which they had committed. The Constitution, in the Court's words, "does not mandate comfortable prisons."

The Supreme Court in *Rhodes v. Chapman* also acknowledged that work and educational opportunities for inmates had diminished at the prison because of double celling and the resultant overcrowding. The Court, however, considered this fact simply irrelevant to the constitutional question before it. The Court observed, "[L]imited work hours and delay before receiving education do not inflict pain, much less unnecessary and wanton pain; deprivations of this kind simply are not punishments."

The conditions of confinement whose constitutionality the Court upheld in *Rhodes v. Chapman* and *Bell v. Wolfish* are to be contrasted with the conditions in Arkansas prisons that the district court found, and the Supreme Court agreed, were unconstitutional in *Hutto v. Finney* (1978). Before the Court in *Hutto* was the question of the propriety of a district court order limiting inmates' confinement in punitive-isolation cells to no more than thirty days as a means of alleviating the unconstitutional conditions in those cells. The cells were only eighty square feet in size, but held four and sometimes up to ten or eleven inmates. The cells contained no windows or furniture, and the toilet within each cell could only be flushed from outside the cell, creating obvious odor and sanitation problems if correctional officers did not oblige inmates by flushing the toilets. Each night, the inmates slept on mattresses brought into the cells, but since the mattresses were intermingled each day, inmates slept on mattresses previously used by inmates with hepatitis and other infectious diseases. The inmates in punitive isolation were also poorly fed, receiving less than 1000 calories a day, less than half the amount required by basic nutritional standards.

The Supreme Court considered the district court's order limiting the duration of an inmate's confinement in a punitive-isolation cell as a reasonable response to the sordid, and unconstitutional, conditions in those cells. Noting that the length of time that an inmate is subjected to certain conditions is relevant to the question whether those conditions constitute cruel and unusual punishment, the Court observed, "A filthy, overcrowded cell and a diet of 'grue' might be tolerable for a few days and intolerably cruel for weeks or months."

In *Wilson v. Seiter* (1991), the Supreme Court clarified that there is both an objective and a subjective requirement that must be met for conditions of confinement to be considered cruel and unusual punishment. In describing the objective component of the eighth amendment, the Court said that an inmate must have been deprived of an "identifiable human need," such as food, warmth, or exercise.

It is clear from the succeeding case of *Helling v. McKinney* (1993), however, that inmates need not be suffering injuries currently from the conditions of their confinement for an eighth amendment claim to lie; sometimes a risk of future harm, if that risk is sufficiently high, will suffice.

The plaintiff in *Helling*, a nonsmoker, was confined in a 48–square-foot cell with another inmate who smoked five packs of cigarettes a day. While the Supreme Court did not itself resolve whether these conditions amounted to cruel and unusual punishment, the Court held that the objective requirement of a cruel and unusual punishment claim would be satisfied if, on remand, the plaintiff proved both that he was exposed to unreasonable amounts of tobacco smoke and that this exposure created risks of harm so serious as to violate society's standards of decency. In other words, the risks could not be ones that society has chosen to tolerate.

As far as the subjective component of a cruel and unusual punishment claim based on conditions of confinement in a correctional facility, the Supreme Court in *Wilson v. Seiter* said that a plaintiff must prove that a defendant acted with deliberate indifference in failing to rectify the problem with those conditions. Four Justices on the Court, however, strongly disagreed with this proposition, arguing that the effect on prisoners of horrendous prison conditions are the same, regardless of the state of mind of the officials maintaining those conditions. Another of the concerns of the dissenters was that correctional officials might duck their responsibility under the eighth amendment to run safe and humane prisons by casting blame on legislatures for failing to appropriate requested funds needed to redress or avert problems in the operation of the prisons. The majority of the Court, however, skirted this critical question of the extent to which the costs of rectifying problems in the conditions of confinement and the lack of funding to do so have a bearing on the existence of the deliberate indifference needed to sustain an eighth amendment claim centering on those conditions.

CHAPTER 16

PAROLE RELEASE AND PROBATION AND PAROLE REVOCATION

In a jurisdiction which has a parole system, a parole board determines how much of an individual's prison sentence will actually be served behind bars. The parole board's decision on when to release someone from prison is based in part on its prediction of the likelihood that a prisoner will successfully reintegrate himself or herself into society and refrain from future criminal activity. When a person is released on parole, however, that person remains under the control of correctional authorities until expiration of the maximum sentence imposed by the sentencing judge.

In recent years, the concept of parole has increasingly come under attack. Four major objections have been asserted against incorporating parole into a sentencing system. First, parole systems can lead to disparity in sentences. Although that disparity can be mitigated somewhat by the adoption of parole guidelines that channel and circumscribe the parole board's exercise of its discretion, disparity remains in the initial decision whether or not to send a person to prison. Second, the uncertainty about when inmates will actually be released from prison that is spawned by parole systems can cause tension, frustration, and even despair in inmates, thereby interfering with attempts to help inmates rehabilitate or habilitate themselves while they are incarcerated and making prisoners more difficult to manage. Third, parole systems, which often enable inmates to be released from prison years before they have served their maximum prison sentences, foster disrespect and even contempt for the legal system. And fourth, the concern about crowding in a jurisdiction's prisons that often drives many parole-release decisions leads to the premature release of many prisoners and consequently the endangerment of the public.

The problems caused by parole have led many states and the federal government in recent years to abandon their parole systems and move towards more determinate-sentencing systems. (Some of the different types of determinate-sentencing systems are discussed in Chapter 5.) The impetus for this systemic change has been the demand for what is called "truth in sentencing."

Parole systems still, however, exist in many states, and even in jurisdictions which have abolished parole, parole boards continue to operate, deciding when inmates who were sentenced under earlier statutory schemes providing for parole release will be released from prison and when they should be returned to prison for violating the terms and conditions of their parole. It is therefore important to understand the constraints placed by the Constitution on parole-release and revocation decisions and on somewhat similar decisions concerning the revocation of probation.

A. PROBATION AND PAROLE REVOCATION

It behooves us to begin with a discussion of the constitutional requirements that govern parole and probation revocation, since the Supreme Court's analysis of the constitutional implications of parole release has been so heavily influenced by its analysis of parole revocation. In *Morrissey v. Brewer* (1972), the Supreme Court addressed the question of whether the due process clause of the fourteenth amendment provides any protection to individuals facing the prospect of having their parole revoked. The Court first had to resolve the threshold question of whether the revocation of parole deprives a person of "liberty" within the meaning of the due process clause. The Court answered this question in the affirmative, noting the "grievous loss" that attends the revocation of parole. While the Court acknowledged that the freedom that a parolee has is conditional and limited, the Court at the same time recognized that parolees enjoy many of the freedoms of an ordinary citizen and that they may spend many more years in prison if their parole is revoked.

The Court in *Morrissey* then turned to the question of what process is "due" a parolee facing the possible revocation of his or her parole. The Court began by noting that parole revocation is different from a criminal prosecution, even though the end result might be the same—incarceration in prison. A criminal prosecution may result in the loss of what the Court described as "absolute liberty," while parole revocation affects only the conditional liberty of a parolee. Therefore, according to the Court, a parolee is not entitled, during a parole revocation proceeding, to "the full panoply of rights" that attend a criminal prosecution.

The Court also noted that the state has an "overwhelming interest" in being able to send parolees who have violated the conditions of their parole release back to prison without having to undergo the burdens of a formal trial. At the same time, however, the Court pointed to two other state interests that supported the extension of a significant measure of procedural protection to parolees during parole revocation proceedings—the government's interest in avoiding erroneous parole revocations and the government's interest in treating parolees fairly, at least in part to avoid the resentment of parolees caused by the perception of unfair treatment and the ensuing interference with their rehabilitation.

The Supreme Court's assessment of the interests at stake during parole revocation proceedings led the Court to conclude that parolees are entitled to the following procedural safeguards before final revocation of their parole. First, when parolees are arrested and detained for suspected violations of the conditions of their parole, they must be afforded a preliminary hearing to determine whether there is probable cause to believe that they violated the terms or conditions of their parole. This preliminary hearing must be held at a place "reasonably near" the place where the arrest or the alleged parole violation occurred and as "promptly as convenient" after the arrest.

Second, parolees must be provided with notice of their impending preliminary hearing, of the parole violations with which they are charged, and of the hearing's purpose to determine whether there is probable cause to believe a violation has occurred.

Third, parolees have the right to attend their preliminary hearing and to make a statement in their own behalf. Fourth, the parolees can submit documents at the hearing and call witnesses to testify about relevant matters at the preliminary hearing. Fifth, the parolees can, upon request, confront and cross-examine adverse witnesses who have provided information supporting the revocation of parole unless such confrontation and cross-examination would jeopardize an informant's safety.

Sixth, the probable-cause determination must be made by someone who is not "directly involved" in the case. In other words, any parole officer who investigated or reported the alleged parole violation cannot serve as the hearing officer responsible for making the probable-cause determination. It is not necessary though for a judge to make the probable-cause determination. Even another parole officer can perform this function as long as the officer has had no direct involvement in the case.

Finally, the hearing officer must summarize the evidence adduced at the hearing, outline which of this evidence was relied on by the hearing officer, and state the reasons for finding that the detention of the parolee pending a final revocation hearing is warranted.

In another case, the Supreme Court clarified that the preliminary hearing, the first step in the parole revocation process, can be skipped if the reason for the contemplated revocation is the commission, while on parole, of a crime of which the parolee has already has been convicted. *Moody v. Daggett* (1976). With the high standard of proof that applies in criminal proceedings—beyond a reasonable doubt, a conviction, by definition, establishes probable cause to believe a parolee has violated the standard parole condition to refrain from criminal activity.

Once it has been determined that there is probable cause to believe a parolee has violated the terms or conditions of his or her parole, the parolee can be sent back to prison to await a final revocation hearing, if the parolee wants a hearing. That hearing must be held within a "reasonable time" after the parolee has been taken into custody for the parole violation, but according to the Supreme Court in *Morrissey v. Brewer*, two months is not an excessive amount of time for the parolee to have to wait for the final hearing.

Morrissey outlined a number of procedural safeguards that must attend the final revocation hearing. Those safeguards include: (1) written notice of the alleged violation or violations of parole; (2) the opportunity to attend the hearing and explain why the revocation of parole is unwarranted; (3) the right to present witnesses and documentary evidence in the parolee's defense; (4) the right to be apprised of evidence that supports the revocation of parole; (5) the right to confront and cross-examine adverse witnesses unless there is "good cause" for not according the parolee these rights; (6) the right to have the final revocation decision made by a "neutral and detached" decisionmaker; and (7) the right to receive a written statement outlining the evidence relied on by this decisionmaker and the reasons for revoking the individual's parole.

In *Gagnon v. Scarpelli* (1973), the Supreme Court held that probationers are also entitled to the procedural protections outlined in *Morrissey* before their probation is revoked. *Gagnon* also answered a question left unresolved in *Morrissey*—whether indigent individuals facing the revocation of their probation or parole have the right to have counsel appointed to assist them during the probation or parole-revocation proceedings.

The Court began by discussing some of the drawbacks of affording appointed counsel in revocation proceedings involving indigent probationers or parolees. If attorneys were appointed to represent indigent probationers and parolees, the government would in turn most likely hire attorneys to represent the government. Revocation proceedings would then be transformed, according to the Court, into adversarial proceedings that are less focused on the rehabilitative needs of probationers and parolees. The proceedings would drag on much longer, and the financial costs to the government, for appointed counsel as well as counsel for the government, would be great.

The Court then refused to adopt an across-the-board rule that indigent probationers and parolees either have or do not have the right to appointed counsel during such proceedings. Instead, the Court held that whether or not there is a right to the assistance of appointed counsel during a revocation proceeding has to be decided on a case-by-case basis. The Court noted though that in most cases, due process does not require the provision of such assistance. The individuals confronting revocation have either been convicted of or admitted committing a crime and any mitigating circumstances that might argue against revocation of probation or parole are straightforward enough not to require counsel for their explication.

At the same time, however, the Supreme Court recognized that the fundamental fairness commanded by due process sometimes requires the provision of appointed counsel to indigents involved in revocation proceedings. The Court in *Gagnon* mentioned two instances when the provision of counsel is presumptively necessary: one, when the probationer or parolee makes a "timely and colorable claim" that he or she has not committed the alleged probation or parole violation, and two, when, although the violation is clear or undisputed, there are substantial mitigating factors which suggest that revocation is unwarranted and those factors are difficult to explain because of their complexity or for other reasons. The Court in *Gagnon* added that if a request for appointed counsel is denied, the reason for that denial must be set forth in the record.

Left unresolved by the Supreme Court in *Gagnon* was the question of the scope of the right to retained counsel during probation and parole-revocation proceedings. Specifically, the question that remains is this: does the right to be represented by a retained attorney extend beyond those instances when indigents have a right to appointed counsel? In other words, is a parolee entitled to the assistance of an attorney during a parole-revocation proceeding as long as the parolee pays for that assistance?

There is Supreme Court precedent that arguably points both ways in answering this question—towards holding that the right to retained counsel is broader than the right to appointed counsel and towards holding that the scope of the two rights corresponds. In criminal trials, defendants have the right to the services of retained attorneys, even in cases where there is no right to appointed counsel. On the other hand, in *Wolff v. McDonnell* (1974), a case discussed earlier in Chapter 11 on page 173, the Supreme Court held that prisoners have no right to be represented by an attorney, whether retained or appointed, in prison disciplinary hearings. What is potentially significant about *Wolff* is that many of the reasons given by the Court in that case for not recognizing a right to counsel during disciplinary proceedings were the same as those asserted by the Court in *Gagnon v. Scarpelli* for limiting the right to appointed counsel during probation and parole-revocation proceedings.

Another question which has not been definitively resolved by the Supreme Court concerns the burden of proof that the government must meet in establishing a probation or parole violation. Most of the lower federal courts and the state courts have held that a violation must be proven by a preponderance of the evidence—in other words, by proof that it is more likely than not that the violation occurred—or by an even lower standard of proof. *Harris v. United States* (D.C.App.1992). The standard of proof that has been applied in revocation proceedings explains why an acquittal of a criminal charge does not bar the revocation of a person's probation or parole for the conduct upon which the charge was based. Just because the government could not meet its burden of proving the individual's guilt beyond a reasonable doubt does not mean that the government cannot meet the lower burden of proof that applies in a revocation proceeding.

Revocation of probation or parole for criminal conduct of which a person has already been acquitted or convicted also does not violate the double jeopardy prohibition found in the fifth amendment and applicable to the states through the due process clause of the fourteenth amendment. When individuals' probation or parole is revoked and they are sent to prison, technically they are being punished and sent to prison for the original crime of which they were convicted, not their more recent criminal conviction.

Apart from the constitutional questions concerning the revocation of probation or parole, there are a number of policy questions concerning not only the procedural aspects of revocation proceedings, but the substantive standards that should have to be met for revocation to occur. Questions regarding the most appropriate way in which to respond to various types of probation and parole violations have become of particularly pressing importance as the nation's already crowded prisons and jails have become increasingly filled with individuals incarcerated following the revocation of their probation or parole. The American Bar Association's Model Adult Community Corrections Act, which was discussed in Chapter 4 on page 78, exemplifies an approach to probation and parole violations which differs from the norm of either ignoring the violations or automatically incarcerating individuals for them. The Act instead establishes a presumption, though a rebuttable one, that imposition of a community-based sanction is the appropriate response to a violation that involves either noncriminal conduct, such as failing to report to a probation officer, or criminal conduct that, if charged, would be either a misdemeanor or a nonviolent felony.

B. PAROLE RELEASE

For a prisoner, a parole board's decision whether or not to release the prisoner on parole is a momentous one. The decision, like the decision whether or not to revoke a person's parole, will determine whether a person is free to live in the community or must instead be isolated and confined in prison, perhaps for many more years. Yet from a constitutional standpoint, parole-release decisions and parole-revocation decisions are, according to the Supreme Court, very different.

In *Greenholtz v. Inmates of Nebraska Penal and Correctional Complex* (1979), the Supreme Court held that just because a jurisdiction establishes a parole system and offers a prisoner the possibility of being released on parole does not mean that a "liberty" interest that would trigger due process protections is implicated when a parole board is making its release decision. The Court cited two reasons for distinguishing parole release from parole revocation. First, the Court said that there is an enormous difference between losing the liberty that one has and not being given the liberty that one wants. Second, the Court stated that the nature of the decisions made during the parole-release and revocation processes is, in the Court's opinion, very different. The Court acknowledged that both processes require the resolution of factual questions and the making of subjective assessments about a person's suitability to live in the community. The Court noted, however, that the question addressed during the first step of the parole-revocation process is purely factual—"Did the parolee violate the terms or conditions of his or her parole? " A negative answer to this question requires a finding in the parolee's favor and obviates the need to turn to the second step of the two-stage process, where the parolee's suitability to remain in the community, despite the violation of parole conditions, is considered. The Court noted in *Greenholtz* that by contrast, when a parole board is making a parole-release decision, no set of facts mandates a prisoner's release from prison on parole. Consequently, because of the more amorphous nature of the parole-release decision, the Supreme Court believed that a prisoner's hope of being released on parole is too tenuous to give rise to a liberty interest.

The Supreme Court in *Greenholtz*, however, recognized that there are protectible liberty interests beyond those that are inherent within the Constitution. A state, through its own laws or regulations, can create a liberty interest encompassed by the protections of due process. See Chapter 12 on pages 187–190.

The Supreme Court in *Greenholtz* in fact found that the applicable state's parole statute in that case did create a protectible liberty interest in being released on parole. That statute provided that a prisoner "shall" be released on parole "unless" certain delineated circumstances existed, such as a "substantial risk" that the prisoner would not abide by the conditions of his or her parole.

While the Supreme Court in *Greenholtz* emphasized that the state statute before it had a "unique structure," in a subsequent case, the Court found that a statute with even more general language than the statute in *Greenholtz* created a liberty interest triggering due process protections. In that case, *Board of Pardons v. Allen* (1987), the statute in question stated that a prisoner "shall" be released on parole "when ... there is a reasonable probability that the prisoner can be released without detriment to the prisoner or to the community" and "only for the best interests of society." According to the Court, the expectation that this statute created that a prisoner would be paroled in certain circumstances gave rise to constitutional protection.

By contrast, the lower courts have held that some parole statutes with slightly different wording do not create protected liberty interests. *See, e.g., Staton v. Wainwright* (5th Cir.1982) ("No person shall be placed on parole until and unless ... there is reasonable probability" certain requirements will be met.); *Averhart v. Tutsie* (7th Cir.1980) ("A parole shall be ordered only for the best interest of society.... A prisoner shall be placed on parole only when" certain outlined circumstances exist.). Because of the way in which the present Court says liberty interests can be created by state law, therefore, a few differences in the words of a statute can potentially have great constitutional import.

A general practice or custom of releasing certain inmates in certain circumstances from prison, however, will not be enough, by itself, to create a liberty interest in such release. In *Connecticut Board of Pardons v. Dumschat* (1981) a prisoner claimed that he was deprived of his liberty without due process of law when his application for the commutation of his life sentence for murder was denied. The prisoner contended that he had a justifiable expectation that his sentence would be commuted, one that amounted to a liberty interest, because the vast majority of inmates with life sentences in the state had their sentences commuted. The Supreme Court, however, disagreed. Emphasizing that the decision whether or not to commute a prisoner's sentence fell within the unconfined discretion of the Connecticut Board of Pardons, the Court observed that a liberty interest was not created just because the Board had been generous towards prisoners in the past in the exercise of that discretion. According to the Court, for a liberty interest to exist, the Board's discretion would actually have to be circumscribed by some statute or government rule.

When a prisoner has a liberty interest derived from state law in being granted parole release, the prisoner, of course, can only be deprived of that interest in accordance with the requirements of due process of law. What due process means in the parole-release context, however, is very different from what it means in the parole-revocation process, in part because of the differences that exist, according to the Supreme Court, between the interests that are at stake in the two processes.

Greenholtz answered only some of the questions about the procedural safeguards that must attend the parole-release decisionmaking process. The Supreme Court first said in that case that inmates who are eligible for parole, but whose chances of being released on parole are slim, have no constitutional right to a formal parole hearing. When the chances of being released on parole are remote, inmates would benefit little from such formal hearings, while the burden to the government of providing such hearings would be great. At the same time, however, the Court emphasized that in Nebraska, the state in which the case arose, all inmates who were eligible for parole had the right to an informal parole-review hearing where they could state why they believed they should be released on parole. The existence of this alternative review mechanism for inmates unlikely to be released on parole was probably significant to the Court because, as Justice Marshall recognized in his opinion partially dissenting from the Court's opinion, the procedures that are constitutionally due in a particular situation may depend on the other procedural safeguards that are already in place.

The Supreme Court in *Greenholtz* also rejected the argument that an inmate denied parole is entitled to be informed of the evidence supporting the parole board's decision. The Court believed that requiring such a summation of the evidence relied upon would transform parole-release hearings into adversary proceedings, fostering ill will between inmates and correctional officials and thereby undermining the long-range rehabilitative objectives of parole. What is a bit curious about this conclusion is that in *Wolff v. McDonnell* (1974), a case dealing with the procedural safeguards that must attend prison disciplinary hearings, the Supreme Court had noted that one of the principal purposes of such hearings is to aid inmates' rehabilitation. Yet in *Wolff*, the Court required a disciplinary decision-maker to provide an inmate with a written statement recounting the evidence relied on and the reasons for the disciplinary action taken.

Although the Supreme Court concluded in *Greenholtz* that inmates denied parole have no right to a statement outlining the evidence upon which the parole board based its decision to deny parole release, the Court at the same time underscored, as it had when discussing the inmates' claim concerning formal hearings, that an alternative procedural safeguard was afforded inmates denied parole in Nebraska. Inmates were apprised, although very generally, of the reason or reasons why the parole board had decided not to release them from prison.

In a dissenting opinion, Justice Marshall vehemently disagreed that these statements satisfied the requirements of due process, particularly since they were so general and given in such a rote fashion as to be almost meaningless. The majority of the Nebraska inmates denied parole were simply told that continuing their treatment, education, or work assignment in prison would significantly increase the likelihood that they would abide by the law upon their release from prison. Justice Marshall believed that the inmates were entitled to a "meaningful explanation" of the reasons why they were denied parole. Requiring such an explanation, in his opinion, would not impose an undue burden on the parole board, since it is not, as he pointed out, "burdensome to give reasons when reasons exist."

Justice Marshall also believed that inmates had a right to be apprised of the evidence upon which the denial of parole was predicated. This statement of the evidence and reasons, in his opinion, would promote care on the parole board's part when rendering its release decision, and it would help to ensure that the decision was not grounded on erroneous information. The statement would also have the added benefit of apprising a prisoner of the steps that he or she should take to increase the prospects of being released on parole. Finally, Justice Marshall argued that the written statement of evidence would aid, rather than impede inmates' rehabilitation by helping, along with other procedural safeguards, to provide them with the assurance that the proceedings in which they had been involved had been conducted fairly.

Perhaps the most clear indicator of the contracted scope of prisoners' due process rights in the parole-release context was the Courts' summary treatment in *Greenholtz* of the inmates' claim that the notice they received of impending parole-release hearings was constitutionally deficient. While the inmates were told the month before their hearing that their parole hearing would be scheduled sometime during the following month, they were not apprised of the date of the hearing until the day on which the hearing was to be held. In addition, they were not apprised of the factors upon which the parole board would be resting its parole-release decisions. While four dissenting Justices argued that the way in which the inmates were notified of the parole hearings nullified their statutory rights to call witnesses to testify in their behalf at the hearings and to receive the assistance of an attorney at the hearings, the Court, in a footnote, cursorily, and in the dissenters' view erroneously, responded that the inmates had not claimed that the present system of notifying them of their upcoming parole hearings seriously prejudiced their ability to prepare for their hearings.

Greenholtz is significant, not only for the rights that it says inmates do not have during parole-release proceedings, but for the possible rights about which it expressed no view. Some of the questions which remain after *Greenholtz* include the following: Do inmates during parole-release hearings have the right to present documentary evidence to the parole board? Do they have the right to present witnesses to testify on their behalf before the parole board? Do they have the right to confront and cross-examine adverse witnesses or the right to check their files to ensure that the information upon which the parole board is basing its decision is accurate? Do the inmates, at least in some circumstances, have the right to be represented by an attorney at the parole hearing or to receive some alternative form of assistance? *Cf. Wolff v. McDonnell* (1974) (is a due process right to assistance from another inmate, a staff member, or a "sufficiently competent" inmate assigned by the staff to provide such assistance when an inmate charged with disciplinary misconduct is illiterate or the case is so complex that assistance is needed to ensure that any defense is adequately prepared and presented). And finally, do the inmates have the right to have the parole decision made by a "neutral and detached" decisionmaker?

In answering these questions, the due process balancing test enunciated in *Mathews v. Eldridge* (1976) will be applied. Under this three-pronged test, which is discussed more fully elsewhere in this book (*see* Chapter 3 on page 39 and Chapter 12 on page 195), the following three factors, you will recall, are weighed when determining whether a particular procedural safeguard is required by due process: the private interest at stake; the way in which and extent to which a governmental interest or interests would be affected if the procedural safeguard were put in place; and the safeguard's value in terms of reducing the risk of an erroneous deprivation of the private interest at stake in the proceeding.

CHAPTER 17

RIGHTS UPON RELEASE

A. RESTRICTED OPPORTUNITIES AND RIGHTS OF RELEASED PRISONERS

Each year, several hundred thousand prisoners are released from prison into the community. The hope, of course, is that these individuals will have learned a lesson from their incarceration and will now become productive and law-abiding members of society. The reality, however, is often otherwise.

Individuals who enter prison uneducated and with few job skills generally leave prison in the same condition. This fact is a particular concern since studies have confirmed that individuals who, upon release from prison, are unemployed or under-employed are much more likely to resume committing crimes. *See, e.g.*, R.H. Finn & Patricia Fontaine, *The Association Between Selected Characteristics and Perceived Employability of Offenders*, 12 Crim. Just. & Behavior 353, 354 (1985) (such offenders are four times more likely to be reincarcerated). Prisoners also usually leave prison with other problems that often contributed to their criminal behavior, such as substance-abuse problems or the lack of coping skills needed when facing the inevitable frustrations of life, such as the ability to control anger. Added to these obstacles impeding released prisoners' successful reintegration into the community is the stigma that accompanies the label "ex-con," a stigma that makes it difficult for released prisoners to find jobs.

With no jobs awaiting them and few job prospects, little money, and serious unaddressed and unresolved personal problems, it is little wonder that prison gates have become nothing more than revolving doors for thousands of released prisoners. One study conducted by the Bureau of Justice Statistics revealed, for example, that 61% of the individuals entering prison had been previously incarcerated. *See, e.g.*, Bureau of Justice Statistics, U.S. Dep't of Justice, *Examining Recidivism* 1 (1985).

The practical obstacles impeding released inmates' reintegration into society are not the only ones. There are also legal obstacles that serve as constant reminders to released prisoners, as well as others convicted of crimes, that they must continue to pay a price for their criminal misdeeds. *See* Office of the Pardon Attorney, U.S. Dep't of Justice, *Civil Disabilities of Convicted Felons: A State-by-State Survey* (1992). Ex-felons are often, for example, statutorily prohibited from serving on juries, and they are also barred by statute from certain jobs. A conviction for a crime involving official misconduct, for example, may foreclose future government employment. The United States Army, Navy, Air Force, Marine Corps, and Coast Guard are also forbidden from hiring convicted felons, although exceptions can be made in "meritorious cases."   10 U.S.C.A. § 504.

Another civil penalty that may attend a felony conviction is a restriction on the right to vote.   The Supreme Court considered the constitutionality of such a restriction in *Richardson v. Ramirez* (1974). In that case, three individuals who were denied the right to vote in California because of felonies of which they were convicted years earlier filed a lawsuit in which they contended that the abridgement of their voting rights violated their fourteenth amendment right to the equal protection of the law. They contended that the curtailment of their right to vote would only be constitutional if the curtailment was necessary for the protection of a compelling governmental interest.   They argued that such a compelling interest did not exist and that in fact, the government's interest in reintegrating ex-offenders into society pointed in the opposite direction—towards extending the right to vote to former felons.

The Supreme Court, however, disagreed that a compelling interest has to be furthered to justify a restriction on the voting rights of ex-felons.   The Court pointed out that another provision in the fourteenth amendment specifically contemplates and condones the disenfranchisement of individuals convicted of crimes.   That provision of the amendment, section 2, provides for reduced representation in Congress when a state denies certain individuals the right to vote.   An exception exists, however, when individuals are disenfranchised because of their participation in a rebellion "or other crime."

In *Hunter v. Underwood* (1985), the Supreme Court distinguished its decision in *Richardson v. Ramirez* and struck down a provision of the Alabama Constitution that prohibited persons convicted of crimes involving "moral turpitude" from voting. The Court found that the constitutional provision had been enacted in order to disenfranchise blacks and in fact had had a disproportionately adverse effect on the voting privileges of blacks. Because of the voting ban's discriminatory intent and its disparate impact on blacks, the Court concluded that the ban violated the equal protection clause of the fourteenth amendment.

B. RESTORATION OF RIGHTS

There are a number of different ways that the adverse collateral consequences of a criminal conviction can be reduced. One way is through a pardon. Federal offenders receive pardons from the President, while in the states, the power to grant pardons may be vested in the governor, the parole board, or a board of pardons. A pardon does not mean that a person was innocent of the crime of which he or she was convicted; a pardon simply removes most or all of the civil disabilities that attend a criminal conviction. In some states though, an individual who has received a pardon must still, when requested, reveal the fact of the conviction on an employment application.

Another common means of mitigating the adverse consequences of a criminal conviction is through the restoration of rights. Under some state statutes, some or all of the rights lost because of a criminal conviction are automatically restored upon the occurrence of a specified event, such as the end of incarceration or the completion of a criminal sentence. In other states, these rights are restored only upon the application of the ex-offender. Whatever the exact mechanism for the restoration of rights, one of their limitations, as with pardons, is that individuals whose rights have been restored must still disclose their criminal convictions when asked about them by prospective employers, thereby diminishing the ex-offenders' chances of successfully obtaining employment.

There are, however, means of limiting the negative effects of a criminal conviction on an individual's employability. Some states, for example, provide for the expungement or sealing of criminal records in certain circumstances, such as when individuals are sentenced to probation or convicted for the first time of a felony. When expunged, criminal records are destroyed. When they are sealed, they remain intact, but access to them is limited. Whether the records are expunged or sealed, the end result is that a person may possibly then, depending on a state's law, refrain from mentioning a criminal conviction when applying for a job.

A few states have taken a different tack to prevent criminal convictions from unduly foreclosing employment opportunities—by generally barring employment discrimination because of prior criminal convictions. The American Bar Association favors the general removal of employment barriers facing individuals convicted of crimes, but at the same time recognizes, as do the states that have enacted discrimination bans, that some employment limitations are reasonable and therefore permissible. *See* Standard 23–8.8, ABA Standards Relating to the Legal Status of Prisoners (1981) (must be a "substantial relationship" between the crime and the responsibilities of the job to which access is denied). A person convicted of child molestation, for example, can be barred from working in a day-care center.

The Constitution also places some limits in certain circumstances on the denial of employment to ex-offenders because of their prior convictions. When a person seeks and is denied a government job, there must, according to the Supreme Court, be a rational connection between the job and the criterion that led to the denial of employment. *Schware v. Board of Bar Examiners* (1957). This due process requirement may sometimes simply not be met when an individual is denied a job because of a criminal conviction that really has no bearing on the individual's capability to perform the job.

PART THREE

PRISONERS' RIGHTS LITIGATION

CHAPTER 18

THE MECHANICS OF LITIGATING INMATES' § 1983 SUITS

A. THE COMPLAINT

The primary vehicle for redressing violations of inmates' constitutional rights by state or local officials is the federal civil rights statute codified in 42 U.S.C.A. § 1983. Section 1983 provides in part as follows:

Every person who, under color of any statute, ordinance, regulation, custom, or usage, of any State or Territory or the District of Columbia, subjects, or causes to be subjected, any citizen of the United States or other person within the jurisdiction thereof to the deprivation of any rights, privileges, or immunities secured by the Constitution and laws, shall be liable to the party injured in an action at law, suit in equity, or other proper proceeding for redress....

The rules and procedures pertaining to the litigation of § 1983 suits are complex. This chapter focuses on only some of the more basic points concerning § 1983 litigation, but the reader is encouraged to turn to other resources that exclusively discuss § 1983 actions for more detailed information. *See, e.g.,* Sheldon H. Nahmod, *Civil Rights and Civil Liberties Litigation: The Law of Section 1983* (3d ed. 1991 & Supp. 1994).

1. Elements of a Cause of Action Under § 1983

There are four key elements that must be established by an inmate to prevail in a § 1983 action. These elements are briefly described below.

1. *Person*—First, a "person" must have violated the inmate's rights. The Supreme Court, however, has not interpreted the word "person" literally; the "persons" who can be sued under § 1983 are not confined to human beings. Municipalities are, for example, "persons" within the meaning of § 1983. *Monell v. Department of Social Services* (1978). The Supreme Court in *Monell* based this conclusion on the fact that at the time that § 1983 was enacted, another federal statute, known as the Dictionary Act, defined the word "person" to include political and corporate entities "unless the context shows that such words were intended to be used in a more limited sense." *See also Smallwood v. Jefferson*

County Government (W.D.Ky.1991) (counties are "persons" subject to suit under § 1983).

According to the Supreme Court though, states are not "persons" subject to suit under § 1983. In *Will v. Michigan Department of State Police* (1989), the Court noted that Congress would have been aware of the immunity of states under the eleventh amendment when they are sued under § 1983 in a federal court. The Court thought it unlikely that Congress had nonetheless intended to make states subject to suit in § 1983 actions filed in state courts. The Court therefore simply interpreted § 1983 as not extending to states at all.

State officials, on the other hand, are sometimes "persons" who can be sued under § 1983 and sometimes not. When sued in their official capacity for damages, state officials are not considered "persons" in the legal sense, since the lawsuit, in effect, is one against the state. Any damages awarded would be paid out of the state's treasury.

On the other hand, state officials can be sued in their official capacity under § 1983 for injunctive relief. *Id.* This type of relief, which requires officials to take or refrain from taking certain actions in the future, is not considered to be directed at the state, even though in reality, compliance with an injunction will often require the expenditure of state funds.

State officials are also "persons" within the meaning of § 1983 when they are sued in their personal capacity. Personal-capacity suits are not considered suits against the state, since any damages awarded are payable by the officials themselves rather than the state. A state may, however, choose to indemnify an official for damages paid to an inmate who prevails in a § 1983 suit.

2. *"Under Color of" State Law*—For an action to lie under § 1983, the "person" sued must also have acted "under color of" state law—specifically, a state statute, ordinance, regulation, custom, or usage. To satisfy this under-color-of-state-law requirement, it is not necessary though that a state law require or even authorize the defendant's unconstitutional actions. In fact, as was discussed in Chapter 8 on page 131, the under-color-of-state-law requirement can be met even if a state law specifically prohibits the defendant's actions. Thus, in *Monroe v. Pape* (1961), the Supreme Court concluded that police officers had acted "under the color of" state law when entering the plaintiffs' home without a warrant, even though the warrantless entry violated the state's constitution and certain state statutes.

The Court noted in *Monroe v. Pape* that all that is necessary for a person's actions to be considered to have been taken "under color of" state law is that they involved the " '[m]isuse of power, possessed by virtue of state law and made possible only because the wrongdoer is clothed with the authority of state law.' " The Court reasoned that § 1983 was designed to provide a federal remedy for the violation of constitutional rights in part because states had often failed in the past to enforce their own laws.

In recent years, governments have increasingly turned to private contractors to operate some or all of certain correctional facilities and programs. The question that arises is whether these private contractors can be sued under § 1983 for violating the constitutional rights of inmates. Specifically, do these private contractors act "under color of" state law? The answer to these questions, after the Supreme Court's decision in *West v. Atkins* (1988), is clearly yes. In *West*, the Court concluded that a private physician who worked in a state prison two days a week could be sued under § 1983. According to the Court, it did not matter that the defendant was not a state employee or that he only worked part-time within the prison. What mattered was his function; he had agreed to assume the government's responsibility, one that the state had delegated to him, of providing inmates with the medical care to which they were constitutionally entitled.

3. *Causation*—A third element that must be established to prevail in a § 1983 action is causation. Only a person who "subjects" another to a constitutional violation or "causes" another to be so subjected can be liable under § 1983.

Many of the questions concerning this causation requirement have arisen in cases concerning the liability of municipalities under § 1983. According to the Supreme Court, a municipality is not liable under § 1983 simply because one of its employees violated someone's constitutional rights. *Monell v. Department of Social Services* (1978). In other words, the doctrine of *respondeat superior* does not apply in § 1983 actions. Under this doctrine, an employer is generally liable for torts committed by an employee that occurred when the employee was acting within the scope of his or her employment.

While the Supreme Court has definitively resolved that there is no *respondeat-superior* liability under § 1983, the Court has been less clear in defining exactly when municipalities will be held liable under § 1983. Most of the Supreme Court decisions discussing municipal liability have been fragmented into a confusing mix of plurality, concurring, and dissenting opinions. *See, e.g., St. Louis v. Praprotnik* (1988); *Pembaur v. Cincinnati* (1986); *Oklahoma City v. Tuttle* (1985). A few clear requirements, however, emerge from these cases.

First, for a municipality to be liable under § 1983, the constitutional violation must have stemmed from an official policy or custom. Second, that policy or custom must have been the "moving force" behind the constitutional violation. Just because a municipality, for example, inadequately trains some of its employees, such as officials working in a local jail, does not mean that the municipality will necessarily be liable under § 1983 if one of those employees violates someone's constitutional rights. To give rise to § 1983 liability, the failure to train adequately must be accompanied by a "deliberate indifference" to the need for more or better training. *Canton v. Harris* (1989).

The existence of such deliberate indifference can be established by showing, for example, that municipal policymakers ignored a very obvious need for more or different training even though deficiencies in the training of municipal employees created a substantial likelihood that they would act unconstitutionally. Alternatively, deliberate indifference may be manifested by the failure to augment training when recurring constitutional violations, such as repeated incidents involving excessive use of force by jail officials, make the need for more training "plainly obvious."

4. *Violation of Federal Rights*—To prevail in a § 1983 suit, the plaintiff must finally prove that the defendant violated the plaintiff's constitutional rights or other rights afforded the plaintiff by federal law. The constitutional rights of prisoners were discussed in earlier chapters of this book.

2. *Bivens* Actions

Section 1983 only authorizes the bringing of a lawsuit for the violation of constitutional rights that occurred "under the color of" state law. There is no federal counterpart to § 1983—no comparable statute to which federal prisoners can turn when their constitutional rights are violated. Nonetheless, these prisoners are not left remediless. In *Bivens v. Six Unknown Federal Narcotics Agents* (1971), the Supreme Court held that the fourth amendment implicitly authorizes suits for damages against federal officials who violate its requirements. The Court has since held that what has

become to be known as a *Bivens* suit can be brought
for the violation of other constitutional rights. *See,
e.g., Carlson v. Green* (1980) (eighth amendment
cruel and unusual punishment); *Davis v. Passman*
(1979) (fifth amendment due process).

3. Jurisdiction

State and federal courts have concurrent jurisdiction over § 1983 suits. In other words, a § 1983
suit can be filed in either a state court or a federal
court. The decision as to in which court to bring
suit will depend on a number of different factors,
including the procedural rules, particularly the discovery rules, that apply in the two courts; the
location of the courts; the time that it will take,
because of docket loads, to move the case through
the different courts; and the extent to which each
court seems receptive to civil rights claims—in this
context, civil rights claims filed by inmates.

4. Sufficiency of the Complaint

Most prisoners' complaints under § 1983 are filed
pro se, which means that the prisoners are unrepre-
sented and unassisted by counsel. A prisoner's *pro
se* § 1983 complaint is often met by a motion to
dismiss the complaint for failure to state a claim
upon which relief can be granted. When ruling on
such a motion to dismiss, the lower courts have,
however, been instructed by the Supreme Court to
liberally construe the prisoner's *pro se* complaint.
Haines v. Kerner (1972). Only when it appears
"beyond doubt that the plaintiff can prove no set of

facts in support of his claim which would entitle him to relief" should the prisoner's *pro se* complaint be dismissed.

The liberal construction of inmates' complaints also occurs when an indigent inmate seeks leave under 28 U.S.C.A. § 1915(a) to file a complaint *in forma pauperis*. If the petition is granted, the inmate is excused from paying the fees and costs that must normally be paid when a lawsuit is filed in a federal district court.

If the court which is deciding whether an inmate can proceed *in forma pauperis* concludes that the inmate's complaint is "frivolous," the court can dismiss the inmate's complaint. 28 U.S.C.A. § 1915(d). The standard applied when determining whether a complaint is frivolous is, however, quite broad, even broader than the standard applied when ruling on a motion to dismiss a complaint for failure to state a claim. A complaint will be considered frivolous only if it has no "arguable basis in law or in fact." *Neitzke v. Williams* (1989). The reason for this exceedingly deferential review of inmates' complaints when they are first seeking to file their complaints *in forma pauperis* is that district courts at this stage generally dismiss complaints *sua sponte*—in other words, on the court's own motion, without an inmate being afforded the opportunity to respond to the court's concerns about deficiencies in the complaint. Even if a complaint is dismissed as frivolous under 28 U.S.C.A. § 1915(d), however, an inmate can later refile the complaint if the inmate is able to pay the filing fee and costs.

In addition to not having the funds to pay filing fees and costs, indigent inmates also cannot afford to pay for the services of attorneys. They are therefore at a severe disadvantage when litigating their civil rights claims unless a court appoints counsel to represent them. Section 1915(d) authorizes courts to appoint counsel to represent indigent parties, including inmates, in federal lawsuits, but this authority is actually exercised in only a small fraction of prisoners' cases. The decision whether or not to appoint an attorney falls within the court's discretion, and the court's decision will be reversed on appeal only for an abuse of that discretion. In determining whether a district court abused its discretion when refusing to appoint an attorney to represent an indigent inmate, an appellate court will look at an array of factors, including the complexity of the case, the extent to which the case appears to have merit, and the plaintiff's apparent ability to prepare and present the case without assistance. *See, e.g., Jackson v. County of Mc-Lean* (7th Cir.1992).

B. AFFIRMATIVE DEFENSES

As is true whenever a lawsuit is being defended against, defendants against whom § 1983 complaints have been filed can assert affirmative defenses to avoid liability. Some of the affirmative defenses that are most frequently raised in § 1983 lawsuits are discussed below.

1. Immunity

a. Sovereign Immunity

The United States cannot be sued without its consent. *United States v. Mitchell* (1983). Congress, however, has given consent to bring constitutional claims against the federal government, which means that federal prisoners can directly sue the government for violations of their constitutional rights. 28 U.S.C.A. § 1346(a)(2).

The assertion of constitutional claims against the states is more problematic. As mentioned earlier, states cannot even be sued under § 1983. *Will v. Michigan Department of State Police* (1989). If Congress were to amend § 1983 to specifically include states as suable defendants, however, the states, if sued, could not invoke an immunity defense. It is true that the eleventh amendment to the United States Constitution, as it has been construed by the Supreme Court, generally bars individuals from suing states in federal court. *Hans v. Louisiana* (1890). Congress, however, has the power, stemming from § 5 of the fourteenth amendment, to override this eleventh-amendment immunity to effectuate the provisions of the fourteenth amendment. *Fitzpatrick v. Bitzer* (1976). Although Congress did not, according to the Court, exercise this power when it enacted § 1983, *Quern v. Jordan* (1979), it can and may choose to do so in the future.

Although states cannot, as of now, be sued under § 1983, they can, ironically, sometimes be liable for a plaintiff's attorney's fees incurred when litigating a § 1983 suit. The Civil Rights Attorney's Fees Awards Act of 1976, 42 U.S.C.A. § 1988, authorizes courts to award attorney's fees to prevailing plaintiffs in § 1983 suits. The Supreme Court has held that when enacting § 1988, Congress intended to exercise its authority under the fourteenth amendment to abrogate the states' eleventh-amendment immunity. *Hutto v. Finney* (1978). The states can therefore be required to pick up the tab for a plaintiff's attorney's fees when state officials were sued in their official capacity under § 1983, litigated their case in good faith, but lost. *Id.*

b. *Official Immunity*

Section 1983 says that *"[e]very* person" that violates another's constitutional rights while acting under the color of state law *"shall* be liable." Despite the all-encompassing and mandatory language of § 1983, the Supreme Court has held that it does not mean what it says. Even when officials have violated the constitutional rights of others, there will be times when they can successfully invoke an immunity defense.

Personal-immunity defenses can be raised by officials sued in their personal capacities for damages. They cannot, however, be invoked by officials sued in their official capacities. *Kentucky v. Graham* (1985).

There are two types of personal immunity—absolute and qualified. Absolute immunity, as its name suggests, totally protects an official from damages liability. Qualified immunity, on the other hand, provides more limited protection. If an official violated "clearly established statutory or constitutional rights of which a reasonable person would have known," a qualified-immunity defense will fail. *Harlow v. Fitzgerald* (1982).

The purpose of official immunity, both absolute and qualified, is to prevent the fear of being sued, as well as the attendant hassles of litigation, from unduly hampering official decisionmaking. Another interest is implicated though when decisions are being made regarding the scope of immunity, if any, that should be extended to a particular type of government official—the interest in vindicating constitutional rights. The Supreme Court has balanced these competing interests by holding that generally, executive officials can avail themselves only of a qualified-immunity defense. *Id.* If executive officials seek even greater protection from damages liability, they have the burden of proving their entitlement to absolute immunity. *Id.*

In *Cleavinger v. Saxner* (1985), the defendants, who were members of a prison disciplinary committee, contended that they were entitled to absolute immunity from damages liability when sued for violating inmates' constitutional rights. They argued that, like judges, they should be accorded absolute immunity, since they too perform an adjudicatory function.

The Supreme Court conceded that prison disciplinary committees perform an adjudicatory function of sorts when they decide whether or not inmates have violated prison rules. Nonetheless, the Court concluded that the prison disciplinary committee members differed from judges in some important respects. For one thing, the prison disciplinary committee members, unlike judges, were not independent. They were employees of the Federal Bureau of Prisons. In the course of making disciplinary decisions, they had to choose between their fellow employees and inmates when deciding who was telling the truth, and obviously, they would feel pressure to find in favor of their colleagues.

Another important distinction that the Supreme Court pointed out between prison disciplinary committee members and judges is in the procedural safeguards surrounding their decisionmaking processes. These safeguards are relevant because they reduce the risk of constitutional errors occurring. While a whole gamut of procedural safeguards attend court proceedings, the Supreme Court in *Cleavinger v. Saxner* noted that most of these safeguards were not included in the disciplinary process in federal prisons. Prisoners faced with disciplinary charges were not represented by counsel or by any other independent nonstaff assistant. They had no discovery rights, no right to confront and cross-examine adverse witnesses, and no right to receive a transcript of the hearing. There was no identified burden of proof that had to be met before prisoners could be found guilty of disciplinary misconduct, and hearsay evidence could be considered by the prison disciplinary committee.

The Supreme Court therefore concluded in *Cleavinger* that the prison disciplinary committee members who had been sued were only entitled to invoke a qualified-immunity defense. At the same time, however, the Court added that prison disciplinary processes can be structured in such a way that disciplinary decisionmakers can be afforded absolute immunity. Administrative law judges can, for example, be used to adjudicate prison disciplinary charges. *See also Procunier v. Navarette* (1978) (prison officials, including the director of the department of corrections and the warden, entitled to qualified immunity).

Since one of the purposes of an immunity defense is to insulate officials from the burdens of litigation, an official's entitlement to immunity will normally be resolved before discovery in a case commences. *Harlow v. Fitzgerald* (1982). For the same reason, an official can immediately appeal an order denying a motion to dismiss on immunity grounds and need not wait until a case is over in the trial court before taking that appeal. *Mitchell v. Forsyth* (1985).

Municipalities, unlike states, cannot invoke the immunity afforded by the eleventh amendment when they are sued in a federal court. *Will v. Michigan Department of State Police* (1989). In addition, while municipal employees may be able to successfully invoke a qualified-immunity defense, municipalities themselves cannot use this defense to

insulate themselves from damages liability. *Owen
v. City of Independence* (1980). Reading § 1983
against its common-law backdrop, the Supreme
Court has explained that at common law, such
qualified immunity was not the norm for municipalities. In addition, the Court has stated that making
a municipality fully responsible for the damages
caused by its violation of constitutional rights would
further the two objectives of § 1983—to compensate
individuals for the violation of their constitutional
rights and to deter such violations through the
imposition of liability.

Based on the Supreme Court's construction of the
common law in effect at the time § 1983 was enacted, however, municipalities are immune from punitive-damages awards. *Newport v. Fact Concerts,
Inc.* (1981). While the Court has said that it is fair
to spread the loss caused by a constitutional violation amongst all of the taxpayers in a municipality,
the Court has qualms about punishing taxpayers for
the wrongdoing of others by requiring them to pay
a punitive-damages award.

What has still not been decided by the Supreme
Court is whether private contractors responsible for
some or all of the operations of a correctional facility can invoke a qualified-immunity defense. *Wyatt
v. Cole* (1992) is arguably of some relevance to this
question. In *Wyatt*, the Supreme Court held that
certain private individuals, sued under § 1983 for
their involvement in the confiscation of the plaintiff's property under an allegedly unconstitutional
state statute, could not invoke the defense of quali-

fied immunity. The Court might find *Wyatt* distinguishable from the situation where a private contractor has undertaken to perform the important governmental function of operating a correctional facility. Much of the language in the *Wyatt* case, however, was sweeping and could be interpreted as foreclosing a qualified-immunity defense for private contractors in the correctional context. At one point, for example, the Court said that "the rationales mandating qualified immunity for public officials are not applicable to private parties." The Court also observed that the principal goal of private defendants is not the furtherance of the public good. However the Court rules on the question of whether § 1983 implicitly includes a qualified-immunity defense for private contractors though, that decision, of course, can be overturned by Congress through an amendment to § 1983.

2. Statute of Limitations

As is true with other lawsuits, a suit under § 1983 must be brought within the time limits prescribed by the applicable statute of limitations. There is no federal statute that dictates a time limit for bringing a § 1983 action, so federal district courts are directed by 42 U.S.C.A. § 1988 to apply the statute of limitations in effect in the state where a lawsuit is brought, unless the application of that statute would conflict with the Constitution or federal law. The statute of limitations to be applied is the one covering actions to recover for personal injuries. *Wilson v. Garcia* (1985). If there are two statutes of limitations in the state—one governing the intentional infliction of personal injuries and a catch-all statute that encompasses all other personal-injury actions, the more general statute of limitations is to be applied. *Owens v. Okure* (1989).

3. Mootness

If a case becomes moot while it is being litigated, the case must be dismissed, even if the case is on appeal. Mootness issues arise with some frequency in prisoner litigation because of the release or transfer of inmates from prisons where a cause of action arose. *See, e.g., Hewitt v. Helms* (1987); *Vitek v. Jones* (1980). There are ways, however, for a prisoner to thwart a motion to dismiss on mootness grounds. First, a transfer or release from a prison will generally not moot a claim for damages relief if such a claim is included in the complaint. *Boag v. MacDougall* (1982). And second, if the prisoner has brought a class-action suit and the class has been certified by the court, the prisoner's departure from the prison will not moot the case. *Sosna v. Iowa* (1975).

4. Exhaustion of Remedies

The Supreme Court has repeatedly held that there is no exhaustion-of-remedies requirement subsumed within § 1983. *See* the cases cited in *Patsy v. Florida Board of Regents* (1982). Section 1983 therefore does not require prisoners to exhaust available state judicial or administrative remedies before bringing suit under § 1983.

A limited statutory exception to this no-exhaustion rule has, however, been carved out in 42 U.S.C.A. § 1997e. Section 1997e authorizes a judge to continue a § 1983 case for up to ninety days while a prisoner exhausts available administrative remedies. For such exhaustion of administrative remedies to be required, however, the remedies must meet certain requirements delineated in the statute. Those requirements include: (1) the participation of staff and inmates in the formulation, implementation, and operation of the grievance system; (2) time limits for written replies to grievances filed and the inclusion of reasons for granting or denying the grievances in those replies; (3) priority processing of grievances in emergency situations; (4) safeguards to prevent retaliatory measures from being taken against inmates who file grievances; and (5) independent review of the disposition of grievances by a person or entity "not under the the direct supervision or direct control of the institution" in question.

In recent years, a number of proposals have been made and continue to be made to expand the exhaustion requirement of § 1997e. The reader is therefore advised to periodically check § 1997e to determine what its present requirements are.

There is not, however, at present, any counterpart to § 1997e that applies to federal prisoners. In addition, the Supreme Court has thus far refused to impose an exhaustion-of-remedies requirement on its own on federal prisoners bringing Bivens actions for damages. In *McCarthy v. Madigan*

(1992), the Court mentioned a number of reasons why an exhaustion requirement for federal prisoners was unwarranted, including the unavailability of damages relief in the grievance process. At the same time, however, the Supreme Court suggested that if the Federal Bureau of Prisons made certain changes in its grievance procedures, the judicial imposition of an exhaustion requirement might follow.

CHAPTER 19

REMEDIES

A. § 1983 SUITS

1. Damages

Damages are frequently sought as a form of relief by individuals who bring suit under § 1983. Damages can be awarded in § 1983 actions to compensate individuals for the harm they have suffered due to the violation of their constitutional rights. To recover such compensatory damages, however, plaintiffs must prove that they were actually injured by the violation of their constitutional rights.

In *Carey v. Piphus* (1978), two students filed a lawsuit under § 1983 after they were summarily suspended from school. The students contended that their suspensions had been effected without following certain procedures required by due process. The federal district court agreed that their constitutional rights had been violated, but refused to award the plaintiffs any compensatory damages because they had failed to introduce any evidence as to how they had been harmed by the violation of their constitutional rights.

The plaintiffs contended that the introduction of such evidence was unnecessary—that a court can appropriately presume that injuries have ensued from the violation of procedural due process rights. They based this argument in part on the fact that one purpose of the procedural safeguards required by due process is to ensure that people deprived of their life, liberty, or property feel that the deprivations have occurred in processes that are fair. Consequently, the plaintiffs argued that when an individual has not been afforded the "process" that is constitutionally "due," a court can assume that the individual has felt distress stemming from the perception of unfair treatment.

The Supreme Court, however, felt that such an assumption is unwarranted. The Court pointed out that sometimes a person will not even be aware of procedural irregularities that attended a deprivation, so these irregularities will not have caused any distress to that individual. In addition, even when distress is felt, often that distress is due to a deprivation that was in fact justified, even though effected without proper procedural safeguards.

The Supreme Court added that no compensation is due for injuries stemming from such a justified deprivation. Thus, if an inmate was confined in segregation following a disciplinary hearing that did not comport with the requirements of due process, the inmate could not recover damages for being confined in the segregation unit if he would still have been found guilty of misconduct and sent to segregation after a disciplinary hearing that met the requirements of due process. The inmate could, however, recover damages for any emotional or mental distress caused by the failure to afford him his procedural due process rights.

The point of *Carey v. Piphus*, however, is that plaintiffs have to actually prove that they suffered such distress; the existence of such distress or other types of injuries will not be presumed. In the absence of such proof, plaintiffs who have established that their procedural due process rights were violated can only be awarded nominal damages. Consequently, the Supreme Court in *Carey* directed that the plaintiffs receive no more than one dollar if the district court, on remand, concluded that the school suspensions were justified.

Punitive damages are also sometimes sought and awarded in § 1983 suits. To be liable for punitive damages, a defendant need not have acted with a malicious intent to harm the plaintiff, although such a malicious intent will certainly support a punitive-damages award. Punitive damages can be awarded as long as the defendant acted with "reckless or callous indifference to the federally protected rights of others." *Smith v. Wade* (1983).

2. Equitable Relief

Plaintiffs who bring suit under § 1983 often seek some form of equitable relief, either alone or in addition to damages. The relief sought may come in several different forms. One form is a declaratory judgment. When entering a declaratory judgment, a court may, for example, declare a state statute or regulation unconstitutional. If the court provides the plaintiff with some type of injunctive relief, the court goes even further—directing a defendant to refrain from taking certain unconstitutional actions in the future or requiring the defendant to take certain steps to avoid future violations of the Constitution.

Injunctive relief can come in the form of a temporary restraining order, a preliminary injunction, or a permanent injunction. The rules governing the issuance of these orders are quite complex. *See* Dan B. Dobbs, *Law of Remedies* 223–76 (2d ed. 1993). Certain key points concerning equitable relief, particularly equitable relief in the correctional context, should, however, be kept in mind.

First, the breadth of a court's equitable discretion in a § 1983 suit is quite broad. Courts, however, typically try to limit their intrusion into the delicate task of running correctional facilities by first requesting government officials to submit plans to alleviate unconstitutional conditions found to exist in those facilities. If the officials fail to submit a plan or an adequate plan, the courts will then intervene, sometimes quite forcefully. Court orders even going so far as to direct the release of some inmates from a facility whose conditions were unconstitutional have been upheld on appeal. *See, e.g., Duran v. Elrod* (7th Cir.1983) (release of pretrial detainees incarcerated only because they could not pay low bonds).

Second, despite the breadth of a court's equitable discretion when enforcing the provisions of the Constitution, there are still limits on the steps that can be taken by a court to redress a constitutional violation through the exercise of the court's equitable powers. *Missouri v. Jenkins* (1990) is a case in point. In that case, a federal district court was confronted with a school district where unconstitutional segregation had persisted for many years. To redress this problem, the school district had proposed a magnet school program that would cost $380 million to implement. The school district, however, was hamstrung in implementing this plan because the state's constitution limited the school district's ability to raise property taxes to pay for the program. The federal district court responded by raising property taxes to obtain the funds necessary to implement the desegregation plan.

The Supreme Court, however, held that in raising property taxes, the district court had abused its equitable discretion because there was a less intrusive alternative to a court-directed tax increase. That alternative was to order the school officials themselves to raise the taxes needed to pay for the magnet school program and then enjoin enforcement of the state constitutional provision that stood in the way of this tax increase. To the Supreme Court, the difference between these two remedies was not just a matter of form, since the school officials themselves, rather than the court, would now have the primary responsibility to take the steps needed to rectify constitutional violations in the operation of the school district.

A third important point to remember about the exercise of a court's equitable discretion in a § 1983 suit is that while a court may, in an unusual case, order the release of inmates from a correctional facility to redress unconstitutional conditions of confinement, a court has no authority under § 1983 to release a prisoner who is challenging, not the conditions of his or her confinement, but the fact or duration of that confinement. In addition, state prisoners challenging the fact or duration of their confinement cannot seek damages stemming from their allegedly unconstitutional confinement in a § 1983 suit unless and until a federal court has issued a writ of habeas corpus, thereby raising doubts about the validity of the conviction or sentence, or the conviction or sentence has been reversed or set aside by a court order or expunged by an executive order. *Heck v. Humphrey* (1994).

In *Preiser v. Rodriguez* (1973), a prisoner brought suit under § 1983, seeking the restoration of good-time credits that he claimed had been unconstitutionally revoked. Issuance of an injunction directing that these good-time credits be restored would have led to the inmate's immediate release from prison. The Supreme Court, however, concluded that the relief that the inmate was seeking was not obtainable in a § 1983 action. Instead, the inmate, and any other inmates challenging the fact or duration of their confinement who sought immediate or earlier release from confinement, would have to seek relief by filing a habeas corpus petition under 28 U.S.C.A. § 2254.

The Supreme Court was concerned that to permit a prisoner to seek release from confinement in a

§ 1983 suit would undermine the comity considerations that underlie the requirement in § 2254(c)
that a prisoner first exhaust available state court
remedies before pursuing habeas corpus relief in a
federal court. The purpose of this exhaustion requirement is to limit the number of instances when
federal courts intrude in the state's domain through
the rather drastic step of ordering the release of a
person from state or local confinement.

3. Attorney's Fees

Plaintiffs who prevail in § 1983 suits can, in the
discretion of the court, recover "reasonable" attorney's fees under 42 U.S.C.A. § 1988. Section 1988
refers to the recovery of attorney's fees by any
"prevailing party" in such a lawsuit, but the Supreme Court has held that only in an unusual case
should attorney's fees be assessed against a plaintiff. Otherwise, the private enforcement of civil
rights laws would be discouraged, in contravention
of the purpose of § 1988. A plaintiff can therefore
be required to pay a defendant's attorney's fees only
when the plaintiff's lawsuit was " 'frivolous, unreasonable, or without foundation, even though not
brought in subjective bad faith.' " *Hughes v. Rowe*
(1980). In addition, a court is supposed to be
particularly hesitant to award attorney's fees
against prisoners who have represented themselves
in § 1983 suits because of the difficulties inmates
face in understanding the complexities of the law.
Id.

To be considered a "prevailing party" within the meaning of § 1988, a plaintiff need not have won the central claim asserted in a § 1983 suit. All that is necessary is that the plaintiff succeeded on " 'any significant issue in litigation which achieve[d] some of the benefit the parties sought in bringing suit.' " *Texas State Teachers Association v. Garland Independent School District* (1989). That benefit may, but need not, have been achieved after going through a trial. In *Maher v. Gagne* (1980), the Supreme Court concluded that the plaintiffs were entitled to attorney's fees even though their lawsuit was resolved through the entry of a consent decree, which is a court order which embodies the parties' settlement agreement. On the other hand, when a plaintiff is awarded only nominal damages, the plaintiff, though technically the prevailing party, should not, according to the Supreme Court, normally be awarded attorney's fees. *Farrar v. Hobby* (1992).

In determining what is a "reasonable" attorney's fee to be awarded under § 1988, what is know as the lodestar figure must first be computed. This figure is calculated by multiplying the number of hours "reasonably expended" by an attorney working on a case times a "reasonable" hourly rate. *Hensley v. Eckerhart* (1983). If the parties cannot agree on what is an appropriate attorney's fee award, then the plaintiff has the burden of proving the reasonableness of the time expended on a case and the hourly rate charged.

The lodestar figure represents the baseline figure from which the final fee award is calculated. One or more of several factors may, however, sometimes lead to an award of attorney's fees which is higher or lower than the lodestar figure. For example, the extent of a plaintiff's success in a lawsuit may lead to an upwards or downwards shift in the fee award. *Id*. The attorney's fees awarded need not, however, necessarily be proportionate to the amount of damages recouped by the plaintiff. *City of Riverside v. Rivera* (1986) ($245,456.25 fee award upheld in a case where $33,350 in damages were awarded).

The fee award can also be adjusted to compensate the plaintiff's attorneys for the delay in receiving payment for their work. *Missouri v. Jenkins* (1989). One way in which to make such an adjustment is to compute the attorneys' fee award using the current market rate for the attorneys' services rather than the rate in effect when the work for the plaintiff was performed.

Sometimes, an attorney will represent a client on a contingent-fee basis. Under a contingent-fee agreement, the attorney does not charge the client on an hourly basis as work is being performed on a case. If the client wins the case, however, and recovers damages, the attorney is entitled to a certain percentage, such as one third, of the damages recovered. If the plaintiff recovers no damages, on the other hand, the attorney is left with no compensation for the work done on the case.

In *City of Burlington v. Dague* (1992), however, the Supreme Court concluded that a fee award should not be shifted upwards to compensate an attorney for assuming the risk of nonpayment when representing a client under a contingent-fee agreement. The dissenters argued that such an upwards adjustment was appropriate and in keeping with the purpose of the fee-shifting statutes to attract counsel to represent plaintiffs who would not otherwise be able to bring suit because of their lack of funds to pay an attorney up front. The majority responded by noting that much of the risk of nonpayment is already subsumed within the lodestar figure. The risk of nonpayment is in part a function of the difficulty of proving that the plaintiff's claim has merit. Surmounting this difficulty will lead to the expenditure of more time on a case, which is reflected in the lodestar, or the hiring of an attorney whose experience and ability in handling such claims is reflected in a higher hourly rate, which is also factored into the lodestar. To adjust the fee award upwards because of the risk of nonpayment would therefore, in the Supreme Court's opinion, result in double-counting.

While the existence of a contingent-fee agreement will not justify the elevation of a fee award under § 1988, a fee award will not be diminished because of such an agreement either. *Blanchard v. Bergeron* (1989). Consequently, the plaintiff's attorney may sometimes receive more money under § 1988 than the attorney is entitled to under a contingent-fee agreement. On the other hand, if the fee award under § 1988 is less than the attorney's fees to be paid under the contingent-fee agreement, the plaintiff can be required to pay additional money to the attorney. *Venegas v. Mitchell* (1990) (plaintiff awarded $117,000 in attorney's fees under § 1988 required to pay attorney 40% of $2.08 million dollar judgment, offset by the fee award, in accordance with the terms of the contingent-fee agreement).

Subsumed within the "reasonable attorney's fee" awardable under § 1988 is compensation for more than just the work of attorneys. The work of paralegals and law clerks is also compensable under § 1988. *Missouri v. Jenkins* (1989). On the other hand, § 1988, as currently drafted, does not provide compensation for the fees of the plaintiff's expert witnesses. *West Virginia University Hospitals v. Casey* (1991). This inability to recover expert-witness fees can greatly impede the ability of inmates to secure the expert witnesses whose testimony will often be needed or extremely helpful in establishing the unconstitutionality of the practices or conditions in a correctional facility. Since there have been some proposals to amend § 1988 to provide for the recovery of expert-witness fees, the reader is advised to continually monitor this statute to determine if such a change is made.

B. MODIFYING COURT ORDERS

Like other types of lawsuits, some inmates' civil rights suits are resolved through a settlement—an agreement between the parties as to the disposition of the case. Some of these settlement agreements, particularly in class-action suits, are embodied in consent decrees. A consent decree, as mentioned earlier, is a binding court order which reflects the parties' agreement.

At times, one of the parties may wish to be relieved of an obligation under a consent decree because meeting that obligation has become burdensome or perhaps even impossible. It is clear that final court orders and judgments can, in certain circumstances, be modified. Rule 60(b) of the Federal Rules of Civil Procedure, for example, authorizes a court to modify a final judgment or order "upon such terms as are just" when "it is no longer equitable" to enforce the judgment or when there is "any other reason justifying relief from the operation of the judgment."

In *Rufo v. Inmates of the Suffolk County Jail* (1992), the Supreme Court elaborated on when modification of a consent decree entered in a case involving reform of a prison, jail, or other public institution is appropriate. *Rufo* involved a consent decree entered after years of sparring in court between pretrial detainees confined in an old, dilapidated, extremely crowded jail and correctional and other government officials. The consent decree, entered in 1979, permitted the defendants to continue to house detainees in the old jail while a new jail was being constructed. The consent decree outlined the agreed-upon design of the new facility and provided for the construction of cells designed to hold only one inmate.

The defendants dragged their heels in implementing the requirements of the consent decree, and as time passed, it became evident that the jail contemplated by the consent decree would not be big enough to meet the county's space needs. The consent decree, with the concurrence of the parties, was then modified in 1985 to permit construction of a larger jail as long as certain other requirements of the consent decree were still adhered to, such as single celling.

Construction of the new jail finally began in 1987. In 1989, while construction of the new jail continued, the sheriff who oversaw the jail's operation moved once again to modify the consent decree, this time to permit the housing of two inmates in a cell. The plaintiffs, however, balked at this proposed change.

The Supreme Court began its analysis of the standards to be applied to consent-decree modifications by noting that the party seeking modification of a consent decree has the burden of proving that such modification is warranted. To meet that burden, the party seeking modification must surmount two hurdles—first, by establishing that there has been a "significant change" in the facts or the law since entry of the consent decree and second, by demonstrating that the proposed modification is "suitably tailored" to the changed circumstance that is prompting modification of the consent decree.

The Supreme Court identified three instances when changed factual conditions might justify modification of a consent decree. The first was when a change in the facts has made compliance with the consent decree "substantially more onerous." The Court underscored, however, that modification is not justified when a party is simply finding it inconvenient to live up to the terms of the agreement.

Second, the Supreme Court said that modification of a consent decree might be in order when enforcement of the decree would be "detrimental to the public interest." As an example of an instance when the public interest might dictate modification of a consent decree, the Court cited a lower court case in which a consent decree had been modified to avert the release of pretrial detainees charged with committing violent felonies.

Finally, the Supreme Court noted the appropriateness of modifying consent decrees that have proven to be "unworkable" because of "unforeseen obstacles." The Court rejected the plaintiffs' argument that modification of a consent decree should not be allowed if the impediments to the decree's implementation were foreseeable, even if not actually foreseen. The Court was hesitant to burden the process through which consent decrees are entered into by in effect asking the parties to make provisions for every possible contingency that might arise during the years and even decades while the consent decree was in effect. The Court added, however, that if a party, at the time the agreement was entered into, had actually anticipated the possibility of the problem occurring in the decree's implementation that had now actually occurred, modification would usually not be appropriate because of the change in the facts. The party seeking modification would have a "heavy burden" of demonstrating that despite the fact that the change in circumstances was anticipated, the party had agreed to entry of the consent decree in good faith and had made a "reasonable effort" to meet the requirements of that decree.

As mentioned earlier, a significant change in the law might also, in some circumstances, support the modification of the terms of a consent decree. For example, if a consent decree requires a party to do something which is now illegal, the consent decree must be modified. The rules that pertain when the change in the law makes legal what the consent decree prohibits are a bit more complex.

The sheriff in *Rufo* argued that the Supreme Court's decision in *Bell v. Wolfish* (1979), which was rendered after entry of the consent decree, justified the modification of that decree. In *Bell v. Wolfish*, you will recall, the Supreme Court held that the double celling of pretrial detainees is not *per se* unconstitutional. *See* page 248. The Court responded in *Rufo*, however, that just because a change in the law makes clear that the parties have obligated themselves to do something more than the Constitution requires does not mean that a consent decree can and should be modified. As the Court pointed out, parties entering into consent decrees have the prerogative to, and often do, take steps that go beyond the minimal requirements of the Constitution. A change in the law that clarifies that the parties in fact did so when they entered into a consent decree is therefore not adequate grounds for unsettling the parties' agreement. Otherwise, consent decrees would be on tenuous grounds, and the incentive of parties to resolve their differences through entry of a consent decree would be substantially diminished. On the other hand, if the parties actually misunderstood the law—in this case, believing that single-celling was constitutionally mandated—and based their consent decree on this misunderstanding, then this misunderstanding might, according to the Supreme Court, support modification of the consent decree.

Once a party seeking modification of a consent decree has proven that there has been a significant change in the facts or the law that warrants changing the terms of the consent decree, the party, as mentioned earlier, must then establish that the proposed modification is "suitably tailored to the changed circumstance." The Court emphasized in *Rufo* that just because the terms of a consent decree might need to be changed somewhat does not mean that the consent decree should then be rewritten to reflect only the minimal requirements of the Constitution. Instead, the changes should be limited to those needed to respond adequately to the change in circumstances. In other words, the consent decree should be reopened "only to the extent that equity requires."

At the same time, however, the Court observed that trial courts should treat with some deference the judgment of government administrators as to how to best respond to the change in circumstances. In addition, the courts should take into account the interests of the public when modifying consent decrees. Finally, while a lack of funds will not justify a failure to rectify a constitutional violation, financial constraints can properly be considered when determining the best way in which to modify a consent decree.

The Supreme Court added in *Rufo* that the two-part test that it was enunciating for consent-decree modifications pertained to the modification of provisions that were at least arguably related to rectifying a constitutional violation. This somewhat rigorous test did not apply to insignificant changes in "extraneous details in the decree," such as the color a building would be painted. While the Court anticipated that normally the parties would agree to such minor changes, the Court noted that if they did not, all that the party seeking modification would have to establish is that there is a "reasonable basis" for the proposed modification.

Many of the court orders that are designed to bring conditions in a correctional facility into compliance with the Constitution govern many different facets of the facility's operation. The question is: what happens when the constitutional violations in one or more areas of the facility's operation being overseen by a court have been rectified, but constitutional problems remain in other areas subject to court supervision?

It is clear that courts may properly end their supervision of some areas of a correctional facility's operation while continuing to supervise other areas. When exercising its discretion to partially end its supervision in a case, the Supreme Court has said that a court should be guided by "the purposes and objectives of its equitable power." Some of the factors that should inform the court's decision include: whether there has been "full and satisfactory" compliance in the area in which the withdrawal of supervision is contemplated; whether ongoing supervision in this area will be needed or helpful to secure compliance in other areas; and whether the government officials have demonstrated their commitment to abide by the requirements of the Constitution. *Freeman v. Pitts* (1992).

Even if a court ends its active supervision over some areas subject to a court order, it still retains jurisdiction over those areas. Consequently, if there is an unconstitutional relapse, the court can resume its supervision in that area. Once the problems that are the focus of a court order have been resolved and the purposes of the order "fully achieved," a court may then, however, withdraw its jurisdiction over the entire case. According to the Supreme Court, the termination of jurisdiction though should only occur when a court finds both that an institution is being operated in conformance with the Constitution and that it is unlikely that the defendants will resume their unconstitutional conduct in the future. On this latter question, courts need not necessarily believe the protestations of officials that they have learned their lesson and will now obey the Constitution. Instead, the courts should look at the extent to which the officials have actually acted in good faith in their attempts to abide by the requirements set forth in the court's orders. *Board of Education of Oklahoma City v. Dowell* (1991).

C. ENFORCING COURT ORDERS THROUGH CONTEMPT PROCEEDINGS AND OTHER MEANS

Lawyers who specialize in prisoners' rights litigation recognize that winning a judgment against correctional officials which requires them to change operations or conditions in a correctional facility is just the beginning of the litigation battle. What often follows are years of haggling over the defendants' compliance with the court's orders.

The defendants are responsible, under 42 U.S.C.A. § 1988, for the plaintiff's attorney's fees incurred in enforcing the court's orders in a § 1983 suit. *Diaz v. Romer* (10th Cir.1992). One of the ways in which the plaintiff may seek to secure the defendants' compliance is by asking the court to hold the defendants in contempt. If the defendants are found to be in contempt of a court order, one common court response is to impose a fine, which continues to accrue until the defendants meet their constitutional obligations. If the defendants have been found in civil contempt, the fine will be paid to the plaintiff, since the purpose of the fine is simply to induce the defendants to comply with the court's orders. On the other hand, if the defendants have been held in criminal contempt, the fine will be paid to the court, since the purpose of the fine is to punish the defendants for their recalcitrance.

Courts may take other measures to ensure that defendants comply with their orders. Federal district courts, for example, sometimes invoke their authority under Rule 53 of the Federal Rules of Civil Procedure and appoint what is called a "master." The master is responsible for reporting to the court at designated intervals about the defendants' compliance with the court's orders, and the master may also assist in the implementation of these orders.

D. OTHER REMEDIES

In addition to civil rights actions brought by prisoners themselves, there are other means by which prisoners' constitutional rights may be enforced. For example, the Civil Rights of Institutionalized Persons Act (CRIPA) authorizes the United States Attorney General to bring suit on behalf of the United States to enjoin the maintaining of "egregious or flagrant" unconstitutional conditions in a state or local correctional facility which are causing inmates "grievous harm" and are being maintained in accordance with a "pattern or practice" of violating the Constitution. 42 U.S.C.A. § 1997a(a). The Attorney General also has the authority to intervene in civil rights suits brought by inmates which involve such unconstitutional conditions. 42 U.S.C.A. § 1997c(a).

The Constitution, however, is not the sole source of protection for inmates. In fact, because of the contracted scope of prisoners' rights under the Constitution, as it has been interpreted by the Supreme Court, the Constitution may be one of the least important sources of prisoner's rights. Prisoners also have rights under state constitutions and federal and state statutes, which can provide rights which go beyond the rights accorded by the federal Constitution. In addition, inmates may be able to bring state common-law claims for the tortious conduct of correctional officials, such as assault, battery, or negligence. State immunity statutes, however, often insulate correctional officials from liability under state law or limit their liability.

Litigation to enforce federal constitutional or other rights is not the only means of ensuring that correctional facilities are safe, humane, and sanitary. States can, for example, adopt health and safety standards for state and local correctional facilities and implement inspection schemes to monitor compliance with those standards. In addition, correctional officials can seek accreditation of their facilities for compliance with professional standards from, for example, the Commission on Accreditation for Corrections and the National Commission on Correctional Health Care. Finally, inmates may be able to seek redress for injurious conditions or practices through inmate grievance procedures. If correctional officials are ever to be relieved from the burdens of litigation, it is imperative, however, that steps be taken to ensure the efficacy of these alternative modes of making correctional facilities safe, humane, and sanitary.

INDEX

References are to Pages.

COMMUNITY CORRECTIONS ACTS
ABA Model Act, 78–79, 265

COMMUNITY SERVICE
Generally, 77

COMPLAINT
Pro se inmate complaints, liberal construction of, 288–290

CONDITIONS OF CONFINEMENT
See Cruel and Unusual Punishment

CONFRONTATION AND CROSS-EXAMINATION
Disciplinary hearings, 177–179
Mental hospitals, inmate transfers to, 193
Parole-revocation hearings, 259, 261
Sentencing hearings, 44–45

CONSENT DECREES
Generally, 308, 312–317
Attorney's fees, 308
Modification, 312–317

CONTACT VISITS
Body-cavity searches after, 210–213
Right to, 152–155

CONTEMPT OF COURT
Civil, 320
Criminal, 320

CONVICTED OFFENDERS, RIGHTS OF
Criminal records, expungement or sealing of, 279
Discrimination, bans against, 279–280
Disenfranchisement, 277–278
Employment, 275–276, 279–280
Pardons, 278
Restoration of rights, 278–280

CORRESPONDENCE
See Mail

COSTS
See Fees

COUNSEL
See Attorneys

HANDS–OFF DOCTRINE—Cont'd
Reasons for abandonment of, 129–132

HISTORY
Burden of proof, sentencing hearings, 48
Prisoners' rights, 128–132

HOME CONFINEMENT
Generally, 68–69
Electronic monitoring devices, 69

IMMUNITY
Generally, 283, 291–297
Eleventh Amendment, 283, 291, 295
Official immunity,
Absolute, 292–293
Qualified, 292–297
Sovereign immunity, United States, 291

IN FORMA PAUPERIS PETITIONS
Frivolousness, dismissal for, 289–290

INCARCERATION
Purposes of, 2–8, 133–134
Conflict between, 7–8

INJUNCTIVE RELIEF
Generally, 303–307
Confinement, release from, 304, 306–307
Taxes, raising of, 305

JAILHOUSE LAWYERS
Incompetent, 168
Prohibition against, 166–168
Reasonable alternative assistance, 167, 171

JURISDICTION
Generally, 288, 318–319
Termination of, 318–319

JURY
Sentencing, 49

LAW LIBRARIES
Access, adequacy of, 170–171

LAW STUDENTS
Interviews of prisoners, 163–165

LAWYERS
See Attorneys

LIBERTY INTERESTS
Constitutionally-derived, 185–187
State-created, 187–190

MAIL
Alternative to media interviews, 140
Attorneys, mail from, 162–163
Books, hardbound, 143
Court documents, withholding of, 162
Due Process, 139
Inmate-to-inmate, 144–147
Nonprisoners, 136–139, 149–150
Union materials,
    Equal protection, 204–205
    First Amendment, 142–143

MARRIAGE
Prisoners, 147–149

MEDIA
Interviews,
    Freedom of speech, 140–141
    Freedom of the press, 141

MEDICAL CARE
Generally, 231–240
Deliberate indifference, 231–234
Disabilities, 236–237
Psychiatric care, 235–236
Right to refuse, 198–201, 237–240
Serious medical needs, 234–235
Systemic problems, 233–234

MENTALLY ILL PRISONERS
Involuntary medication, 198–201, 237–240
Psychiatric care, right to, 235–236
Transfers to mental hospitals, 186–190, 193–196

MIRANDA WARNINGS
Criminal cases, statements of prisoners, 181–182
Disciplinary proceedings, admissibility, statements made without, 181

MUNICIPAL LIABILITY
Eleventh Amendment, 295

RACIAL SEGREGATION
See also Discrimination; Equal Protection
Prisons, 201–203

RECIDIVISM
Rates, 3–5

RELIGION, FREEDOM OF
Generally, 155–160
Constitutional, 155–159
Religious Freedom Restoration Act, 160

REMEDIES
Generally, 301–322
Attorney's fees, 291–292, 307–311, 319
Damages,
　　Compensatory, 301–303
　　Confinement, fact or duration of, 306
　　Nominal, 303, 308
　　Punitive, 296, 303
Enforcement of court orders, 319–320
Equitable relief, 303–307
Exhaustion of, 298–300
Grievance procedures, 321–322
Master, appointment of, 320
Modification of consent decrees, 312–317
State common law, 321
State constitutions, 321
Statutes and regulations, 321

RESTITUTION
Generally, 7, 74–76
ABA Guidelines, 75–76
Seventh Amendment, 75
Victim-offender mediation programs, 7

RETALIATION
For litigation, 171

SEARCHES AND SEIZURES
See Fourth Amendment

SECTION 1983
See also, Affirmative Defenses; Attorney's Fees; Court; Exhaustion of Remedies; Immunity; Jurisdiction; Municipal Liability; Remedies
Causation, 285–287

VICTIM–OFFENDER MEDIATION PROGRAMS
Restorative justice, 6–8

VISITATION RIGHTS
Contact visits, 152–155
Liberty interest, 188–189

VOTING RIGHTS
Convicted offenders, 277–278

†